# THE SOCIOLOGY
# OF PUBLIC
# ISSUES

# THE SOCIOLOGY OF PUBLIC ISSUES

Steven L. Nock
Paul W. Kingston
UNIVERSITY OF VIRGINIA

Wadsworth Publishing Company, Belmont, California
A Division of Wadsworth, Inc.

Sociology Editor: Serina Beauparlant
Editorial Assistant: Marla Nowick
Production: Cece Munson, The Cooper Company
Print Buyer: Randy Hurst
Interior and Cover Designer: Cynthia Bassett
Copy Editor: Steven Bailey
Technical Illustrator: Carl Brown
Compositor: Weimer Typesetting Company, Inc.
Signing Representative: Bob Podstepny

Printed in the United States of America
1 2 3 4 5 6 7 8 9 10—94 93 92 91 90

**Library of Congress Cataloging-in-Publication Data**

Nock, Steven L.
    The sociology of public issues / Steven L. Nock & Paul W.
Kingston.
        p.  cm.
    Includes index.
    ISBN 0-534-12096-2
    1. Sociology.  2. Social problems.  3. United States—Social
conditions.  I. Kingston, Paul W.  II. Title.
HM51.N63  1989
301—dc20                                              89-14698
                                                          CIP

# Contents

# Preface

Everyday life is often said to be the laboratory for sociology. This is certainly so, but it takes some direction to *see* the sociology around us. That is the goal of this book—to show beginning students that sociology can distinctly illuminate public issues. News reports of these issues rarely mention sociology, but there *is* conspicuous sociology in the news. Indeed, most public issues directly interest sociologists, and just as they draw our professional attention, public issues can prompt student interest in sociological thinking.

The subject matter of our introductory courses includes much that is familiar to students—crime, the family, politics, religion, and organizations. This familiarity, however, is both a blessing and an obstacle to our efforts as teachers. We can refer to the social world and assume that there is common understanding and interest. Yet students are often so "close" to the subjects of our discussions that they may not recognize their sociological importance or question their own preconceptions. As sociology instructors, then, we need to draw on students' natural curiosity and help them understand their world in a distinctive way.

We hope this book will stimulate in students what C. Wright Mills called a "sociological imagination"—that is, an ability to see private troubles as *public issues* and public issues as *private concerns*. By applying sociological analysis to familiar public issues, we want to show students that a sociological imagination can be valuable, both personally and intellectually. As students engage these issues, we hope that the principles of sociology will become more clear and exciting.

We have often begun and concluded our own introductory sociology courses by telling students to examine newspapers and magazines for illustrations of sociological principles. We have told them that the course was a "success" if they could interpret these news accounts in a new, more penetrating light. But rather than simply urging students to read about their world in a sociological perspective, we are now convinced that it is useful to do it *with* them. We hope that our examples can help them to develop their own interests and abilities.

In every case, for every issue examined, we reach conclusions. We have tried to balance our presentation with all "sides" of an argument. At the same time, we argue that certain sociological interpretations are better than others. We evaluate. We condemn. We praise. We do so because informed sociologists have opinions. Sociology can rarely lay claim to undisputed "truth," but sociologists should not refrain from expressing an informed opinion. That is our intellectual responsibility.

Students should realize that sociology has the potential to inform debates, but that it cannot remove all ambiguities. Disagree with us! We hope that our interpretations will challenge you and your students' thinking.

Are we biased? Yes, of course. Issues are not inherently interesting or important. What we decided to write about reflects our value judgments—our biases—about what is interesting and what is important. And on the matters we do discuss, we have personal views (sometimes *very* different) on what *should* be done. We are aware that these personal preferences may influence our judgments. No one is immune from these influences. We consciously strive, however, to distinguish empirical from normative statements—that is, statements of "what is" from statements of what "should be." We expect that people of every ideological persuasion will agree with many of our empirical sociological analyses while disagreeing with others. These essays are not intended to advance a particular political agenda.

Public issues are ideal for teaching sociological principles because they are both complex and intriguing. We have chosen some topics because they are particularly contentious, others because they dramatically allow us to develop sociological principles or theories. All topics, however, address important social issues. Reasonable people disagree about them. A sociological analysis may resolve some of that disagreement or, at least, clarify the reasons for disagreement.

The title of this book, *The Sociology of Public Issues*, calls for some explanation. A public issue is a matter of public concern, political debate, or widespread public interest. For our purposes, a precise definition is not needed, and we do not need to explain how some matters become defined as "issues." We simply looked at the news media to see what commands public attention—matters that should be familiar and interesting to students. The full importance of some issues, however, may not be readily apparent to students until they examine them sociologically. And that is one motivation for writing this book.

There is another reason we wanted to write this book. We are both sociologists who trained in the early 1970s. Both of us entered sociology because it promised a rewarding opportunity to study the problems of our society. For us, sociology largely means an analysis of contemporary society. In the issues of the day, we believe, lies the attraction of sociology for students. Students should be able to use sociology to understand *their* contemporary world, something not typically emphasized by sociology textbooks.

Finally, as teachers of introductory sociology courses, we need a book like this one. We use introductory textbooks and expect to continue using them, although we want to add depth and make their content more alive by intensively engaging only a few topics. Our book, then, is primarily intended as a supplement to the textbooks that most instructors use. It elaborates central topics in standard texts and applies general principles to current concerns. *The Sociology of Public Issues* may also be used as a primary source in an introductory course. It does not presuppose a background in sociology, and we provide short explanations of key concepts that may be unfamiliar to students. In any case, we hope to stimulate discussion, questions, and argument by using familiar issues.

After reviewing the leading textbooks, we selected issues that closely related to the concerns and organization of those books. Thus, each chapter of this book complements a chapter in a larger text. We have omitted certain topics as unnecessary or unworkable, but have included chapters for all topics that we view as the core substance of most introductory sociology textbooks.

We have purposefully avoided elaborate references and footnoting because we want these chapters to be read as short essays. Where statistics are necessary, we use them and provide source references. Assertions and arguments that are commonly accepted within the discipline, however, generally are not referenced. The decision to write this way reflects our intentions about how to use this book. Students should read the relevant chapter in their main textbook *before* reading our essay. That text will provide a larger analytical context and needed citations.

We view sociology as an exciting way to examine and understand the social world. We hope these essays will convey the excitement that we, as sociologists, experience when we read the newspaper, listen to the evening news, or deal with our fellow citizens.

# Acknowledgments

Our strongest thanks go to Sheryl Fullerton, then Sociology Editor, who initially saw the promise of our idea. Of course, we can't extoll her editorial judgment without obvious bias, but we can draw attention to her record of developing sociological texts that break out of the usual mold. For several years, she relentlessly pursued the project—always encouraging us with a clear understanding of the concept. More personally, we can say that she valuably helped us, at each stage of the way, move from general intentions to a completed volume.

Serina Beauparlant, the current sociology editor, ably and smoothly took up the reins on the project when Sheryl was promoted to Executive Editor. She took the time to learn the history of this project and took care to hear our intentions for it. When we suggested changes in design, she understood and helped us accomplish those changes. We enjoyed a truly collaborative relationship with her.

All authors can truly envy, as well, the friendly, professional and efficient help we received from others at Wadsworth, including Marla Nowick, who kept us apprised of all our tasks, and Robert Kauser, who handled permissions. Cece Munson deserves great credit for her fine work as production manager. She transformed a manuscript into a book that faithfully reflected our understanding of its purpose. Steve Bailey edited our writing with proper respect for clarity and convention and a generous inclination to let our own voices speak. Cynthia Bassett, who designed the book, enabled our material to be presented clearly and beautifully.

Our intellectual debts are many because we necessarily ventured outside of our academic specialties in writing these essays. Specially due thanks are the following colleagues at the University of Virginia: Mark Cooney, Thomas Guterbock, James Hunter, Jim Hawdon, Walter Newsome, Daphne Spain, and Gresham Sykes. We also thank Janie Iven (MADD National), John McCarthy (Catholic University), and Craig Reinarman (Northeastern University) for providing materials and advice.

Wadsworth arranged to have reviewers who brought lively minds, seasoned expertise, and good judgment to the task. We certainly can't pretend to have met all of their challenges, but the book is surely better because of the comments of these reviewers: Karen Denton (University of Utah), Paul C. Friday (Western Michigan University), Christopher Hunter (Grinnell College), Martin N. Marger (Michigan State University), John S. Miller (University of Arkansas, Little Rock), James Spates (Hobart and William Smith Colleges), and Theodore C. Wagenaar (Miama University).

We also thank the participants in the roundtable discussion at the American Sociological Association meetings two years ago, in which many very valuable ideas were presented. The participants were Ben Agger (SUNY—Buffalo), Louis Anderson (Kankakee Community College), Richard Peterson (Cornell College), Howard Robbey (Trenton State College), and Beth Ann Shelton (SUNY—Buffalo).

# THE SOCIOLOGY
# OF PUBLIC
# ISSUES

CHAPTER 1

# Methods

## Sociological Research and Public Issues

**T**he audience for sociological research routinely extends beyond the academic world. This research affects how the larger public thinks about issues and even what it considers to be an issue.

*How many homeless are there? What are their backgrounds and their outlooks?* Journalistic accounts feature not only gripping stories of individuals, but also reports of systematic attempts to count the homeless population, to detail their problems (for example, the percentage with drug or alcohol dependency), and to measure the effectiveness of programs to assist them. The widespread expectation that scientific evidence *should* inform public discussions is underscored by the fact that journalists emphasize the need for more good research on the homeless.

*Do early education programs such as Head Start improve the academic performances of disadvantaged children?* Of course, that is the hope. But policy makers and the citizens who pay for the programs want "proof," seeking it in statistical studies that compare the academic achievement of students who went through the program with those who did not (but who were otherwise similar in background).

Researchers present their findings before governmental committees, legislators cite these studies in position papers, and the popular media summarize the results for common consumption.

*Do Americans favor affirmative action programs to improve opportunities for blacks and other minorities?*

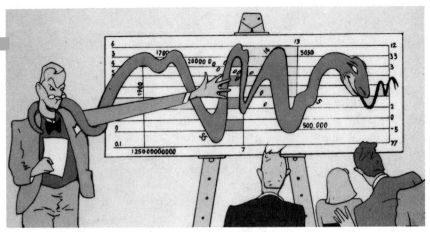

©Istvan Banyai

Statistics can both inform and distort discussions of public issues. Some analyses are demonstrably better than others, however, because they are based on sound research procedures. Your aim should be to evaluate carefully and accept what meets rigorous methodological standards.

Assessment of public opinion, which is a key force in our democratic system, is not left to the intuition or the guesses of presumed experts ("As a fellow I know said, . . ."). On affirmative action and virtually all public concerns, the media present the results of sample surveys ("*x*% of Americans think . . ."), which scientifically measure our collective mood. And, of course, no group is more attentive to these results than politicians. To some extent, public opinion polls have become modern-day substitutes for town meetings.

In short, discussion of public issues rarely proceeds without some reference to social science research. At the same time, however, this research itself has become an issue, especially when it attempts to quantify what goes on in social life.

There is good reason for skepticism. Informed citizens can diligently follow an issue and read totally opposite but "scientific" conclusions. And it's only a small jump to the conclusion, "People can 'prove' whatever they want to." This hardly suggests that social science has much to offer. With this attitude, people can justify holding on to their unexamined opinions: "Your opinion is no better than mine just because you cite some statistics."

To the contrary, we argue that people can *say* almost whatever they want with a "scientific" gloss. And they often do. Some judgments, however, are demonstrably better than others because they are based on sound research procedures. Research can be systematically evaluated and valuably inform us about public issues.

In the short space of this chapter, we have no pretensions of presenting a minicourse in research methods, but we can raise some basic questions that may help you become a better consumer of much sociological research.

We look first at the critical matter of defining terms in measurable ways—that is, "Who Counts What." Then, because public opinion polls are so prominent, we focus on two concerns that pertain directly to evaluating their meaning: "Who Is Asked" and "What Is Asked."

# Who Counts What?

A few years ago, one could not eat breakfast cereal without literally coming face-to-face with a burning social issue: On milk cartons were pictures of missing children. By printing such photographs and "hot-line" numbers, milk producers had joined a national crusade against child abductions.

Americans seemed to be in an epidemic of fear. School and law-enforcement officials recommended that parents create identification files for their children with photographs, dental records, and fingerprints. Day-care centers instituted elaborate checkout procedures. The familiar parental injunction to children "Don't talk to strangers" took on new urgency.

This fear was reflected in public opinion surveys. In reviewing survey data about missing children, sociologist Joel Best reported that 89 percent of Illinois parents thought stranger abductions were a "very" or "quite" serious problem. Thirty-seven percent of adults in California saw "a great deal of danger today of children being abducted by a stranger." And three-quarters of the respondents in a national survey of youths aged 8 to 17 were very concerned about these kidnappings.

Why the sudden emergence of this problem? Undoubtedly, part of the answer was the widespread media coverage of a few heartbreaking cases—Eton Patz, Adam Walsh, and 28 serial murders in Atlanta. Yet these cases developed into a "problem" because people cited alarming estimates of 50,000 stranger abductions per year. These numbers were used to justify the view that "something needs to be done."

These activists were politically astute in buttressing their case with numbers. If an issue can be quantified, it often becomes more compelling. Numbers symbolize understanding, an objective scientific perspective that transcends the distortions of raw emotion. Numbers help to legitimize the "seriousness" of an issue and the competence of those who try to "rectify" problems—as long as they are not contradicted by more believable numbers.

Virtually all policy debates in contemporary America involve battles of numbers. Not only do the proponents of a particular policy try to convince others that the "facts are on our side," but also that their issue is "bigger" or "more important" than other issues that also seek public attention. The predictable outcome is that the numbers that are cited to "explain" an issue often tell widely different stories.

Clearly, the incentive for political activists is to cite numbers selectively. Of course, the possibility of outright fabrication cannot be ignored. Perhaps more frequent, however, it is the uncritical acceptance of numbers that justifies a person's sense of "truth" as well as a reflexive dismissal of figures that contradict this truth. It is not too cynical to say that political activists tend to have far more concern for promoting their own causes than in being reflective about the quality of their data.

Even so, once numbers are invoked, activists often cannot control the introduction of other numbers into public debate. This battle of numbers may not produce ultimate truths, but it does undermine unreasonable claims and can point the way to a more objective understanding.

As a case in point, consider what happened to the estimates of 50,000 made by missing children organizations. No one knows how presumed "experts" settled on this figure. But just when this number seemed to become widely accepted, journalists noted that the FBI reported 67 investigations of child abductions by strangers in 1984. These official numbers carried so much more weight that many observers concluded that the whole issue was trivial.

But even the FBI figures cannot be taken as the final word. Here we see what Joel Best has called "a touching faith in official statistics"—and, we might add, an unwillingness to probe their meaning. Were there "only" 67 abductions? The FBI does not have jurisdiction in all kidnapping cases, and it has been widely criticized for its reluctance to open cases. Although the FBI reports proved valuable in alleviating much of the fear that accompanied the 50,000 estimate, they suffer from their own distortions.

Indeed, at this point, any astute observer of this numbers battle would have wondered if the participants were talking about the same thing. Were they comparing apples to apples, apples to oranges, or even apples to elephants?

In short, *what is a missing child?* The question seems straightforward, but it is not easy to answer. Do we include children who are taken, willingly or not, by noncustodial parents? By any reckoning, parental "abductions" are much more common than are abductions by strangers. Should we include runaways?

Let us assume that we want to focus on stranger abductions. Should we include only successful kidnappings or include attempted kidnappings as well? How long must a child be gone before she or he is designated missing? A half hour? three hours? overnight? Who is a stranger?

Obviously, we need a clear *operational definition*—that is, an explicit way of measuring a concept. We need to define the concept "stranger abduction" in measurable terms. Both the words "stranger" and "abduction" must be considered. We could define a "stranger abduction," for example, as any abduction of someone under age 18 by a person other than a parent that lasts at least 24 hours. In principle, researchers could use this definition and count the number of occurrences.

Nonetheless, neither this definition nor *any other* definition can claim to be right, only more or less useful. Other researchers could propose their own definition, perhaps shortening the abduction period to twelve hours because they think our definition is overly restrictive. Some people may prefer to use our definition instead of someone else's and vice versa. But in either case, they will be able to see how the same data can lead to different estimates of the problem.

Not surprisingly, now that the fearful figure of 50,000 has been discredited, the National Center for Missing and Exploited Children (NCMEC) in Washington, D.C., is pressing the results of a study that used very inclusive definitions: kidnappings and attempted kidnappings, of both short- and long-term duration. Extrapolating from the figures for two cities with high crime rates (Houston, Texas, and Jacksonville, Florida), NCMEC arrived at a national figure of almost 30,000. Such a large number keeps the issue alive.

If only those abductions that resulted in murder or lasted 24 hours are included, however, the national estimates using these extrapolations come to little more than 1,000. But Houston and Jacksonville are unusually violent, so even this estimate is probably high.

At this point, the battle of numbers has become a struggle over operational definitions. No research can avoid defining concepts in measurable terms. That is an essential component of empirical research. Nonetheless, such seemingly technical, even picky, considerations can have important implications for policy.

*What* is counted affects *how many* are counted—and thus how the seriousness of a problem is perceived. This is true for the issue of missing children as well as many other public issues. One important challenge is to judge whether all the relevant terms are reasonably defined.

## Who Is Asked?

A few years ago, best-selling author Shere Hite produced a massive analysis, *Women and Love: A Cultural Revolution in Progress* (1987), in which she argued that women were overwhelmingly and deeply frustrated in their relations with men, both emotionally and sexually. Her book was laced with bitter quotes from some of the 4,500 women who responded to her lengthy survey. In addition, she reported summary statistics of their responses—for example, women initiated 92 percent of all divorces; 95 percent of the women experienced "emotional and psychological harassment" from the men they love, and 70 percent of women married at least five years had at least one extramarital affair. With this quantification, her analysis has the trappings of social scientific research (Hite is neither a sociologist nor a professional survey researcher).

If Hite is right, women can do little more than despair, and men should feel a crushing burden of guilt. Should you accept this bleak picture of relations between the sexes? In thinking about this question, you probably think first about whether your personal experiences (or those of your friends) fit Hite's conclusion. Of course, you are most intrigued by your sample of one (or just a few), but you also know that you cannot tell whether your experience is typical. More analytically, you probably also wonder how 4,500 women could "speak for" millions of others. Hite's respondents, after all, are only a minuscule fraction of American women.

But you *cannot* dismiss Hite's analysis simply because she did not listen to enough voices. A survey of 4,500 women *can* provide highly accurate estimates of what all women in the general population think and do. Even smaller samples can prove valid.

At this point, we must explain a few terms so that you can follow our critique of Hite's work. A *sample* represents observations about some "members" of a larger *population* (for example, all adult American women or all companies with sales in excess of $1,000,000). For the sample to provide accurate information about the population, the sample must be *representative*—that is, the members of the sample must be like the members of the population in key respects. In Hite's case, that means the proportional distribution of responses within the sample of 4,500 women (for example, the percentage within various age categories or the percentage with happy marriages) must correspond to the same proportions in the population of all women.

Obviously, the "representativeness" of a sample cannot be directly judged for many items in a survey because the distributions within the population are unknown—hence the need for the study. Using established statistical principles, however, social scientists have developed methodological procedures that make it possible to generalize from small samples to larger populations.

The only way to ensure representativeness is to use a *random sample*. In such a sample, all members (and all combinations of members) of the population to be studied have an equal chance of being included in the sample. But if some types of members of the population are more likely to be included in the sample than others, then the sample cannot be used to find out what the population is like.

The process of *estimating* the characteristics of a population from sample results is known as *inference*. (We discuss this process in the accompanying box, "Making Inferences.") Suffice it to say here that researchers can use statistical laws to make very good estimates from samples, and with specified levels of confidence in these estimates. But these laws apply *only if the sample is random*.

As the box explains, Hite's sample is much larger than needed for making good estimates. The real issue is her method of selecting the respondents in her sample—and, relatedly, the sample's representativeness.

Unfortunately, Hite's data collection procedures were seriously flawed. She distributed 100,000 questionnaires to various organizations, church groups, and a "wide range" of other women. Do you see the initial bias? Imagine that *all* questionnaires were distributed to group members and then were returned. These 100,000 questionnaires may reflect the views of women in organizations (assuming that all types of organizations were proportionately contacted), but Hite could not say

# Making Inferences

An inference involves estimating an unknown value from the results of a sample of observations such as those in public opinion polls. In these polls, a *sample* of individuals (typically, 1,000 or so) answers questions, and the answers are used to estimate the responses of the entire public (the *population*).

Suppose we are trying to estimate the proportion of American voters who will vote Democratic in an upcoming election. If 47 percent of a sample of registered voters say they plan to vote Democratic, that is the best guess about how all registered voters feel. But it is *probably wrong*. It is unlikely that *exactly* 47 percent of all registered voters feel this way. The questions to ask are: (1) How close to the real value is the sample result likely to be (how much error is there)? and (2) How likely (how *probable*) is it that the sample result is close to the real value?

These two concerns are the basis of inference and are known as *error* and *probability level*. Although we cannot fully explain these matters here, we can relate how researchers use statistical laws to interpret survey results.

## Error

For the same topic (for example, presidential vote), each random sample will give somewhat different results—one sample may indicate that 48 percent of respondents intend to vote Democratic, another 49 percent, and yet another 52 percent. But if each sample is random, we know that these results are just as likely to overestimate as underestimate the real value. We can also determine how close to the unknown value our result is likely to be.

Applying statistical laws, survey analysts use a formula to calculate the average error—that is, the extent to which any particular sample result is likely to differ from the unknown value that is being estimated. This statistic is called the *standard error*. Because a researcher does not know how good her partic-

continued

ular sample is, she must assume that it errs by the average amount.

If we want a close estimate, we should have a small standard error. But getting a small error is difficult because two factors influence it: the actual split of voters in the population and the sample size.

For example, if 100 percent of voters planned to vote Democratic, every sample of voters would give exactly the same results—there would be absolutely no error. If the actual split were 50/50, however, every sample would probably give slightly different results. The more even the split in the population (the closer to 50/50), the larger the standard error. Nothing can be done about this.

The other factor that influences the error is the sample size. The larger the random sample, the smaller the standard error, and hence the more confident we are in the sample's results. To reduce error, then, researchers must increase their sample size. This is true no matter what the split in the population or the size of that population.

## Probability Level

Statistical principles also state that 95 percent of all truly random samples produce estimates that are no more than two standard errors from the unknown value being estimated. By convention, statisticians refer to two standard errors as the *error margin*.

Suppose that our sample estimates that 49 percent of voters will vote Democratic and that we calculate the error margin as 2 percent. Because 95 percent of all random samples produce estimates that are no more than 2 percent from the real value, we know there is a 95 percent chance (*probability*) that the true value is no more than 2 percent above or below 49 percent.

In other words, there is only a 5 percent chance that the true figure in the population is outside the range of 47 percent to 51 percent. This range is called the *confidence interval*.

Because this point is counterintuitive, note that error margins (and confidence intervals) have nothing to do with the *size* of the population or the proportion of the population that is sampled. Only the sample size affects these margins. As the sample increases, the error decreases.

To show how sample size affects estimates, we calculate the error margins for the percentages of voters who plan to vote Democratic using different sample sizes:

| Sample Size | Error Margin (%) |
|---|---|
| 300 | 5.6 |
| 600 | 4.0 |
| 900 | 3.3 |
| 1,200 | 2.8 |
| 2,400 | 2.0 |
| 4,800 | 1.4 |

These margins are the same whether the population is all U.S. voters or just voters in Cincinnati. If we sample 600 Americans randomly and find that 47 percent plan to vote Democratic, our error margin of 4.0 percent says that we are 95 percent confident that between 43 percent and 51 percent of American voters actually feel that way. If we need a better estimate, we will need a larger sample.

For many research purposes, a sample size of 1,000 to 1,200 is sensible—reasonable accuracy at an affordable cost. Below that size, the error is simply too great to permit reliable estimates. Above that number, small gains in precision are offset by higher costs of the additional sample size.

When evaluating the results of any survey, the following questions should be asked.

1.   Is the sample a *random* one? If not, ignore the results or be highly skeptical of them and look for better evidence. (Confidence intervals and probability levels are meaningless on non-random samples.)

2.   What is the *error margin*? For matters such as "calling" an election, a small margin is needed because the real results probably will be close. On other issues, larger margins can be tolerated. Error margins that exceed 4 percent do not have much precision.

3.   What is the probability level? The convention is to report the error margin (or confidence interval) at the 95 percent level. (This is often shown as "statistically significant at the .05 level.") One need not be much of a gambler to accept results at this probability level. Some researchers, however, report findings at the 90 percent level, which means there is a 10 percent chance that the true result is outside the confidence interval. A probability level below 90 percent involves a large gamble, and the results should be ignored.

anything about the nonjoiners, who may well have different views on relations between the sexes. It is not clear what Hite's study has sampled, but it did not start as a sample of *all* American women.

We also know that the *response rate* was far less than complete: only 4.5 percent. Are these actual respondents like the other 95.5 percent of potential respondents (much less the population)?

In itself, a low response does not necessarily mean there is a *response bias*—that is, a tendency for certain women (for example, those who are angry) to complete the questionnaire and for others to throw it in the trash. It is possible that the few who responded are like the many who did not, but a low rate raises concerns about bias, and Hite's response rate is very low by the standards of sociological research.

Who do you think would take the time to write out answers to more than 100 questions such as, "Did you ever grow to hate a lover?" The woman with a reasonably happy marriage or the woman on the verge of divorce? We suspect that there is some self-selection and that the malcontented are disproportionately heard.

So, is Hite right or wrong? She *might* be right in concluding, "What is going on right now in the minds of women is a large-scale cultural revolution." But she cannot validly reach this conclusion by using the results of her survey. Without a representative sample, she is left with many anecdotes, often poignant, that may or may not tell us about women in general.

Moreover, we have good reason to question her analysis because many of her "findings" contradict studies that were based on nationally representative samples. For instance, look at Table 1.1 to see how married men and women assess their marriages. The results there come from the 1987 General Social Survey (GSS) produced by the National Opinion Research Center (NORC). As a random sample, the GSS conforms to all of the accepted standards for including representative respondents. In addition, the interviewers who conduct the survey make repeated efforts to contact all people in the sampling frame in order to ensure a high response rate (about 75 percent), reducing the likelihood of a response bias.

A quite different picture emerges from these data. Both women and men overwhelmingly report happy marriages. Of course, you should be skeptical of looking at responses to one question as *the* barometer of marital happiness in America. (See our comments about multiple indicators in the following section, "What Is Asked.") You can be confident, however, that a high proportion of all American women are willing to *say* they are happy in their marriages. On the other hand, you cannot be confident that the responses in Hite's survey are typical of what American women would say on a questionnaire.

Our methodological criticism here does not mean Hite is wrong in her main conclusion, although we strongly suspect that she presents an

**Table 1.1**  Marital Satisfaction, Men and Women*

| Satisfaction | Women (%) | Men (%) |
|---|---|---|
| Very happy | 69 | 62 |
| Pretty happy | 30 | 35 |
| Not too happy | 1 | 3 |
| | 100 | 100 |
| | (372) | (420) |

*Respondents were asked the question, "Taking all things together, how would you describe your marriage?" They were then given the three choices indicated in the left column. Numbers in parentheses indicate number of respondents.

Note: The slight differences in the responses of men and women are not statistically significant at the conventional .05 level.

Source: 1987 General Social Survey, National Opinion Research Center (NORC)

overly bleak view. Rather, we believe that the issue she addresses is too important to be considered with shoddy research. Not only is it essential to use a random sample, but also we must ask appropriately subtle questions, an issue to which we now turn.

# What Is Asked?

Imagine that certain politicians want to enact laws that reflect public opinion on business taxation issues. They know that the general public does not think much about the intricacies of depreciation allowances, investment credits, and capital formation. But the politicians want to know the public's general views on business taxes so that specific proposals can be evaluated; thus they turn to the polls.

Conveniently enough, many political lobbyists supply these politicians with survey results. Not surprisingly, these surveys show that Americans want exactly what a particular lobby wants. The surveys do not lie; they just ask questions that are likely to be answered in a particular way.

To see the effect of questionnaire wording, first consider this question: "Do you agree or disagree that large corporations should start paying their fair share of taxes before there are any increases in any taxes that ordinary working and middle-income Americans pay?"

Almost everyone agrees on this. To disagree, one would, in effect, be saying, "I'm in favor of businesses paying an *un*fair amount." Proponents

# A Consumer's Checklist

A good national survey sample will have:

☑ *Information collected from a random sample* (or a systematic sample that has been designed to create a random sampling) of the population to be studied.

This means that all people within the population to be studied (for example, all American adults) have an equal chance of being included within the sample.

☑ *A sample size of at least 1,000.* Somewhat smaller samples may be considered, although they have larger confidence intervals. (See "Making Inferences.")

Sample sizes of approximately 1,500 are very adequate for making estimates. Substantially larger samples do not greatly increase accuracy (that is, reduce the size of the confidence interval).

☑ *A high response rate* (the higher, the better). Be wary of results that are based on surveys that have response rates of less than 50 percent.

Watch out for:

☒ *Magazine-sponsored polls* of their readers. These may be large in size, but they are probably subject to response bias.

☒ *Television call-in polls.* Same defect as above.

☒ *Most commercially conducted market research.* These often have very low response rates and nonrandom sampling procedures (for example, shoppers in the mall on Friday morning are asked to fill out a questionnaire).

☒ *Overnight tracking polls,* which are primarily used to follow shifts in political opinion at election times. Small samples and low response rates create problems.

☒ *Any survey that does not include details about the sample.*

of heavier tax burdens for businesses predictably interpret the results to "demonstrate" popular support for their view. The sponsor for this survey was the Citizens for Tax Justice, a labor-oriented group against tax breaks for business.

This game can be played by both sides. Consider this question: "Should Congress pass a law that could hobble economic growth?"

Of course, almost everyone will say "No." Few people would say, "I'm for hobbling the economy." It is not surprising, then, that probusiness groups interpret the results to "demonstrate" support for *their* view. The sponsor of this survey was the U.S. Chamber of Commerce, the largest organization of American businesses.

With *loaded* questions, such surveys do not really help a politician get a feel for popular opinion or help common citizens know what their fellow citizens believe. Indeed, the wordings are so distorted that any sensible reader should dismiss them out of hand. These polls start with a prejudice and end with a statistic.

In many instances, however, and with no political motivation, the wording of questions critically shapes both responses and the inferences drawn from them.

Suppose we want to know whether the public supports governmental action to improve the lives of poor people. Government antipoverty efforts, of course, are generally called "welfare," although many specific programs fall under this label (for example, Food Stamps, Medicaid, and Aid to Families with Dependent Children). Reasonably enough, one thus might want to assess public sentiment about welfare.

The NORC GSS noted above, which is a state-of-the-art survey based on a random sample of the American adult population, may prove instructive. Responding to a series of questions about government spending, 19 percent said that we spend "too little" on "welfare." This response suggests there is very little public enthusiasm for greater government involvement.

In the same survey, however, 65 percent of respondents said that "too little" was spent on "assistance to the poor." How "welfare" and "assistance to the poor" differ in meaning to the people answering the questions is hard to say. Nonetheless, it is very clear that the difference in wording leads to very different impressions about public sentiment.

The word "welfare" seems to trigger disregard for the poor; the phrase "assistance for the poor" activates concern. And when respondents are asked about spending for "*caring* for the poor," they appear even more generous. NORC researcher Tom Smith analyzed this matter in his aptly titled article, "That Which We Call Welfare by Any Other Name Would Smell Sweeter."

So what can we conclude about public attitudes toward governmental assistance for the poor? There is no unambiguous answer, but the discrepancy in responses can be interpreted to suggest public ambivalence. A spirit of generosity seems to be mixed with reservations about the value of current efforts to combat poverty. Neither liberals (who favor greater governmental effort) nor conservatives (who are skeptical of governmental involvement) can claim a clear mandate for their views.

More generally, this discrepancy illustrates the need for *multiple indicators*—that is, responses to several questions addressed to the same general concern. Complex issues such as attitudes toward the poor have many dimensions. On this matter, for example, it might be useful to know the general public's concern for the poor, reactions to specific programs, views on the "deserving" and "undeserving" poor, and desire to spend money on the poor relative to other policies. No single question can really get at the full complexity of public opinion.

The use of multiple indicators, of course, can complicate a researcher's task. The data often do not fall into neat patterns and tell a coherent story—and so it should be. Contradictions, ambivalences, and subtle nuances are all part of public opinion. It is essential to recognize that survey responses do not speak for themselves. Sociologically informed thinkers accept the ambiguities of these responses and try to interpret their meaning.

The complexity of public opinion is readily evident in the heated issue of abortion. (For further discussion of this issue, see chapter 12.) No responsible researcher can simply claim that Americans are "for" or "against" abortion—or, to use the language each side prefers for itself, the prochoice or prolife positions.

Americans make distinctions that are crucial to recognize. Public opinion cannot be squeezed into one of two molds—for and against.

The NORC GSS again provides valuable data. Respondents were asked, "Please tell me whether or not *you* think it should be possible for a pregnant woman to obtain a *legal* abortion if . . . "; seven different circumstances then were described (for example, a woman becomes pregnant as a result of rape). Responses are indicated in Table 1.2.

Most Americans do not support abortion "on demand," although a large minority endorses this view. Majority sentiment is also against abortion when a pregnancy is ended because it "complicates" a woman's life financially or emotionally. At the same time, substantial majorities support abortion when health is at stake and when a pregnancy has been forced on a woman.

Obviously, no single survey question can reflect all these distinctions, and no newspaper headline is likely to summarize them accurately. When correctly used, however, this set of questions can valuably inform public debates about how the abortion issue should be resolved.

Again, the general point is that on many issues, asking several questions *and* considering the responses to all of them is essential. It is a

**Table 1.2**  Abortion Attitudes

| Reasons | Those Favoring Legal Abortion<br>Percent |
|---|---|
| For any reason | 38 |
| If there is a strong chance of serious defect in the baby | 77 |
| If the woman is married and does not want more children | 40 |
| If the woman's own health is seriously endangered by the pregnancy | 86 |
| If the family has a very low income and cannot afford more children | 44 |
| If the woman becomes pregnant as a result of rape | 77 |
| If the woman is not married and does not want to marry the father | 41 |

Total sample size is 1,467.

Source: 1987 General Social Survey, NORC

matter of constructing questionnaires wisely (asking the right questions) and interpreting their subtleties (recognizing complexity and distinctions).

# Final Encouragements and Cautions

Quantitative social science will surely continue to illuminate and distort public discussion of many issues. It is wrongheaded to either embrace quantification wholeheartedly or dismiss it out of hand. The aim should be to evaluate it carefully and accept what meets rigorous methodological standards.

We are particularly concerned, however, that many people are inclined to discount such research because it often cannot be definitive or because the reality it reveals is not what people want to hear. Whatever methods it uses, sociology can promise neither unambiguous truth nor comforting messages. But, as we hope the chapters here indicate, sociology can provide distinctive understandings that go beyond or even challenge "common wisdom." To realize this potential, we must tolerate ambiguity, keep open minds, and press for ever better research.

Although good research can improve our knowledge, there are several things it *cannot* do. Sociology cannot tell us whether an issue is "important"; whether some social arrangement is "just," "desirable," "good," or their opposites; or what "ought" to be done. Sociology can only hope to tell us *what is*. The evaluation of this reality is a matter of personal values.

For example, in principle at least, sociologists could document the number of homeless and explain why they exist. After reading this research carefully, we might conclude that this account is accurate. Others might read this account and agree. But we might still disagree with our fellow citizens about what *should* be done. Some of us may see the numbers as a mandate for action, while others may conclude that the homeless are "undeserving" or are too few to worry about.

In each case, these reactions involve *normative* judgments—that is, judgments that are based on personal values about what should be. An empirical statement (what is) cannot logically determine a normative position (what should be).

Even so, we are much better able to evaluate what should be done if we first know what *is*. Moreover, we can much more effectively act on our beliefs if we have a good sense of the effects that various actions might have. To us, these reasons more than justify the often difficult task of using empirical social science to understand our society.

# References

Best, Joel. "Missing Children, Misleading Statistics." *The Public Interest* (92): 84–92, 1988.

Converse, Philip, and Michael Trangott. "Assessing the Accuracy of Polls and Surveys." *Science* (234): 1094–1098, 28 Nov. 1986.

Hite, Shere. *Women and Love: A Cultural Revolution in Progress.* 1987. New York: Knopf.

Smith, Tom W. "That Which We Call Welfare by Any Other Name Would Smell Sweeter: An Analysis of the Impact of Question Wording on Response Patterns." *Public Opinion* (51): 75–83, 1987.

# Suggested Readings

Babbie, Earl. *The Practice of Social Research.* 1986. Belmont, CA: Wadsworth. An excellent text on the logic and techniques of sociological research.

Best, Joel. "Missing Children, Misleading Statistics." We draw on this informative article that details the role of numbers in debates about missing children.

Converse, Philip, and Michael Trangott. "Assessing the Accuracy of Polls and Surveys." Two acknowledged experts on polls effectively summarize the pitfalls in surveys while making a strong case for their value.

CHAPTER 2

# Socialization

## Gender, School, and Jobs

**A**s do most college students, you often think about which career you will enter when you graduate, and you may already have made a decision. Nothing could seem more personal because of your individual talents, interests, and preferences for matters such as where to work and for how long. Even if you are not entirely clear about your future, you probably have some idea about the general types of jobs you would prefer. You realize that your job will be an important feature of who you are, how you view yourself, and how others view you.

Counselors, parents, and others will tell you to choose wisely, to find something that "fits" your personality. But as sociologists, we must tell you that your choice is much less individualistic than you might imagine. There are clear patterns in the types of jobs held by certain *types* of people. In this chapter, we address the fact that men and women consistently select different types of work.

Approximately 42 percent of all employed persons are women. Thus, if men and women selected the same types of jobs equally, we should find that approximately 42 percent of each occupation is held by females. But this is not at all what we find, as Census Bureau statistics show. Only one in twenty engineers, one in ten architects, one in five natural scientists, and one in three computer scientists are women. On the other hand, virtually all secretaries, communications equipment operators, and social workers are women. Three-fourths of

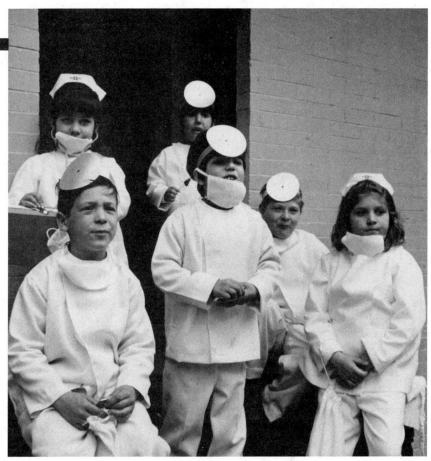

©Abigail Heyman

Boys learn to become doctors; girls learn to become nurses. "Gender lessons" start early and continue throughout life. Career "choices" are much more socially determined than we like to think.

**Table 2.1**    Percentage of Employed Persons Who Are
Females

| Profession | Percent Females |
|---|---|
| Architects | 6 |
| Engineers | 11 |
| Computer scientists | 30 |
| Natural scientists | 20 |
| Physicians | 16 |
| Secretaries | 98 |
| Operators (phone) | 92 |
| Social workers | 94 |
| Grade school teachers | 72 |
| Health therapist | 77 |

Source: *U.S. Statistical Abstract*, 1986, Table 680

primary and secondary school teachers and health therapists are women
(see Table 2.1).

Many high-paying, prestigious positions place a premium on quantitative reasoning and technical skill—and are overwhelmingly male. Do
women choose not to pursue these opportunities for prestige and
money?

Undoubtedly, some of the higher concentrations of women in certain
types of jobs and their low concentrations in others reflect historical
events and discrimination. But men and women also do appear to *choose*
different jobs. What accounts for these differences? And what is the
sociological meaning of these "choices"?

To explore these questions, we analyze a particular sociological puzzle: Why are women so underrepresented in jobs that require a mathematical turn of mind? This puzzle is particularly relevant to consider as
the use of computers spreads so rapidly throughout the working world.
A facility with computers is essential for many good jobs. The question
we ask is whether this new technology represents a distinctive obstacle
for women. If so, computers will perpetuate and perhaps even aggravate
the sexual segregation of the workforce as shown in Table 2.1.

# Learning to "Choose"

The sociological perspective emphasizes that males and females are
taught to want different things—for example, to value different aspects
of jobs. From birth, boys and girls are treated differently and are ex-

pected to behave differently. In short, they are *socialized* to become different in many ways. Their selection of careers or jobs reflects the effects of socialization. Because of their social experiences, individuals tend to make certain choices about jobs.

People differ in a myriad of ways. There are obvious differences in physical characteristics: height, weight, strength, color, physique, and attractiveness. Obvious, too, are differences in nonphysical traits such as income, education, language, religion, attitudes, values, and beliefs.

Despite the wide range of differences among people, however, only some are truly important from a sociological perspective; that is, people are *treated differently* depending on their possession of *certain* traits. We do not ordinarily treat short people much differently from tall people, strong people differently from weak ones. But we do treat males differently from females, the rich differently from the poor, and people of our own race differently from others. In short, only certain differences have social consequences.

Indeed, the biological fact of being born male or female has tremendous implications for an individual throughout his or her life. Imagine that your sister has had a new baby. You would probably ask, "What is it?" Of course, she could answer that question in many ways—a bald one, a loud one, a healthy one. But she knows that you are asking about the baby's sex, and you know that she knows this. Right from the start, we make a fundamental distinction between males and females.

Members of all societies recognize sex to be an important distinction; but unlike many other physical differences, sex is the basis for treating people differently and *expecting different behaviors* of people. The distinction between the biological fact of being male or female is translated into the social distinction between masculine and feminine traits; that is, one is *born* male or female, but one *becomes* masculine or feminine. Sex is biological, while gender is the set of learned characteristics that are associated with sex.

This observation fits with our everyday experiences. We recognize that females are expected to dress, groom, and speak differently from males. What is not so obvious, however, is that gender has such a wide range of consequences. Although each of us thinks of our choices in life as our own (we take pride in our own individuality), these choices are frequently the result of our sex. We learn what is and is not appropriate or acceptable for our sex. As a consequence, males and females consistently make different types of decisions. We learn such lessons well and act on them so routinely that we take these differences for granted. Males and females may not feel that they are forced to make the life choices they do, but we must recognize the very powerful but often subtle influence of socialization.

*Socialization* refers to the process by which individuals learn the ways of a society or group so that they may function within it. One very important part of socialization is the entire set of gender traits that one learns. Quite simply, boys and girls are socialized differently so that each may grow up to function as a member of his or her gender.

The easiest way to demonstrate the profound importance of sex role, or *gender socialization,* is to examine failures of the process. Males who act effeminately or females who act in a masculine manner have often been considered deviant, provoking disapproval or scorn from many others. Although some may wish it were otherwise, Americans are like members of all other societies in the world, expecting men and women to behave differently.

Gender socialization illustrates the most basic sociological principle: Human behavior is caused, in part, by the particular social environment in which one lives. Individuals may experience their lives as a series of personal decisions, the exercise of "free will." But from a sociological perspective, such free will or individual choice is often little more than illusion. That is, the choices that the individuals make reflect the choices they have been taught to make by parents, teachers, and peers—in short, by the agents of socialization. Free will is often the exercise of learned decisions. Men and women may report that they want to be different, but that desire is something that they have been taught.

In this chapter, we consider an important difference between boys and girls: their decisions about which types of courses to take in school and which types of degrees to earn. Additionally, we are concerned with differences between males and females in learning about and using computers. After considering the facts about such differences, we examine evidence that suggests that these differences are predictable consequences of socialization.

## Boys and Girls in School

Although the school experiences of boys and girls differ in many ways, the differences in the courses they take and the programs they complete are among the most important.

Because computers are increasingly important in our society, the person who does not know how to use them or is not aware of their capabilities will have an obvious disadvantage in finding a high-paying job or a rewarding career (Linn, 1985). So what evidence suggests that boys and girls differ in their exposure to computers?

From high school through college, boys are both more likely than girls to take courses that use computers and be exposed to computer use in other ways. A national survey of high school seniors in 1984 showed that 31 percent of boys had used microcomputers, but only 21 percent of girls (U.S. Department of Education, 1982, 1986). At the same time, girls were more likely than boys to have used a word processor, the new secretarial tool.

Even more telling are the results of a nationally representative survey of 61,500 households conducted by the U.S. Bureau of the Census in 1984. This survey showed that approximately 11 percent of all children ages 3 to 17 used computers at home (15 percent had them available), and 28 percent used computers at school. In total, approximately 30 percent of children less than 18 used computers.

Boys and girls differed markedly in their use of computers at both home and school. Boys are much more likely than girls to use a computer if one is in the home (80 percent of boys, 66 percent of girls), and they are more likely to use a home computer for school use.

Significant differences also are found in the use of computers at school. Although similar numbers of boys and girls use computers at school in some way, the applications differ considerably. Girls are more likely to have experience with word processors and are far less likely to have experience with writing computer programs. Girls are also less likely to have used statistical packages (U.S. Department of Education, 1987, Tables 260 and 261).

These differences in secondary school experiences are even more pronounced among college students. Among those who have computers in their homes, 63 percent of males, but only 43 percent of females, use them. Overall, four in ten male college students use computers, but only one-quarter of female students do.

It is not surprising to learn, then, that males and females differ in the fields to which they are attracted in college. In 1986, 52 percent of college students were women. Given that approximately one-half of all college students are women, one would expect that approximately one-half of the majors in any field would be held by women. But only 14 percent of engineering majors (including those in computer science) were women, only 42 percent of mathematics majors were women, and just 27 percent of physical science majors were women. Women do not "choose" technical or science degree programs in the same proportions as do men (U.S. Department of Education, 1988, Table 127). Women are more likely than men to major in English, humanities, or other liberal arts. Thus, it seems that the differences between boys and girls in their exposure to and use of computers parallel the differences in the fields they choose to study. Males are more likely to choose technical fields that require mathematics and computers.

# Explanations for Male–Female Differences

How are we to account for such differences? Why do boys and girls have such different experiences? What accounts for boys' greater use of computers and the difference between boys and girls in the fields they choose in college?

# Biological and Genetic Differences

One argument is that males and females differ in their mental abilities. According to this argument, males are born with superior abilities in things such as mathematics. Many theories suggest the reasons for such differences, but all propose that biological differences between males and females are at least partially responsible.

Evidence to support such theories is mixed, neither consistently supporting nor refuting the notion of physiologically rooted differences. Clearly, even if true, such factors cannot be given complete credit for gender differences in occupational selection. If biology were that important, there would be little question about it, but no study shows more than a modest difference in ability, and it is difficult to say whether these differences result from nature or nurture. Moreover, scientists have certainly not been able to agree about the effect of biology on the sexual division of labor.

If biology matters for job performance, it makes a difference of degree, not of kind. That is, biology might favor males over females to some degree in certain mental tasks that require mathematics or mathematical logic, but if such differences exist, they are small.

In other words, both men and women differ among themselves in any particular type of mental ability. If the skills needed for computers are innate, we know that there would be males born with and without the ability to master such skills. So, too, for women. In fact, there would be a wide range of ability for both sexes.

If a biological or genetic difference does exist, then the average for males is different from the average for females. For either sex, however, there is a wide range of abilities.

Suppose that, on average, males have more of the genetic abilities that would be required in using a computer than do females. The two bell-shaped curves shown in Figure 2.1 represent these male and female abilities. The average differences are shown by the two vertical lines, each of which represents the average for a sex. Individuals of great ability are rare; thus, on the right side of the curves, there are few males or females of high ability. There are also few individuals at the low end of the ability scale, but near the middle, the number of individuals increases. In fact, more people are at the average than at any other point.

From this figure, it is clear that slightly more males than females—but only slightly more—have higher abilities. Is such a small difference enough to account for the finding that only 14 percent of engineering majors are women? Probably not, because the magnitude of the difference between males and females is so great it could not be accounted for by the small difference in mental ability that might exist.

In sum, biological or genetic causes of gender differences in school performance or occupational choice cannot be dismissed: No one has

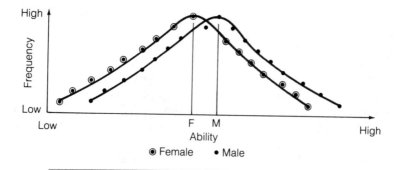

**Figure 2.1**   Male and Female Ability Curves

been able to prove whether they exist. On the other hand, they cannot be accepted as a full explanation. Many sociologists, however, accept the idea that certain physiological *potentials* exist that differ by sex and that may or may not be activated by the physical or social environment. Females may possess a greater potential for certain abilities than do males, but whether such potentials are developed depends on the environment. It is not a question of "nature *or* nurture," but one of *how much* nature and *how much* nurture are involved. To deny the existence of either is to ignore the accumulated evidence from both the physical and social sciences. Nonetheless, the social environment *is* involved, which means that socialization is a major factor in gender.

## Socialization

Is it possible that boys and girls are socialized differently with respect to such things as computer use? Although no one would deny that parents and teachers treat boys and girls differently, how can we explain differences in computer use in these terms? Are parents and teachers responsible for such differences?

Some parents and teachers probably do expect boys and girls to differ in their abilities, perhaps believing that boys are better at mathematics and encouraging them to develop such abilities. Girls, however, receive little encouragement in these pursuits. It is also probably true that the reactions of parents and teachers to boys' and girls' efforts differ. Perhaps when girls experience the inevitable frustration and difficulty that are encountered when working with computers, parents and teachers see this as evidence that girls have less ability than boys with such things. Thus, girls may be allowed to fail where boys are not. In discussing mathematical ability and the differences between boys and girls, Sheila Tobias writes: "At some point, a girl *will* encounter very difficult math. At which point she will say 'I always knew there was this point—everyone told me girls couldn't do math' " (Tobias, 1978).

Most parents and teachers, however, do not directly teach boys and girls different things about computers. Instead, many subtle but cumulative differences appear in the way that boys and girls are treated. Not all that is acquired during the socialization process is intended. Indeed, much of what we become is not intended, and general unintended lessons may have important consequences for such specific matters as computer use.

Social scientists generally agree that the orientation of boys and girls to others and to rules is the most important difference in their upbringing. Girls are taught the primary importance of *relationships* with others; boys, however, are taught the primary importance of *mastery*, or achievement—they learn the importance of *rules* and how to use them in order to achieve. This pervasive difference accounts for many of the obvious and subtle gender differences we observe. Lenore Weitzman summarizes this point of view:

> Our definition of femininity *requires* reactions from other people. The young girl cannot assess whether she is attractive, nurturing, or helpful without continual interaction and feedback from others. She is forced to be dependent on people to court their acceptance in order to obtain those experiences that help establish sex-typed behaviors.
>
> In contrast, the boy is encouraged to be self-reliant. Many masculine sex-typed behaviors, especially those involving physical skills, can be developed alone. A boy is taught to stand up for himself and engage in certain behaviors because he, as a person, feels that is appropriate. In fact, men who stand by their individual principles despite opposition and the scorn of others often become cultural heroes (Weitzman, 1979, p. 18).

Differences in the upbringing of boys and girls start right after birth and continue through childhood. Sociologist Lenore Weitzman describes several studies that support this conclusion. In one, eleven mothers each played with a six-month-old child. Six of the women were told the child was a boy, and five were told it was a girl. The researchers then observed which of three toys—a doll, a train, and a fish—the mothers offered the child. Although each mother claimed she did not distinguish between boys and girls at that age, the women who thought the child was a girl most often offered "her" a doll to play with. The women who thought the child was a boy offered "him" a train. Weitzman concluded, "This research vividly illustrates socialization at its earliest stages. It indicates that sex role socialization begins before the child is even aware of a sexual identity." Similarly, studies of children's picture books show that boys are portrayed as active and adventuresome, while girls are shown to be more passive. Girls receive their status through relationships to people (husbands or children) and boys through their achievements and mastery (Weitzman, 1979, pp. 3–8).

This difference between the sexes is reinforced by teachers in school. Studies show that teachers' reactions to students differ depending on the gender of the student. In particular, teachers respond to boys' use and mastery of rules. For girls, other aspects of their work matter more often to teachers. Most positive feedback to boys comes from the intellectual quality of their work. This is less true for girls, who are more often praised for intellectually irrelevant aspects of their work such as neatness. Negative feedback follows a similar pattern. For boys, only one-half of work-related negative feedback relates to intellectual inadequacy; the remainder is for failure to obey *rules of form.* For girls, approximately 90 percent of negative feedback is related to intellectual performance, and little pertains to violations of rules of form.

## A Different Voice

In her book, *In a Different Voice* (1982), psychologist Carol Gilligan argues that the result of such differential experiences produces a different way of looking at the world. Boys and girls focus on different things in their attempts to understand what is around them. Gilligan's research suggests, for example, that boys and girls develop consistently different standards by which right and wrong are evaluated because significant others respond differently to boys and girls. She illustrates this difference by studying the way that sixth-grade boys and girls resolve moral dilemmas. The one that Gilligan used was developed by Lawrence Kohlberg, who studied moral development. The following situation was presented to the sixth graders.

> A man's wife was dying of cancer and there was only one drug that might save her. The pharmacist who had discovered the drug was charging ten times its cost to him, or $2000 for a small dose. The sick woman's husband tried to borrow the money, but he could raise only about $1000. He told the pharmacist that his wife was dying and asked him to sell it cheaper or let him pay later. The druggist refused. In desperation, the man broke into the drugstore and stole the drug for his wife. Should he have done that? (Kohlberg, 1969)

After hearing each child's response, Gilligan probed to find out why the answer was given—that is, how the child arrived at his or her answer. Comparing the responses of the boys with the girls shows how differently they view the world.

Gilligan describes the answers given by Jake and Amy, two 11-year-olds. Jake is convinced that the man should steal the drug because the dilemma is between the value of property and life. "For one thing," he says, "a human life is worth more than money, and if the druggist only makes $1000 he is still going to live, but if [the man] doesn't steal the drug, his wife is going to die." Jake explains his choice by noting that if the man were caught, "the judge would probably think it was the right thing to do," and although the man broke the law, "the laws have mistakes" (Gilligan, 1982, p. 26). Jake believes his choice is the one that others would make, that most people would see this as the right thing to do. Jake has made a distinction between two sets of rules—those of law and those of morality—and has decided that the latter are more important in this situation. Jake acknowledges the druggist's right to receive payment for his property, but he sees the wife's rights to be more important.

When presented with the same dilemma, Amy gives a very different answer:

> I think there might be other ways besides stealing it, like if he could borrow the money or make a loan or something, but he really shouldn't steal the drug—but his wife shouldn't die either (Gilligan, 1982, p. 28).

When she is asked why he should not steal the drug, she does not refer to the law but rather the effect that theft could have on the relationship between the man and his wife. She further explained:

> If he stole the drug, he might save his wife then, but if he did, he might have to go to jail, and then his wife might get sicker again, and he couldn't get more of the drug, and it might not be good. So, they should really just talk it out and find some other way to make the money (Gilligan, 1982, p. 28).

Amy's answer shows that she focuses on the long-term *relationship* between the man and his wife. To her, the wife's life depends on the continuing relationship between the woman and her husband. Gilligan writes, "Amy's moral judgment is grounded in the belief that, 'if somebody has something that would keep somebody alive, then it's not right not to give it to them'; she considers the problem in the dilemma to arise not from the druggist's assertion of rights but from his failure of response" (Gilligan, 1982, p. 28). Amy is convinced that the problem is with the druggist, and that he simply needs to be shown the consequences of his refusal to give the man the drug. And if the man cannot do that, someone else can.

To Jake, it seems clear that a judge would understand that stealing the drug was the right thing to do. Thus, Jake sees the solution in the rules and logic of laws—impersonal standards that can be applied to this particular situation. To him, the rules are clear: laws against stealing are less important than moral rules governing human life.

To Amy, however, the solution is quite different. She is equally confident that a solution could be found, but it does not involve stealing the drug. Amy believes that the man and the druggist could work something out if they talked it over long enough. "Thus in [the man's] dilemma these two children see two very different moral problems—Jake a conflict between life and property that can be resolved by logical deduction, Amy a fracture of human relationship that must be mended with its own thread" (Gilligan, 1982, pp. 29–31).

In summary, we can see that boys and girls arrive at adolescence with different world views through many influences—parents, teachers, and peers. Boys are more concerned with rules and the logics that pertain to them, and girls to relationships and their maintenance.

## World Views, Computers, and Occupational Choices

So what does all this have to do with the courses that students take or their experiences with computers?

In her intensive study of student computer use, sociologist Shery Turkel (1984) found two types of computer users. The first are those whose approach Turkel describes as "hard mastery." Hard masters implement their will over the machine through realization and execution of a programmed plan. Such a planner's approach suggests that one knows what needs to be done, designs a plan to accomplish it, and instructs a computer to carry out the plan.

"Soft mastery," however, is more interactive. Soft masters know what they want the computer to do, but they are less structured in accomplishing it. Their programs are less bound by rules and more by results. A soft master will try something, watch the consequences, try something else, watch the consequences, and continually revise instructions through an interactive process (Turkel, 1984, pp. 104–105).

Hard masters see the world as something to be controlled. In fact, Turkel believes, such people have a high need for control. As children, these individuals played with toys that could be manipulated—erector sets or blocks, for example. Soft masters see the world as something to which they need to adapt and not something they need to control. As children, they played with toys that were not manipulable—dolls or toy soldiers, for example.

Turkel found that girls tend to be soft masters, while boys tend to be hard masters. Girls, she found, establish a *relationship* with the computer, using a program as a language with which to communicate. Boys use computer programs to *control* the machine, seeing the system as a set of unforgiving rules. Turkel's explanation for these findings reflects Gilligan's discussion of different voices.

Turkel argues that girls are taught the characteristics of soft mastery through socialization. Negotiation, compromise, and give-and-take are stressed as virtues, both in the toys that girls play with and the games they play. Boys are taught that decisiveness and the imposition of will are virtues. Girls *experience* their programs, imagining themselves to be part of the program. Boys, however, are *outside* their programs, using them to enforce control.

We began this chapter by stating that many choices result from socialization. Day after day, week after week, boys and girls learn to see the world differently. They focus on different aspects of their worlds. As a result, their choices reflect learned differences.

When we remember the differences between boys and girls in the fields they select and their applications of computers, such differences are easily understood as reflective of the differing world views of the two sexes. Mathematics, engineering, science, and statistical applications demand the exercise of formal logic and the imposition of inflexible rules. Faced with the need to select a course of study, young college students think about their possible futures. Young men choose those majors that reflect their learned appreciation for structure, rules, and logic. The humanities, social sciences, and writing stress relationships among individuals, where communication is essential and rules are secondary. Such areas are more desirable to women because they stress activities that girls have been taught to appreciate.

When we asked whether and how boys and girls use computers, we found that girls were less likely to use them and to use them for less structured purposes than were boys. Even when seeking the same outcome as boys, however, girls tended to be soft masters where the boys tended to be hard masters, differences that are wholly reflected in differing world views; one stresses relationships, and the other formal logic and rules.

Computer use, of course, is a small part of an individual's entire education, but the differences seen in computer use illustrate a fundamental difference between boys and girls in their gender. Such a difference can be traced through the entire life course of individuals—in education, jobs, and relationships. Such differences arise quite early, but are continually reinforced throughout life. Socialization is a continuous process that begins at birth and ends at death.

## Conclusion

This chapter began by noting the significant differences between boys and girls in the types of careers they choose, the programs they select in college, and their exposure to computers. We conclude by asking again why such differences exist.

First, such differences are not entirely, or even largely, natural in any biological sense of that word. Although biology may be involved in the differences between males and females that have been discussed in this chapter, its role appears to be secondary to that of socialization.

Second, such differences are not entirely the result of large differences in the *specific training* that boys and girls receive. There are clear differences between boys and girls in their exposure to and use of computers in school. But the similarities in the grade-school training of boys and girls are just as impressive. Both sexes take comparable mathematics and science courses, for example. The specific skills taught in primary and secondary schools are not fundamentally different for boys and girls. Instead, the differences are found in the world views that are imparted in school and elsewhere.

Boys and girls develop strikingly different views of their worlds. Such world views spring from diverse sources—teachers, parents, peers, and the various media. Their lessons, although subtle, are nonetheless consistent. Boys learn to focus on rules, logic, and their mastery. Girls learn to focus on relationships and communication among people. These different world views influence the different choices that males and females make throughout their lives.

Clearly, there is no simple way to eliminate the different choices that boys and girls make. We know, for example, that very few engineers are females. One might be tempted, then, to suggest that girls be encouraged to take more courses that are specifically related to engineering. But that is not the solution. Girls choose fields other than engineering because they see the world in ways that engineering does not. If the goal is to produce more female engineers, it is not enough to teach specific skills. Instead, an entirely different view of the world is required. To produce more female engineers, we must focus not only on what happens in school, but also on events at dinner tables, playgrounds, on television, in magazines, in church, and in movies—that is, in all areas of socialization.

Whether it is desirable to strive to eliminate gender differences in world views is ultimately a question of individual values. Each person must decide whether such a goal is desirable. Undeniably, some gender differences will continue to exist, but the modern workplace mixes males and females together and demands comparable performance from both. In all likelihood, the influx of females into traditionally male domains—as well as the influx of males into traditionally female pursuits—will mean that employers will learn the advantages of a mixed work force, one with people of differing world views, and each one with a valuable contribution to make.

# References

Gilligan, Carol. *In a Different Voice*. 1982. Cambridge, MA: Harvard University Press.

Kohlberg, Lawrence. "Stage and Sequence: The Cognitive Developmental Approach to Socialization," in D. Goslin, Ed., *Handbook of Socialization Theory and Research*, pp. 143–163. 1969. Chicago: Rand McNally.

Linn, Marcia C. "Gender Equity in Computer Learning Environments." *Computers and the Social Sciences* (1): 19–27, 1985.

Tobias, Sheila. *Overcoming Math Anxiety.* 1978. New York: Norton.

Turkel, Shery. *The Second Self.* 1984. New York: Simon and Schuster.

U.S. Bureau of the Census. "Computer Use in the United States," CPR series P–23, #155. 1984. Washington, DC: U.S. Government Printing Office.

U.S. Department of Education, Center for Educational Statistics. "High School and Beyond," 1982 survey. Washington, DC: U.S. Government Printing Office.

U.S. Department of Education, Center for Educational Statistics. "High School and Beyond," 1986 survey. Washington, DC: U.S. Government Printing Office.

U.S. Department of Education, Center for Educational Statistics. *Digest of Educational Statistics.* 1987. Washington, DC: U.S. Government Printing Office.

U.S. Department of Education, Center for Educational Statistics. *Digest of Educational Statistics.* 1988. Washington, DC: U.S. Government Printing Office.

Weitzman, Lenore J. *Sex Role Socialization.* 1979. Palo Alto, CA: Mayfield.

## Suggested Readings

Gilligan, Carol. *In a Different Voice.* A psychologist argues that males and females interpret reality and morality differently. Females stress relationships, while males stress rules and hierarchies in their respective understandings of the world.

Turkel, Shery. *The Second Self.* A sociologist analyzes the role of computers in shaping how we think about the world.

CHAPTER 3

# Organizations

## Entrepreneurs and
## Bureaucracy Bashing

**E**ntrepreneurs are hot—innovative business people commanding respect, envy, and fascination. Entrepreneurs have even been hailed as modern-day economic saviors, bringing prosperity to all of us as they make their own fortunes.

Before the 1980s, media coverage of business was confined to dutiful reports of economic indicators ("The GNP rose . . ."). The inside world of business drew little attention. A world of meetings, memos, and money pursued by faceless men in grey flannel suits seemed much too dry. But now entrepreneurs such as the following are featured on the covers of national magazines:

*Steven Jobs,* the founder of Apple Computer. A college dropout who was more comfortable in jeans than in a suit at the office, this visionary organized the creative talents of many young technical minds, only to lose control during a corporate struggle. Jobs is viewed as the model for all entrepreneurs in California's "Silicon Valley," the home of much of the U.S. computer industry.

*H. Ross Perot,* the founder of Electronic Data Systems (EDS), one-time controversial director of General Motors (GM), and swashbuckling rescuer of hostages in Iran. An IBM dropout, Perot launched EDS with $1,000, then sold it to GM for $2.5 billion.

*T. Boone Pickens,* down-home corporate raider. He used his Texas oil money to fund corporate take-overs and threatened take-overs, amassing a fortune in all the stock

Reuters/Bettmann Newsphotos

Entrepreneur Steven Jobs launches his latest
innovation—the NeXT, a computer featuring optical
disk and vocal synthesizer technology. Jobs is the most
famous example of the brash, young entrepreneurs
who made fortunes in California's "Silicon Valley" by
developing computer-related technology.

trading. Along with other raiders such as Carl Icahn, Pickens has threatened the security of executives at many large corporations.

The entrepreneurial bandwagon is rolling. Would-be entrepreneurs can turn to new specialized magazines that glorify their role and offer practical advice. Television specials look at the contributions of entrepreneurs to U.S. progress with hardly a critical second thought. And universities, increasingly attuned to what is hot, have new course offerings, even whole centers, that are devoted to entrepreneurial studies.

In keeping with this cheerleading spirit, David Lambro (1986) writes, "a new kind of hero has emerged for our time, the entrepreneur, whose national and international appeal offers greater promise for a healthier, happier, and more prosperous society for us all."

Along with this enthusiasm for the entrepreneur have come increasingly sharp attacks on the corporate manager and the large corporation, particularly its "bureaucratic" ways. For example, in *The Spirit of Enterprise* (1984), George Gilder gives the charge full force: "Among the legions of lawyers, financiers, bureaucrats, and masters of business strutting into the American economy from the nation's leading schools, nothing has been so rare in recent years as an Ivy League graduate who has made a significant innovation in American enterprise."

What the United States needs, in this view, are the following changes:

- more entrepreneurs and fewer managers, who are portrayed as rule-bound paper-pushers

- more daring and less bureaucracy, which is characterized as inefficient hierarchies plagued by red tape and in-fighting

- more innovation and fewer big corporate businesses, which are seen as stodgy behemoths unresponsive to a changing environment.

The glorification of entrepreneurs captures our sociological attention because it implicitly advances a theory about what makes economic organizations effective. The "great man" and the unstructured organization are key elements of this theory. We will argue, however, that this theory is at best incomplete and often wrong. Before making this case, we will first clarify what we mean by the term "entrepreneur" and consider why this figure currently enjoys such approval.

## Defining the Species

What makes a person an entrepreneur? For all the currency of the term, its meaning has little precision. This is true in everyday conversation as much as in academic discussion.

Neither the vice president in charge of claims at an insurance company nor the owner of a local hardware store is likely to be called an entrepreneur. Each of these businessmen may be shrewd, hardworking, and highly paid, but those are not enough. Rather, entrepreneurs are economic innovators, businesspeople who see new possibilities or new ways of doing things and put these ideas into action.[1] Entrepreneurs are not distinguished by their affiliation with any particular type of business (small or large, high- or low-technology, profitable or not), and they do not necessarily hold any particular title within a business organization. Businesspeople are entrepreneurial to the extent that they break routine—that is, introduce a new good, develop a new method of production, discover a new market, locate a new source of materials, or organize operations in a new and more efficient way.

Entrepreneurs are necessarily leaders, people who are able to translate ideas into practical action that will work in the economic marketplace. For this reason, an entrepreneur usually owns and personally directs his or her own business rather than running someone else's as a hired manager. Ownership allows the innovator to say, "This is my show, and here's how we're going to do it."

On the other hand, the corporate manager (who is, in actuality, only a highly paid employee of the stockholders) can be intensely entrepreneurial. Perhaps the most noted "corporate entrepreneur" in our business history is Alfred Sloan, the man who forged many small manufacturers into General Motors, an organizational colossus. He was also a mass marketing innovator par excellence.

The very size of large corporations, however, means that recognizable entrepreneurs generally are unlikely to emerge from within their ranks. An entire corporation, or even a division within it, may have a record of innovation, but these efforts usually cannot be attributed to the actions of a single individual. Innovations within large corporations often result from collective efforts, a point we will elaborate on later. And even when a new idea is the brainchild of an individual, it is absorbed by the larger organizational structure during its implementation.

In short, the entrepreneur is generally not a large corporate animal, although some corporate executives certainly have entrepreneurial qualities and some corporations have an organizational commitment to innovation. Even if the definition of the species is still imprecise, public attention focuses on innovators who direct their own companies. As we think sociologically about our economic future, these people and their organizations deserve special attention.

---

[1]   Our definition here follows the classic statement by economist Joseph Schumpeter; more than any other scholar, he brought attention to the role of the entrepreneur in capitalist development.

# Misplaced Individualism

Entrepreneurs are not new to the U.S. business scene, of course. Neither is admiration for their ingenuity and success. Our business history is replete with accounts of their exploits. Thomas Edison, Henry Ford, John D. Rockefeller, and Andrew Carnegie are all familiar figures who did much to shape our nation's economy.

They are "ultimate" Americans. More accurately, they personify the characteristics that Americans like to see in themselves: daring, hardworking, imaginative, and successful. These are "can-do" types, rugged individualists, even mavericks.

In the late 1970s and early 1980s, the U.S. economy was beset by high inflation and recession. With these economic troubles, many Americans had lost confidence in our institutions, a point dramatized by President Carter's pronouncement on television that the nation suffered from a "malaise." Searching for a way out of this crisis, Americans sought answers in their traditional ideals, in a return to what they believed had created earlier success. The idea of entrepreneurial rejuvenation fit the cultural mood. Entrepreneurs promised to make things right again, not only rejuvenating the economy, but also doing so in the traditional "American Way"—by hardworking *individual* effort. As Roger Kaplan has written in the *Harvard Business Review* (1987), "entrepreneurial zeal [became] a kind of moral therapy."

The celebration of the entrepreneur is rooted, then, in American individualism. But while understanding the appeal of men such as Jobs or Perot, we should still ask whether individual efforts at innovation promise economic renaissance.

Underlying this celebration is a sociological theory about economic change that is much like the Great Man theory in history, which holds that the main ebbs and flows of civilizations reflect the actions of a few decisive individuals. To understand modern Russia, one must understand what Lenin and Stalin did. Similarly, the force of Gandhi's personality is key to understanding the complexity of modern India. Few historians, however, advance such a theory in a pure and unqualified way. But popular accounts of historical and contemporary events tend to overemphasize the role of a few prominent individual personalities. They neglect to see how individual actions were shaped by social forces and vitally depended on what so many other people did. This is so as much in business as in other realms of life.

Thomas Edison, every American learns, brought the convenience of electricity to our lives. Often overlooked, however, is that his inventions transformed life because an existing industrial and governmental structure created a demand for these inventions and a means to promote them. Faceless technicians made the necessary practical applications, and countless managers created huge organizations that were capable of delivering the energy. Not to deny Edison's particular genius, as sociologists we would say that the context was ripe for an Edison to emerge and that his own success depended on this context.

Seeing contemporary economic innovation in such a sociological light is even more important. The key to success is not individual genius but the translation of ideas into marketable products by coordinated *groups*.

As Robert Reich has documented (1987), Americans have led the way in developing many of the "big ideas" for modern technology: videocassette recorders, basic oxygen furnaces, microwave ovens, integrated circuits, and computerized machine tools. The list goes on and on, indicating no shortage of creative Americans. On the other hand, other nations have turned our big ideas into their own big profit, often better than we have.

As we have painfully learned, the road between an initial innovation and production, especially production that responds to evolving demands, is long. Great "breakthroughs" that by themselves can sustain a company are rare. Ideas travel quickly and are easy to borrow. Companies remain competitive only if they can continuously refine the products from their breakthroughs. This is often a matter of small steps, advances building on advances; for example, adding remote controls, stereo sound, split-screen capabilities, and so on, to the videocassette recorder.

The agents of these incremental innovations are workers at various levels of organizations. Companies are successful in this high-technology economy to the extent that they *collectively innovate;* that is, a successful company encourages employees throughout the firm to work together to refine products, seek new uses for existing technology, and extend the capacities of those technologies that are currently in use. The task of developing and managing all the related refinements in products and services is simply beyond the capacities of a few great leaders, no matter how visionary or energetic they might be.

Robert Reich (1987) is right when he argues that we need to celebrate the "team as hero," not the lone innovator or the star chief executive officer (CEO). We must recognize and promote the organizational team as the source of key innovations in a high-technology economy. At the same time, we need to go beyond bureaucracy bashing when analyzing the organizational obstacles to innovation.

## Two Cheers for Bureaucracy

Bureaucracy is a dirty word—not four-letter, but dirty all the same. In exasperated tones, people often say something such as, "That's bureaucracy for you." Usually they mean that an organization is inefficient, inflexible, difficult to deal with, or just inhumanly cold. And to call someone a "bureaucrat" is to question a person's initiative, imagination, and human feeling.

Bureaucrats are drones, paper pushers, rule mongers—the very opposites of the high-voltage, risk-taking, convention-breaking entrepreneurs. In searching for a remedy for the ills of American business, then, many people call for a personality transfusion: Take bureaucrats out and put entrepreneurs in. The latter will "save" us from bureaucracy and its red tape and inertia.

Do we really want to rid ourselves of bureaucracy? To answer this question, we must first see what distinguishes it from other forms of organization.

Following the lead of Max Weber, sociologists identify the following elements as common to all bureaucracies:

- *Hierarchy of authority.* Positions are fixed in a hierarchy, with those at the top directing those below through a clear chain of command.

- *Specialization of labor.* Workers handle particular tasks for which they are specifically trained, and a defined division of labor establishes responsibilities for each position.

- *Rules and regulations.* Formal statements set out job responsibilities, work procedures, promotional criteria, and other policies. The "right" way is what the rule book says.

- *Extensive records.* Bureaucracies are systematically committed to documenting what they have done and are doing, thus the reams of files, reports, and data bases.

- *Universalistic standards.* Workers are evaluated on their job-related performance—what they do, not who they know or what they are (for example, a white male). Deviations from this ideal occur, of course, but formal procedures guarantee that the commitment to rewarding merit has real backing.

Now think where we would be if we had organizations that:

- could not commit their full energies in a particular direction because no one individual or group had the right to tell another what to do;

- assigned people to tasks for which they were untrained (computer programmer today, advertising director tomorrow);

- allowed each worker to decide what her responsibilities were ("It's not my job") or how to complete a task ("I didn't feel like checking their credit rating");

- could not find any evidence of having provided a billable service or had no record of current inventories; and

■ promoted the manager's cousin, a college drop out, to the head of finance, over the MBA who had ten years of experience.

These organizations would be thoroughly *non*bureaucratic, and our society would be a mess. In no time at all we would be clamoring for the efficiency, reliability, predictability, and fairness of bureaucracies! Indeed, many of our complaints about bureaucracies are actually complaints that the organization is not bureaucratic enough: The boss promotes his do-nothing cronies or clerks ignore the policy that all customer complaints are to be reported to the manager.

Still, it is possible to argue that bureaucracy can be taken "too far." Although there is some truth in this view, many of the alleged bureaucratic "extremes" remain misunderstood. This is seen most often perhaps in the attack on rules, the source of bureaucratic red tape.

In their best-selling "how-to" book *In Search of Excellence,* Thomas Peters and Robert Waterman (1982) extoll the entrepreneurial zeal of one CEO who directed his company to throw out its policies and procedures manual. This abandonment of rules supposedly would create a "bias for action"—a freedom from constraints and a willingness to innovate.

Dramatic, yes, but grossly inefficient. This CEO and these management consultants overlook the fact that all large organizations require "rules"—commonly accepted understandings of how others will act in specific situations. These rules can be formal, written statements or informal, but unless they exist, groups cannot accomplish collective tasks. Workers need to be able to count on what others will do. Uncertainty is paralyzing.

In a nonbureaucratic organization, workers can informally meet and personally negotiate acceptable procedures. The process, however, is time-consuming, and the resolutions apply only to those workers who are involved in the negotiations. Written rules speed up business life, have force even when workers do not personally get along, and live on after specific workers leave their jobs.

Perhaps most paradoxically, written rules expand the realm of freedom, the ability to innovate—to act entrepreneurially. By knowing clearly what is all right to do or not to do, innovative employees can forge ahead without fear of breaking implicit rules. They can act with confidence within the guidelines established by written policies. "Good" rules leave room for discretion on matters that can improve organizational efficiency.

This last point is well argued by Wilfred Brown, himself a successful manager (see "Rules and Initiative").

The problems that face the potentially innovative employee in a bureaucracy are not generally caused by an excess of rules. More typically, the problems result from the presence of a few bad rules or the absence of appropriate rules.

# Rules and Initiative

**M**any managers feel that "freedom" lies in the sort of situation where their supervisor says to them: "There are not many regulations in this place. You will understand the job in a month or two, and you make your own decisions. No red tape—you are expected to take command; make the decisions off your own bat as they arise. I am against a lot of rules or regulations, and we do not commit too much to paper." In my experience a manager in such a situation has virtually no "freedom to act" at all. He starts making decisions and his boss sends for him to say: "Look here, Jones, I am sorry to tell you that you have made two rather serious mistakes in the course of reorganizing your work. You have promoted one man to supervisor who is not the next man due for promotion in the factory, and you have engaged five additional machinists, a decision you should have referred to me because we have some surplus men in this category in an adjacent factory." Now Jones might well say: "You said there were no regulations but, in fact, you have already mentioned the existence of two. . . . Please detail these regulations to me precisely, so that I can work to them in the future. . . ."

In practice, Jones probably says nothing of the kind, because he does not think in this way; to him regulations are stumbling blocks in the path of those wishing to display initiative. He will proceed, over the years, to learn, by making mistakes, of the whole array of regulations which, by the very nature of Executive Systems, do in fact exist. . . . Jones is thus in a situation where he does not know what decisions he can or cannot make, and when in doubt he is likely to follow a course of doing nothing at all. . . .

It is much more efficient to delineate as precisely as possible to a new subordinate all of the regulations he must observe and then say: "You must take all the decisions that seem to you to be required, so long as you keep within the bounds of that policy. If, keeping within those bounds, you take decisions which I think you should have referred to me, then I cannot criticize. . . ."

In fact, it is only by delineating the area of "freedom" in this way that a subordinate knows when he can make decisions. . . .

Source: Brown, Wilfred. *Exploration in Management.* 1960. New York: Wiley. Pp. 97–98.

We might also add that the rule-bound structure of bureaucracies does *not* seem to create the stereotyped bureaucratic personality, a timid "overconformer" who slavishly follows rules for their own sake. Certainly we have all encountered workers in bureaucracies who fit this description. They simply tell us "That's policy," without questioning the sense of the policy or showing any interest in addressing the problem. In several sophisticated studies, however, sociologist Melvin Kohn (1971) has undermined the accuracy of the stereotype.

Kohn has found that when compared to other types of workers, bureaucrats are slightly *more* intellectually flexible, open to new experiences, innovative, and morally self-directed. This research does not mean that all or even most bureaucrats have the vision and fire of entrepreneurial superstars. At minimum, however, it does indicate that extreme negative views of bureaucrats are exaggerated and that innovation can be welcomed in bureaucracies.

So why do we give only two cheers for bureaucracy, not the full chorus of three?

As we suggested, many companies have taken certain bureaucratic tendencies too far. The extreme division of labor and the resulting isolations of levels and departments can be counterproductive. Everyone may know his or her own task but not be able to see the forest for the trees. The tendency is to push parts of problems onto someone else; no one has the incentive or ability to see whole issues and to work together to resolve them.

A steeply sloped pyramid of authority can create further problems. Too often, even though they are close to specific problems and know best how to solve them, lower level workers lack the authority to make the necessary changes. Those at the top of the pyramid hold tightly to their prerogatives to make decisions, although others could do better if given the chance.

By denying power to lower level workers, bureaucracies undermine their initiative. A predictably common reaction is, "Why bother? No one listens anyway." When workers do not feel that a decision is theirs, their commitment—a vital component in the success of many business projects—can be harder to motivate.

We agree with sociologist Rosabeth Kanter's recommendations (1983) that the typical corporate bureaucracy be reformed to reduce the segmentation of work and the concentration of power at the top. This means creating special work teams to handle projects, developing new avenues for "upward" and "sideways" career moves, and increasing the discretion of employees at all levels. Above all, it means granting power to more people so that they have the means and incentive to innovate.

In this way, entrepreneurial orientations can be incorporated *within* the bureaucratic organization. (Many organizational analysts have taken to calling this orientation *intra*preneurship to indicate that innovation is internal.) These recommendations are distinctly sociological. Innovation does not depend on the infusion of new personality types (those who have some innate entrepreneurial spirit). The restructuring of organizational form to foster the innovative potential of many workers is essential. The goal should be to infuse an entrepreneurial spirit within bureaucracies, not to abolish them or hold faith in the alleged virtues of a few great men.

## Organizational Size

Along with the celebration of the entrepreneur has come an attack on bigness. Entrepreneurs are daring and nimble, guiding their *small* companies across the business battlefield, seizing new opportunities, outmaneuvering their competitors, decisively acting on their gut instincts as to the right move. The small firm thus is seen as the ideal vehicle for entrepreneurs to translate their ideas into action; they are responsive, maneuverable, and directly subject to personal command and vision.

These virtues are lacking, it is often now alleged, in the large corporation, which is portrayed as a lumbering dinosaur unadapted to the turbulent and changing business environment. It cannot gear up to move decisively, and cannot change directions when needed. It is simply too big for any one leader to control. Ideas lose force and energy as they spread through layer after layer and division after division. The result is organizational inertia.

Indeed, some management specialists have even predicted the extinction of large corporations in the forseeable future, doomed by the requirements of a high-technology economy. Although huge productions of standardized goods such as household appliances and textiles dominated the past, economic success now has become ever more dependent on the rapid development and promotion of new ideas and their related products. According to this view, the small firm is more adapted to the new environment, while the large corporation is tied to declining economic forces.

We think, however, that those who promote the "small is beautiful and big is bad" line have overstated their argument. Yes, we recognize the success of Steven Jobs and other technological wizards in the computer industry, and we also can easily imagine that small firms can maneuver more quickly than large firms. But it is highly arguable that small organizations are inherently superior to larger ones and that large organizations have become technologically obsolete.

Our point is that both big and small can be beautiful (and both can be ugly!). One need not choose between them but instead recognize the distinctive and complementary virtues of each.

The limits and strengths of small organizations become dramatically clear as we consider the computer and computer-related industries. These industries exemplify the high-technology world and have been the launching pad for many fabulously successful entrepreneurial careers.

Out of garages and small shops, young American engineers—some corporate dropouts—made technological advances on shoestring budgets. In feverish competition with each other, these engineers moved into uncharted technological territory. Although unconstrained by corporate red tape, they were also often unsophisticated about the business strategies of marketing and finance. Many failed from the start, and others succeeded briefly only to be passed by others; a few, such as Apple Computer, sustained their success.

Perhaps this daring and imagination is unlikely to be matched within a large bureaucratic organization where people jealously guard their own turf and resist changes that challenge their authority. One virtue of smallness is that the innovator is free from the organizational constraints that stifle creativity, and innovation is obviously important for continued economic success.

These small firms, however, have been good primarily at developing the pioneer models of new technologies. They have been less successful in producing and promoting refined products that are suitable for wide use or in moving from one generation of a technology to the next. Moreover, large firms have made computer technology widely accessible, and their laboratories account for many advanced technologies.

Although inherently flexible, small firms cannot take advantage of *economies of scale*. In many industrial processes, when inputs such as materials, equipment, and labor are increased, the outputs can increase by an even greater amount. Thus, a large elaborate production process that is designed to turn out huge numbers of microchips, for example, can produce a chip at a lower *unit cost* than can a smaller operation. A machine operator can set controls for $x$ chips in the same time as $10x$ chips, thereby reducing the labor costs for each chip.

Small firms also cannot take advantage of *concentrated resources*. Some ventures simply require large and immediate expenditures to be successful—for example, the huge expenses of research and development programs or the implementation of sophisticated marketing and distribution systems. Large firms can much more readily afford these initiatives than can small firms.

These advantages of large firms are more than just theoretical considerations. One recent estimate suggests that from 1974 to 1984 the minimally efficient plant scale for the production of semiconductors rose from approximately $25 million to at least $200 million, an investment that only large companies can make. Indeed, if we look at who is succeeding in the semiconductor industry, we see the emerging winners to be large Japanese companies. Since 1980, the world market share of computer chips held by U.S. companies has dropped from 60 percent to 40 percent. In the same time, Japanese firms have doubled their share to almost half.

Six Japanese firms are responsible for this success in semiconductors, and the same six dominate Japanese computer, telecommunications equipment, and consumer electronics production. Thus, as many Americans idealize the virtues of smallness, our main economic competitor draws on its large companies to compete successfully in the international marketplace.

In organizational structure, these Japanese firms are almost fully *vertically integrated.* That is, within its own organization, the firm incorporates divisions that produce all the necessary supplies to create a finished product as well as to market and distribute it. In this way, they remove themselves from dependence on suppliers and can develop integrated product lines that work well with each other. Smaller U.S. companies cannot offer this latter advantage, a fact that hinders their competitiveness.

Small "start-up" firms will still be able to exploit new markets in computer-related industries. They can draw on low-cost small computers and electronic control systems to create products that fill niches in the information technology sector. But they can do this only because they can use products such as semiconductors, personal computers, and software that are mass produced cheaply by large companies. The continuing vitality of many small high-technology firms, then, requires the success of large firms.

Their critics have been right in claiming that many large companies have been slow to innovate. This point is dramatically made clear as U.S. firms lose their market shares in many industries, including high technology, to foreign competitors. (Their response often has been to seek government protection to ease their troubles.) This poor performance, however, does not mean that bigness is inherently bad or technologically obsolete.

The conclusion instead should be that many large U.S. businesses have been bad performers. They have not effectively capitalized on the potential organizational virtues of large size. The contrast with Japanese firms is telling.

Nevertheless, in the forseeable future, large companies will continue to play a prominent part in our economy. We need the mass production of standarized goods, and many initiatives require commitments of money and labor that only large organizations can afford. For many economic tasks, bigness is not just a virtue, it is a necessity.

Small companies can complement these efforts by offering personalized services and developing specialized products, often by using or modifying the products of large firms. In markets with narrow, distinctive demands, the virtues of smallness—flexibility and responsiveness—come to the fore. As the demand for services expands and new market niches are created by new technologies, small firms have a promising future.

But the challenge is creating both large and small companies that are committed to quality and innovation. Innovation on either scale can stimulate innovation on the other. The nation's economic health requires that we reap the distinctive benefits of both small and large organizations.

More generally, the challenge is to think organizationally to generate and institutionalize entrepreneurial spirit throughout the economy and the rest of society.

# References

Brown, Wilfred. *Exploration in Management.* 1960. New York: Wiley.

Ferguson, Charles. "Beyond Entrepreneurialism to U.S. Competitiveness." *Harvard Business Review* (66): 55–62, May–June 1988.

Gilder, George. *The Spirit of Enterprise.* 1984. New York: Simon and Schuster.

Kanter, Rosabeth. *The Changemasters: Innovation and Entrepreneurship in the American Corporation.* 1983. New York: Simon and Schuster.

Kaplan, Roger. "Entrepreneurship Reconsidered: The Anti-Management Bias." *Harvard Business Review* (65): 84–89, May–June 1987.

Kohn, Melvin. "Bureaucratic Man: A Portrait and an Interpretation." *American Sociological Review* (36): 461–74, June 1971.

Lambro, David. *Land of Opportunity: The Entrepreneurial Spirit in America.* 1986. Boston: Little, Brown.

Perrow, Charles. *Complex Organizations: A Critical Essay.* 1979. Glenview, IL: Scott, Foresman.

Peters, Thomas, and Robert Waterman. *In Search of Excellence: Lessons from America's Best Run Companies.* 1982. New York: Harper & Row.

Reich, Robert. *Tales of a New America.* 1987. New York: Times Books.

Schumpeter, Joseph. *The Theory of Economic Development.* 1961. New York: Oxford University Press.

# Suggested Readings

Ferguson, Charles. "Beyond Entrepreneurialism to U.S. Competitiveness." This strong defense of large firms and coordinated industrial policy focuses primarily on computer-related industries. The article responds directly to George Gilder's earlier article, "The Revitalization of Everything: The Law of Microcosm," *Harvard Business Review,* March–April 1988, which celebrated the small firm.

Gilder, George. *The Spirit of Enterprise.* This is a spirited advocacy of the entre-preneur, laissez-faire capitalism, and traditional individualism.

Kanter, Rosabeth. *The Changemasters: Innovation and Entrepreneurship in the American Corporation.* Kanter insightfully uses sociological insights to ad-vance a program for corporate reform. Based on fascinating case-study materials.

Perrow, Charles. *Complex Organizations: A Critical Essay.* This is a sophisticated discussion of organizational theory and a powerful argument about the efficiencies and dangers of bureaucracies.

Reich, Robert. *Tales of a New America.* Reich develops the theme "team as hero" and analyzes developments in the contemporary economy.

# CHAPTER 4

# Deviance and Social Control

## Drug Tests and Witch Hunts: The Creation of Social Deviance

**B**y many accounts, drugs are *the* social problem of the United States, the worst problem facing our nation. Drugs undermine our moral values, destroy our children, and make the workplace unsafe. Drugs are responsible for crime, make our nation less competitive than other industrialized nations, and are responsible for the dismal performance of many children and young adults in school. Drugs lead young people to turn against their parents, friends, and teachers and commit suicide. Drugs destroy entire communities, forcing residents to hide behind their own doors in fear. A major cause of many serious psychiatric disorders, drugs destroy the health of young and old alike. They make people squander money that could be used for food, rent, and clothing for their children. Drug use is even partly responsible for the rapid spread of AIDS.

No wonder that our nation has declared a "war" on drugs. Politicians and parents are convinced that drugs are a menace to our very way of life. Moreover, the problem appears to be worsening. Younger and younger people are being lured into drug abuse by criminals whose only motive is greed. Not only are the pushers a threat, but also users—or, more properly,

The Bettmann Archive

In the Salem "witchcraft trials" of 1692, women were condemned to death if they failed a test—for example, if a supposedly "bewitched" girl stopped having "fits" when an accused woman was ordered to touch her, the woman was convicted as a witch. The current emphasis on drugs as Public Enemy Number One is remarkably similar—faulty tests label deviants, and moral uncertainty, not any objective danger, fuels the crisis.

abusers—must share the blame. Even nonusers who express any degree of toleration for "recreational drug use" are condemned as "soft on drugs," contributing to the growing crisis. More lives are ruined by cocaine addiction each year. Elementary school children sneak out from class to puff on marijuana joints. We seem to have an epidemic that threatens our way of life. The sky, it appears, is falling!

Drug use is deviant behavior, and drug users are deviants. So what can be done? How can we combat this deviance? One attempted solution has been the passage of stricter laws that stipulate harsh penalties for the sale or use of drugs. In 1988, for example, the U.S. Congress passed legislation that mandated the death penalty for certain categories of drug offenses.

But laws have not had much effect on drug use in the United States. No matter how strong the law, how harsh the penalty, drugs continue to flow into this country and people continue to use them. So perhaps another solution is needed.

By mid-1988, one-quarter of all Fortune 500 corporations and every branch of the federal government and military had programs to test people for illegal drug use. Such testing requires that individuals provide samples of body fluids (urine or blood) to their employer on demand or risk losing their jobs. The federal program began in September 1986, when President Ronald Reagan issued Executive Order 12564 which called for a drug-free workplace. With the power of federal law, this order required that all government agencies establish programs to test employees for illegal drug use. Drug-testing in the workplace now is a fact of life for millions of Americans, the overwhelming majority of whom approve of the practice.

Drug-testing is also being proposed for high schools and colleges. The Henry P. Becton Regional High School in East Rutherford, New Jersey, announced a policy of mass urinalysis in 1986 to determine whether students used illegal drugs or alcohol. College athletes commonly submit to random drug-tests both during and after their competitive seasons. Although court challenges to such practices continue to be brought, and often won, more often drug testing goes unchallenged and even praised as a way to combat "national enemy number one." Most Americans accept drug testing: "Why should I oppose it? I have nothing to hide. I don't use drugs." We seem willing to accept a fundamental change in our traditional notions of guilt and innocence: With drugs, people are presumed guilty until proved innocent. Drug tests are justified as contributing to the public safety, and several cases of disaster have been attributed to railroad engineers and truck drivers under the influence of drugs.

In this chapter, we consider drug use as deviant behavior. We ask why users of certain substances are called "deviants," while users of other, equally mind-altering drugs are not. We analyze drug testing as a means of *social control*—that is, a way of enforcing certain patterns of acceptable behavior. Why has the United States declared a "war on drugs" and labeled users as deviants? Why have Americans accepted drug tests as a legitimate weapon in this war? Finally, how serious is the national threat posed by drug use?

# Drug Users as Social Deviants

Almost everyone agrees that something about drug users marks them as different. They are not the same as the rest of us. Drug users are deviants. But what makes them deviant?

No one has offered an objective definition of a deviant—that is, what *type* of person a deviant is. No single thing distinguishes the type of person who commits deviant acts from one who does not—not appearance, physical characteristics, mental state, religion, or anything else. Deviants are of all shapes and sizes, races and religions, levels of intelligence, social classes, and occupations.

Nor has anyone been able to objectively define deviant *behavior*. Deviant behaviors share no single common characteristic. The behavior seen today as deviant might be seen tomorrow as acceptable, perhaps even praiseworthy. The behavior punished severely in one society is normal in another: A man who has sex with an unmarried woman in the United States faces no significant legal sanction, but in fundamentalist Muslim countries the behavior is punishable by death.

Further complicating the issue is that deviants do conform to most rules. A person rarely departs entirely from most customary modes of behavior. By defining a person as a deviant, we focus on only a small part out of the larger repertoire of his or her behaviors. It is that small part, however, that *really* matters. Once a person has been defined as deviant, he or she is treated as being wholly different, not just different in one or two respects. This is true just as much with drug use. Everything about the user is suspect. He is no longer viewed as a competent person, regardless of the quality of his work or mind.

To illustrate the problem in defining deviance in any society, imagine that you are a newly arrived foreigner who is trying to learn the rules of this country. You soon discover that using marijuana is punishable by law, but that using beer is not. Addiction to substances such as cocaine or heroin is not only unfortunate, but also illegal and deviant. Addictions to other substances—nicotine and alcohol—hardly evoke collective outrage. Although marijuana and beer have similar physical and psychological consequences, their uses evoke different reactions. Beer is celebrated on television, advertised everywhere, and associated very closely with sports. But marijuana is strictly forbidden. Its possession is illegal, and an athlete who is found to use it will be suspended from competition. How can this be?

Turning to the history of various substances, you discover that things once seen as legitimate and legal—marijuana and opium, for example— no longer are. But other behaviors that were once outlawed or forbidden—the possession and consumption of alcohol and women smoking cigarettes—are now legal and accepted.

Finally, it becomes clear that determinations of deviance are not based on a person's actual behavior. Two persons may use and be affected by the same illegal drugs, but only the one whose drug use is discovered will be termed deviant. Most drug users, however, are not discovered by their actions but by chemical testing.

We can draw several conclusions from this analysis. First, although deviance pertains to only a select portion of a person's behaviors, the label applies to the whole person. Second, deviance cannot be objectively identified, which is particularly the case with drug use. Identical behaviors may have different consequences depending on their cause (for example, beer, wine, cocaine, or marijuana). Third, nothing about a particular substance makes its use deviant. Addictive and intoxicating substances are advertised and distributed legally in the United States— tobacco and alcohol, for example. Fourth, problematic behaviors usually do not get drug users in trouble; generally, their failure to hide drug use from authorities is the cause. Finally, the actual danger that a drug poses to both an individual and a society has little to do with the sanctions associated with its use. Relatively safe drugs that have minor physical or psychological effects are banned while more powerful and destructive ones are condoned or at least tolerated. These observations lead naturally to one question: What makes the use of certain substances deviant?

# Why Are Certain Substances Illegal?

## The "Social Menace" Explanation

This explanation holds that only certain mind-altering substances are illegal because they are the only truly threatening substances to individuals or society. According to this argument, marijuana is prohibited but alcohol is not because marijuana poses the more serious threat.

This explanation, however, makes little sense. Marijuana is not the social problem that alcohol has been. Scientific evidence (President's Commission on Mental Health, 1978, for example) as well as casual observation support this conclusion. Marijuana is not as intoxicating and does not produce the same degree of physical injury that alcohol does. People do not lose consciousness from smoking marijuana while "passing out" is a common and serious consequence of alcohol poisoning. The damage to lungs from marijuana smoke, although serious, is less than that from tobacco. By contrast, alcohol damage is pervasive, causing irreversible damage to the brain and other organs.

Other societies that are similar to ours—Holland, for example—have decriminalized marijuana and have managed just fine.

## The "Stepping Stone" Argument

Mild mind-altering drugs such as marijuana are widely believed to lead to the use and abuse of more serious and destructive substances, acting as a "stepping stone." The person who smokes marijuana is alleged to be more likely to turn to cocaine or heroin than one who has never used it. Indeed, any type of drug might serve as an introduction to more deleterious substances.

This argument, however, provides no strong evidence of being either true or false. Many drug addicts have admitted using marijuana before heroin, for example. But the more legitimate question is not "How many drug addicts used marijuana before using more serious drugs?" but rather, "How many marijuana users become addicts of more serious drugs?" There is only one acceptable method of demonstrating that X causes Y. Those *exposed* to X must be compared to those *not exposed* to X. If everything else about these individuals is the same, except that some have and others have not experienced X, then differences in the appearance of Y may be attributed to X. Thus, if people who have smoked marijuana are compared to those who have not, and the former are found to be more likely to go on to other drugs than the latter, it is logical to assert that marijuana led to the use of other drugs (if we assume, also, that marijuana users and nonusers are alike on all other factors). To find that a large percentage of heroin users smoked marijuana says absolutely nothing about whether marijuana leads to heroin use, because it is possible that an equally high percentage of nonusers of heroin smoked marijuana. In short, there must be a "control group" to which an "experimental group" is compared in order to establish a cause-effect relationship. Because marijuana use is presumed to be the proximate cause of more serious drug abuse, we must ask, "What percentage of people who once used marijuana are addicts?" not, "What percentage of addicts once used marijuana?"

National surveys that have followed high school seniors for nine years after graduation have revealed that drug use diminishes after high school. Students who used drugs in high school or college decrease their use over time. For example, approximately one-third of high school seniors in 1978 admitted smoking marijuana in the previous thirty days, but only one-fifth reported such use nine years later (National Institute on Drug Abuse [NIDA], 1987, Figure 42b). Indeed, use of almost all types of drugs is greatest among high school and college youths and declines thereafter (NIDA, 1987, Figure 39). The exceptions to this rule are cigarettes and alcohol, which do not drop off with time. If marijuana use led to more serious drug abuse, one would expect to find usage *increasing* with time or at least remaining constant, not decreasing as it does.

One drug, however, is indisputably linked to the use of illicit drugs. Discussing high school seniors in 1986, NIDA noted:

> Of the pack-a-day cigarette smokers, 95% have used an illicit drug and 81% have used an illicit drug other than marijuana. Two-thirds (67%) of the pack-a-day smokers were actively using illicit drugs (in the prior thirty days) versus only 10% of those who never smoked. Current marijuana use was eight times as high among pack-a-day smokers as nonsmokers, and daily marijuana use 20 times as high. Daily use of some illicit drug other than marijuana is 13 times as high (NIDA, 1987, p. 249).

Because most regular smokers began smoking on a frequent basis in junior high school (NIDA, 1987, p. 248), when daily use of illicit drugs is low—cigarette smoking would appear to lead to illicit drug use. The other possibility is that some third factor leads young people both to smoke and to use illicit drugs. But no one has called for urine tests to determine whether students have been smoking cigarettes even though such tests might help prevent the later use of illicit drugs. Because the greater majority of young, regular smokers go on to use illicit drugs, knowing whether someone is such a smoker would permit school officials to intervene and possibly prevent subsequent drug use. There have been no calls for such a program in the United States, even though the federal agency charged with preventing drug abuse—NIDA—has made its findings on cigarette smoking available to the public for several years.

## The "Growing Problem" Explanation

According to this argument, the recent war on drugs results from drug use as a "growing problem." It makes sense that a society would forbid those forms of deviance that it views as growing threats. According to this explanation, a certain amount of deviance is tolerable as long as it does not become a serious threat to social order. Every state in this country, for example, has a law forbidding homosexuality. Sodomy laws, however, are rarely enforced because the "problem" is not viewed as a menace to society.

Undeniably, Americans view drug use as a growing problem. National surveys in the late 1980s have consistently revealed that most people view the "drug problem" as a serious, if not the most serious, threat to our way of life and national security.

The evidence concerning drug use, however, presents a different picture. Understandably, it is difficult to measure the use of illegal drugs. Few individuals volunteer information about their illegal activities. But anonymous questionnaires distributed to large national samples of high school students and young adults every year since 1975 present probably the best evidence we have on drug use in the United States. Conducted by the University of Michigan's Institute for Social Research, these studies are funded by NIDA. To the extent that self-reports on drug use are in error, they probably underreport. But the researchers who conduct these studies have concluded that such underreporting is consistent from year to year. Although the precise percentages of users may be higher than these studies reveal, the trends noted year to year are valid.

Figure 4.1 shows self-reported drug use for the 15,000 to 16,000 high school seniors who have been sampled around the country since 1975. The number over the bar for each year indicates the percentages of students who used any illegal drug and those who used marijuana

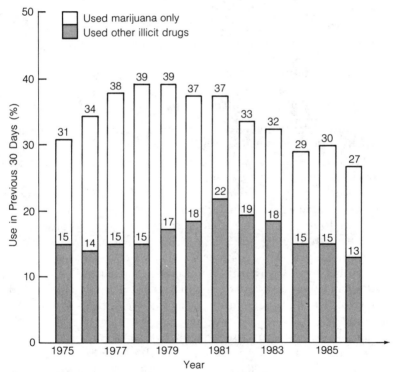

NOTE: "Other illicit drugs" include hallucinogens, cocaine, heroin, other opiates, stimulants, sedatives, or tranquilizers.

**Figure 4.1** Trends in 30-Day Prevalence of Illicit Drug Use, 1975–1986 (all seniors) *Source: Adapted from National Institute on Drug Abuse. "National Trends in Drug Use and Related Factors among American High School Students and Young Adults, 1975–1986," p. 38.*

only in the previous 30 days. In 1975, for example, 31 percent of high school seniors admitted to using an illicit drug in the preceding 30 days. Of these, one-half (15 percent) had used marijuana only. As the figure shows, illicit drug use has declined since 1979. Many drugs are included in these statistics, but NIDA has noted that the use of all illicit drugs except cocaine has declined. From 1979 to 1984, cocaine use leveled off, neither increasing nor decreasing. But since that period, cocaine usage has seen a modest increase, attributable largely to the availability of "crack," a form of cocaine that can be smoked.

A brief comment about measuring drug use is in order. NIDA asks respondents to report whether they have "ever used" an illicit drug, whether they have used such a drug "in the past 30 days," "in the past year," and whether they use any drug "almost daily." Depending on the measure used, a different set of percentages results. Consider those who report the use of marijuana, the illicit drug used most often in the United States:

| High School Class of 1986 | Usage (%) |
|---|---|
| Ever used marijuana? | 50.9 |
| Used in past 12 months? | 38.8 |
| Used in last 30 days? | 23.4 |
| Used daily in last 30 days? | 4.0 |

Obviously, a large percentage of people try illicit drugs at some point in their lives. Few, however, are daily users. Of the remaining types of usage ("within the last year," "within the last month"), the latter most appropriately suggests some regularity.

The same study has followed students who graduated from high school, both those who enrolled in college and those who did not. NIDA researchers found "very little difference between those enrolled in college versus high school graduates of the same age not enrolled in college, in their annual prevalence of illicit . . . drug use" (NIDA, 1987, p. 203). Students, however, do report somewhat greater use of alcohol but a considerably lower use of cigarettes. Only 13 percent of college students smoke daily, while 30 percent of their noncollege peers smoke (NIDA, 1987, p. 204).

Table 4.1 shows drug use as reported for 1980 through 1986 by college students who were interviewed after graduation from high school. Students were asked whether they had used any of the drugs listed within the previous thirty days.

Quite clearly, no indication of "increasing" drug use is seen. Based on the data presented in this table and other analyses, NIDA has concluded that:

1.  the proportion of college students who use *any* illicit drug dropped steadily from 1980 to 1984; since 1984, however, use has not dropped as rapidly;

2.  the use of illicit drugs *other than marijuana* has declined steadily from 1980 to the present;

3.  the trends since 1980 among those in college tend to parallel both those for the age group as a whole and those for high school seniors.

These cumulative findings led the NIDA researchers to conclude that "for most drugs, there has been a decline in use over the [time interval] studied" (NIDA, 1987, pp. 228–229).

We have all heard or read stories about railroad engineers or truck drivers plowing into other trains or automobiles or ignoring warning signals and causing death and injury because they were stoned on marijuana or high on cocaine. On March 7, 1988, *U.S. News and World Report* ran an article reporting that "After an Amtrak train hit a maintenance vehicle in Pennsylvania in January, injuring 25, tests showed a switch operator had used marijuana, cocaine, and amphetamines. In the most serious mishap, 16 passengers were killed when an Amtrak train plowed

---

**Table 4.1**  Trends in 30-Day Prevalence of
12 Types of Drugs
(College students 1–4 years beyond high school)

| | Use in previous 30 days (%) | | | | | | |
|---|---|---|---|---|---|---|---|
| | 1980 | 1981 | 1982 | 1983 | 1984 | 1985 | 1986 |
| Marijuana | 34.0 | 33.2 | 26.8 | 26.2 | 23.0 | 23.6 | 22.3 |
| LSD | 1.3 | 1.4 | 1.7 | 0.9 | 0.8 | 0.7 | 1.4 |
| Cocaine | 6.9 | 7.3 | 7.9 | 6.4 | 7.6 | 6.9 | 7.0 |
| Heroin | 0.3 | 0.0 | 0.0 | 0.0 | 0.0 | 0.0 | 0.0 |
| Other opiates[a] | 1.8 | 1.1 | 1.0 | 1.1 | 1.4 | 0.7 | 0.7 |
| Stimulants[a] | 13.4 | 12.3 | NA | NA | NA | NA | NA |
| Sedatives[a] | 3.7 | 3.4 | 2.5 | 1.1 | 1.0 | 0.7 | 0.6 |
| Barbiturates[a] | 0.9 | 0.8 | 0.9 | 0.5 | 0.7 | 0.4 | 0.5 |
| Methaqualone[a] | 3.1 | 3.0 | 1.9 | 0.7 | 0.5 | 0.2 | 0.1 |
| Tranquilizers[a] | 2.0 | 1.4 | 1.4 | 1.1 | 1.2 | 1.4 | 1.8 |
| Alcohol | 81.8 | 81.9 | 82.8 | 80.3 | 79.1 | 80.3 | 79.7 |
| Cigarettes | 25.8 | 25.9 | 24.4 | 24.7 | 21.5 | 22.4 | 22.4 |

[a]Only drug use that was not under a doctor's orders is included here.

NA: Data not available

Source: Adapted from National Institute on Drug Abuse. "National Trends in Drug Use and Related Factors among American High School Students and Young Adults, 1975–1986," p. 207.

into Conrail locomotives that had run through a stop signal. Evidence is mounting that the modern menace of employee drug abuse *threatens to turn train trips into fatal adventures*" [emphasis added]. Undoubtedly, drug use among rail workers is a problem and accidents occur as a result. But the publicity surrounding these particular cases was unusual, an effect of the national war on drugs, which has brought calls for drug testing. Less noticed, the facts surrounding these cases, and which seemed to justify drug testing, were later called into question.

Five months after these railroad disasters, the toxicologist who said that his drug tests had shown evidence of recent marijuana use by the train crew pleaded guilty to falsifying blood analysis reports from train wrecks. Prosecutors showed that claims of *recent* drug use were unsupported. The toxicologist *had* found evidence of marijuana use in the crewmen's urine, but he reported that use as recent (that is, within the previous six hours) and supported his findings as verified by blood analysis. As a result, the U.S. attorneys prosecuting the train conductors never mentioned drug use in their charges. The media, however, still blamed drugs for the disasters (Hoffman, 1987, p. 123).

Given all the evidence, we discover a curious set of contradictions. Just as the United States launched several new wars on drugs, drug use was declining regularly and consistently, according to the very federal agency that is charged with combatting drug use. At the same time that many wanted mandatory drug tests, fewer people were using drugs. Although national surveys showed that drug use was among the biggest concerns to Americans, drug use was lower than it had been for almost a decade. Clearly, drug use is not a growing problem in the United States.

## Deviance Defines Social Boundaries

In contrast to the explanations just discussed, sociologists take a strikingly different view of drugs and deviance. Sociologist Emile Durkheim suggested that crime and deviance perform a needed function for people in a society by drawing them together—that is, by uniting them against a common enemy. A society's declaration that a certain type of behavior is unacceptable defines what people in that society stand for. As Kai Erikson states, "The deviant individual violates rules of conduct which the rest of the community holds in high respect; and when these people come together to express their outrage over the offense and bear witness against the offender, they develop a tighter bond of solidarity than existed earlier" (Erikson, 1966, p. 4).

Any society, no matter its size, is more than a collection of individuals: It is a *moral community*, a group of people who share certain values about right and wrong, good and bad, acceptable and unacceptable. Moral communities have collective goals and accepted means of reaching those goals. Members of any group must see themselves in fundamental agreement with the important values espoused by that group. Without such consensus, there is no real community; nothing makes this group different from any random collection of individuals. The moral community is based on shared norms, values, and laws.

A society has not only geographical boundaries, but also *moral boundaries*. These define the limits of acceptable behavior and belief. At some point, people may stray beyond those boundaries and think or act in ways outside the acceptable range. A society then must act to both define clearly and maintain its boundaries. People must know where the boundaries of their community lie and then impart this information to new members.

One method of boundary maintenance is the definition and treatment of deviance. A deviant is one who has acted in ways beyond a community's moral boundaries. When deviants are confronted by the community (for example, when they are arrested or punished), all members can see the line between acceptable and unacceptable behavior—that is, the moral boundaries. Members are then able to describe what makes them special or unique. "*We* do not do that sort of thing!"

That deviance serves this purpose is apparent: Disputes over deviant behavior are almost always given prominent attention. In the past, executions were public. So, too, were whippings, dunkings, and other punishments. Although sentences are no longer carried out in public, they remain a prominent topic for all media.

> A considerable portion of what we call "news" is devoted to reports about deviant behavior and its consequences. . . . Deviant forms of behavior, by marking the outer edges of group life, give the inner structure its special character and thus supply the framework within which the people of the group develop an orderly sense of their own cultural identity (Erikson, 1966, pp. 12–13).

The moral boundaries of any community are continually in flux. New members bring new ideas about what is right or wrong. Attitudes, beliefs and circumstances all change. What worked in the past does not always work in the present. In short, there is a need to continually redefine and establish boundaries. Somehow, people must arrive at a consensus on what is acceptable for members of their community or society.

If we accept that deviance performs this valuable function for a group, we must ask, "In some curious way, does our society actually create deviance?" Are those agencies that are devoted to preventing and punishing deviant behavior somehow producing it? For example, is it possible that the mechanism designed to uncover drug abuse—that is, urine testing—actually creates it? Do urine tests discover drug abuse that does not truly exist in order to force a public discussion about drug use, confronting us with the question of what is and is not acceptable? To answer this question, we must briefly consider the political climate that surrounds drug use in the United States.

## The Political Reality of Drug Use

Consider the following and who might have said it.

> Branding most psychoactive drug users as criminals or mentally disturbed when their behavior has no measurable adverse result is to divert resources to the eradication of a *nonproblem* and to divert attention from those truly suffering from the adverse effects of drug misuse.
>
> To classify all psychoactive drug use as misuse or abuse is the same as equating light or moderate use of alcohol with the problems associated with alcoholism.
>
> [We] recommend that all possible efforts be made legally, medically, and socially to make distinctions between that psychoactive drug use with minimal social costs—experimental, recreational, and circumstantial—and the more dysfunctional intensified and compulsive use patterns.
>
> The social costs of the use of all illicit drugs including heroin, hallucinogens, and cocaine, is far less than either alcohol or tobacco.
>
> [We] believe the most important and immediate goal is to decriminalize personal possession and use of small amounts of marijuana. Public policy consideration should be devoted to the decriminalization of personal possession for private use of small amounts of other psychoactive substances.

Such "radical" proposals and statements appear to be the work of people who are "soft on drugs." Who else would recommend the decriminalization of marijuana and small amounts of other psychoactive drugs? Actually, these conclusions came from the President's Commission on Mental Health, an assembly of experts on the subject of drugs and drug abuse (President's Commission on Mental Health, 1978, pp. 2105, 2110, 2112). These recommendations, however, were made in 1978 for President Jimmy Carter. At that time, the political climate was more lenient toward drugs, stressing the need to distinguish between harmful and "recreational" use and thus calling for the decriminalization of certain drugs. Let us now examine the situation in the late 1980s.

By 1986, the tone of political discourse had changed completely. Gone was any distinction between acceptable and unacceptable drug use: *all* drug use was condemned. The concept of decriminalization had been completely rejected. Indeed, the White House itself called for a policy of "zero tolerance" whereby any amount of illegal substance—even one marijuana seed—would justify arrest of persons and seizure of property by federal agents. The Drug Free America Act of 1986 and the Anti–Drug Abuse Act of 1986, two major pieces of federal legislation, announced the war on drugs. Citing "billions of dollars of lost productivity in the workplace" and "widespread drug use among students, not only in secondary schools, but *increasingly* in elementary schools" [emphasis added], these bills called for "drug testing to create a healthier educational environment and increase productivity" (The Drug Free America Act of 1986) and harsher penalties for those possessing or selling any illicit drug.

What happened between 1978 and 1986 to produce such a shift in official opinion about drug use? Was new medical knowledge made available that indicated new and significant problems from drug use? Had drug use increased significantly? Were there increases in drug-related injuries, deaths, and crimes? The answer to all these questions is, "No." Drug use was decreasing. Crime rates were going down. Fewer than 4,000 Americans have died in any year because of illicit drug use, fewer than those who die each year from accidental drownings (*Statistical Abstract of the United States*, 1987, Table 120) and significantly fewer than die from cigarette smoking or alcoholism. Again, what happened to produce such a large change in the "official" position on drugs?

What changed was the perception of the United States, its role in the world, and the unique position it occupies. In short, the *boundaries* that define who we are became unclear.

Two themes dominated the political scene in the mid- and late 1980s. First came a concern about the declining competitiveness of U.S. business and industry. A huge and growing trade imbalance placed the United States in the embarrassing position as the world's largest debtor nation. Increasingly, U.S. business lost market shares to Japan and other industrialized nations. Even within the United States, automobile and electronics manufacturers could not compete for consumer dollars. More manufacturing moved to less developed nations—Mexico and Central America, among others—where labor costs were lower. And the quality of many U.S.-made goods was universally recognized as poorer than comparable products from other countries, while often being more expensive.

The second theme that came to dominate political discussion was the loss of educational excellence. National commissions routinely condemned our public schools as ineffective. William Bennett, the secretary of education, told Americans in 1987 and 1988 that colleges and universities were "ripping off" students by charging for poor quality instruction. By some estimates, one-quarter of high school students dropped out of school before graduating. Standardized tests showed that American students did not perform as well as students in most other developed nations. High school and college curricula were criticized for having too much "fluff" and lacking sufficient emphasis on such basics as mathematics and science.

These concerns forced Americans, especially politicians, to ask, "What's going on? What's happening to us?" Our economic and educational institutions, which were long the envy of the rest of the world and the core of our society, were seen to be failing. The United States, it seemed, was not what it had once been. It was time to shore up our foundations, or, stated differently, examine our *boundaries.*

# Drug Use as Symbolic of American Problems

The greatness of this nation has been viewed as the result of hard work, commitment and dedication to excellence, the acceptance of responsibility, and adherence to discipline and deferred gratification, what has been commonly called the Protestant Work Ethic. Americans believe that "You don't get something for nothing—no pain, no gain." If our greatness was jeopardized, it was because these traits and values were no longer so dearly held.

Drug use symbolizes the very opposite of these collective beliefs. It symbolizes the rejection of authority through a willingness to break the law, immediate gratification, pleasure before sacrifice, and "something for nothing." Drugs allow euphoria without effort. Drug use's great symbolism has been described by sociologist Troy Duster: "When we hear that someone is addicted to drugs, we seldom think of the physiological problem first. Instead, we conceive of an immoral, weak, psychologically inadequate criminal" (Duster, 1970). Seen in this way, the problems with our economy and in our schools are easily diagnosed: If workers and students do not have the correct values anymore, it must be because they are using drugs. The remedy, therefore, is equally obvious: To cure our economy and schools, we must stop the use of drugs.

We must remember at this point that no hard evidence has ever linked our competitiveness with drug use in the workplace. Similarly, the performance of the entire population of students in America cannot be linked directly to drug use by a minority of students. But that is not important. The war on drugs is a battle against the perceived loss of *moral values*—that is, the values that drugs have come to symbolize, not against the specific behaviors caused by illicit substances. The war on drugs seeks to reestablish moral boundaries. It is not coincidental that a major strategy in our war on drugs is the patrolling of our national borders—our physical boundaries. Congress has authorized the military to patrol our borders in order to interdict drug smuggling. Our focus on physical boundaries is symbolic of a more profound concern about our moral borders.

Central to any war is the identification of the enemy—in this case, the drug user. Because drug users cannot be identified by their deviant behavior, some type of test is required to identify them. Is it not strange that our nation has launched a massive effort to identify those individuals whose actual behaviors are not seen as problematic, whose performance is not obviously deficient? Not at all! We are waging a moral crusade. A person's innermost values and beliefs are rarely obvious to others, but by the logic of this crusade, discovery of illegal drug use reveals much about his or her morals.

## Historical Precedent

In 1692, much the same sort of social experience occurred among the Puritans in Salem village, in the Massachusetts Bay Colony. All around Salem were signs of decadence: England had just revoked the colony's charter, members of the community openly challenged the authority of their ministers, ministers argued that people had turned their backs on God, and Puritans in England had dismissed the experiment in New England as a failure. The Puritans in the New World were losing their identity as a unique religious community.

The threat was not economic competitiveness or educational excellence but loss of religious identity and uniqueness. The Puritans saw themselves as a special people wholeheartedly committed to specific religious principles. When this unique identity was threatened, the culprit was found in the religious realm: Satan must have bewitched the residents of Salem village.

Witchcraft was clearly evident in Salem. Several young girls had come under the influence of a maid from Barbados, who told them stories of voodoo and curses. To the community's horror, these hysterical girls were discovered one day crawling on the ground and barking like dogs. Local doctors concluded that witchcraft was the cause of their behavior. The girls were swept up in the resulting hysteria and named many local people as witches. What followed came to be called the "Salem Witch Hunts."

The Puritans faced the same dilemma that we now face with drug users. One could not tell witches by watching them because nothing about their behavior revealed their deviance. Clearly, tests were required. Those who were accused of witchcraft by the girls were then "tried." The evidence in these trials came not only from the accusations leveled by others, but also from the tests themselves. The Salem girls would attend the trials of each of the accused, where they acted as "bewitched" as they had before, howling like dogs and claiming to see spirits in the courtroom. The judges required each of the accused to touch the girls. If the girls' "fits" ceased, it was "irrefutable evidence" that the accused was indeed a witch, and a death sentence was imposed. The episodes lasted about two years, during which time many villagers were tried and executed. How can such a bizarre event be explained?

Kai Erikson has noted that the witch hunt hysteria occurred when "the sense of mission which had sustained [the Puritans] no longer existed and the people of the Bay were left with few stable points of reference to help them remember who they were. For a few years, at least, the settlers of Massachusetts were alone in the world, bewildered by the loss of their old destiny but not yet aware of their new one, and during this fateful interval they tried to discover some image of themselves by listening to a chorus of voices which whispered to them from the depths of an invisible wilderness" (1966, pp. 155–159).

## Urine Tests and Witch Hunts

The tests that were used to identify the Salem witches, of course, were shams, providing no evidence of true witchcraft. But what about urine tests? Are they any better? Consider the facts about modern drug tests.

The federal Centers for Disease Control in Atlanta and NIDA both sent urine samples to drug-testing labs throughout the United States to determine their accuracy. On average, one-third of urine samples that contained drug traces were identified as free of drugs—that is, the tests produced "false negatives." More worrisome, however, was that an equally high percentage of "false positive" errors were found: Urine samples that were free of drug traces were found to contain illegal drugs (*U.S. News and World Report,* October 20, 1986).

Even the manufacturer of the most commonly used urine test, the Enzyme-Multiplied Immunoassay Technique (EMIT), has advised against its use for mass screening, acknowledging a 5 percent rate of false-positive errors. And that rate was found with laboratories in which all conditions were controlled (urine temperature, age, and pH). Even higher error rates are possible, according to the manufacturer, when tests are performed in less controlled environments. Depending on whose estimates are believed—the test manufacturer's or the federal government's—when 100 people are tested for drugs, between 5 and 30 will be falsely identified as drug users. To answer a question posed earlier, yes, we are creating deviance where it does not exist. We are identifying as drug users people who do not use drugs. And we are using a test that fails to do what it was designed to do.

## Conclusion

Faced with crises that appear to result from moral decay, we have sought to restore our moral strength. At a time when our uniqueness and mastery are questioned, we seek to rediscover our identity. Drug use has come to symbolize the moral decay that is blamed for our uneasiness. The war on drugs is an attempt to redefine ourselves as a nation. The problem areas of greatest concern during the 1980s were schools and the economy. No wonder that our war on drugs focused on these two areas, with calls for urine testing of students and workers.

The discussions and debates about drug use reveal the moral values that we hold dear. The battle to rid ourselves of illicit drugs is a way of defining what is and is not acceptable. Where are the boundaries of our moral community? Which values are acceptable and which are not? It is neither the use of a substance nor the behavior caused by that substance that bothers people. It is what the use *symbolizes* that troubles us. The drug user seems to reject those values that we hold central to our self-image. By creating deviance and getting tough on its practitioners, we affirm our commitment as a moral community to a set of values and beliefs that we feel are in danger of being lost.

# References

Duster, Troy. *The Legislation of Morality.* 1970. New York: Free Press.

Erikson, Kai T. *Wayward Puritans.* 1966. New York: Wiley.

Hoffman, Abbie. *Steal This Urine Test.* 1987. New York: Penguin Books.

National Institute on Drug Abuse, U.S. Department of Health and Human Services. "National Trends in Drug Use and Related Factors among American High School Students and Young Adults, 1975–1986." Publication (ADM) 87–1535. 1987. Washington, DC: U.S. Government Printing Office.

President's Commission on Mental Health. *Liaison Task Panel on Psychoactive Drug Use/Misuse, vol. IV.* 1978. Washington, DC: U.S. Government Printing Office.

U.S. Congress. *The Drug-Free America Act of 1986.* House Document 99–266. Washington, DC: U.S. Government Printing Office.

# Suggested Readings

Erikson, Kai. *Wayward Puritans.* Sociologist Erikson analyzes the "crime" waves that hit the Massachusetts Bay Colony during the Puritan experiment. He argues that these waves were methods of creating and locating deviance in order to place significant symbolic issues on the agenda for public discussion.

Hoffman, Abbie. *Steal This Urine Test.* A political and social activist presents evidence on the invalidity of urine tests. He argues that America is in a drug hysteria at a time when drug use actually is diminishing.

# CHAPTER 5

# Inequality

## Understanding Contemporary Poverty

THE WASHINGTON POST
FRIDAY, JULY 31, 1987

## Number of Poor Americans At Lowest Level Since 1980

By Spencer Rich
THE WASHINGTON POST

In July 1987, headline news was made when the federal government announced that the poverty rate in the United States had dropped to its lowest level since President Ronald Reagan had taken office. The official rate for the previous year was 13.6 percent, 1.6 percent lower than its peak in 1983. That meant that approximately one in seven Americans was officially poor.

Why was such a small change in the poverty rate such big news? Poverty is a tangible sign that *something* is wrong. But what? Is there something wrong with our attitude? With the way poor Americans are brought up? Or is there something wrong with our economy, legal system, and educational institutions?

Contrary to popular perception, most poor people in the United States are white. Large numbers of families are "officially" poor at some point in their lives, but except in some rural areas, few families remain below the official poverty line for an extended period of time.

# Rising Tide

## The Poverty Rate Falls

The White House could not have been more delighted. A generally vigorous economy, low inflation and a decrease in unemployment helped lift 1.8 million Americans out of poverty last year—or at least out of the category that the Census Bureau defines as poverty, which is annual cash income of less than $10,609 for a family of four. The bureau reported last week that the proportion of needy Americans decreased by nearly a full percentage point, to 14.4%, the first reduction after five years of steady increases. Said Gordon W. Green Jr., assistant chief of the Census Bureau's population division, "The reduction in poverty last year occurred basically for all demographic groups." In a statement from California, Ronald Reagan said, "I believe these numbers are further proof that the greatest enemy of poverty is the free enterprise system." The President,

as ever, was optimistic: "The success of 1984 does not mean the battle against poverty is over; it does mean that America, after a difficult decade, is once again headed in the right direction." The Administration sees the drop as a vindication of Reagan's economic policies and a sign that a rising economic tide has actually lifted all boats, even the ones in danger of sinking.

Democrats, who have maintained that Reagan's budget cuts have increased poverty, did not see the bureau's report as an endorsement of Reaganomics. In a joint statement, Democratic Congressmen Charles B. Rangel of New York and Robert T. Matsui of California noted that the 1984 poverty rate was higher than for any year from 1970 to 1980, that the rate for black children under six increased and that the gap between rich and poor was not getting narrower.

Because Americans pride themselves on their affluence and opportunity, poverty is news. It challenges our ideals and tells us about our society—how things are or are not working. Poverty almost seems "un-American." Although many of us prefer to overlook its harsh reality, poverty cannot be easily ignored. As a dramatic indicator of our nation's welfare, the fact of poverty fairly demands public scrutiny.

Consider President Reagan's response to an earlier reduction in the poverty rate as reported in *Time* magazine. Reading on, however, one notes that other elected officials had markedly different reactions.

Indeed, reasonable people disagree about the nature of the problem and what should be done to alleviate it. Some believe that its solution, even elimination, is possible. Others believe that our society must learn to live with poverty. In large measure, such disagreements reflect differing beliefs about human nature, the role of government, and the meaning of justice.

Even with these fundamental disagreements, everyone seems to agree that our existing policies do not work and should be overhauled. But before we can debate the details of particular programs, we will find it useful to see the underlying issues from a sociological perspective. What exactly is poverty, and what does it tell us about our society? What causes it? What is the debate between liberals and conservatives all about? Will the poor always be with us, as the Bible advises? Or is it possible to reduce or eliminate poverty?

In this chapter, we examine how our society has responded to the question, "What is to be done about the poor?" In one form or another, this question has been asked by virtually every politician, clergyman, philosopher, and national leader—not to mention most taxpayers. Although the answers to this age-old dilemma are debated endlessly, we must recognize that they are often based on specific definitions of who is poor and what accounts for poverty.

## Explaining Poverty

When Americans explain poverty, they often express the belief that the poor are deficient people (see Table 5.1). The poor are incompetent money managers and lazy workers with little talent and are given to immorality and excessive drinking. The popular belief thus attributes poverty to *flawed individual characteristics*, primarily the attitudes of the poor (for example, an unwillingness to work hard), although their abilities also are cited as inadequate. Presumably, then, if people had the right attitudes or abilities, they would not be poor.

A sociological theory underlies these popular beliefs about the causes of poverty. This "flawed character" explanation has been elaborated within sociology as the Culture of Poverty theory. In this view, certain people have become trapped in a subculture, a group life, that emphasizes fatalism, instant gratification, and little control over impulsive behavior. These negative values limit effective participation in the larger society. Because these values are transmitted from parents to children, future generations are destined to remain in the culture of poverty. A distinct class of poor people is thus created.

Many economists also emphasize the individual deficiencies of poor people to explain poverty. The perspective titled the Human Capital theory assumes that people are rewarded for their productivity: The greater one's ability and training, the higher the pay. In this view, poverty results from low individual productivity. The poor lack the skills (what economists refer to as "human capital") that are needed to compete effectively in the labor market.

Although popular explanations emphasize the individual deficiencies of the poor, many Americans also point to failures in the system. As

**Table 5.1**  Reasons for Poverty, 1980

| Reason | Percent of Respondents Indicating Very Important |
|---|---|
| Lack of thrift and proper money management skills | 64 |
| Lack of effort by the poor themselves | 53 |
| Lack of ability and talent | 53 |
| Their background gives them attitudes that keep them from improving their condition | 46 |
| Failure of society to provide good schools for many Americans | 46 |
| Loose morals and drunkenness | 44 |
| Sickness and physical handicaps | 43 |
| Low wages in some businesses and industries | 40 |
| Failure of private industry to provide enough jobs | 35 |
| Prejudice and discrimination against blacks | 31 |
| Being taken advantage of by rich people | 20 |
| Just bad luck | 12 |
| N = 1507 | |

Table 5.1 shows, a large minority of us attributes poverty to low wages, insufficient jobs, and discrimination—factors that cannot be controlled by or blamed on poor people. This "flawed system" perspective reflects another sociological theory.

Unlike the Culture of Poverty theory, *structural theories* emphasize that many people have extremely limited opportunities to move ahead.

In this view, poverty is the product of an economy that consistently fails to generate enough jobs that pay wages above the poverty level. Because many people lack the opportunity to support themselves, there is a large population of poor. Why are certain groups such as rural blacks so disproportionately poor? Structural theories emphasize differences in opportunity. Rural blacks and other disadvantaged groups have less access to good training or high-paying jobs—at least they have fewer chances at them than middle-class whites, for example. This explanation of poverty shifts the focus from the individual to the system's deficiencies.

Later in this chapter, we will evaluate these competing explanations, but first we will consider why the issue of poverty generates so much emotion and why the flawed character explanation is so widely believed.

## American Ideology

Debates about poverty have other purposes, which are perhaps more important than their consequences for the poor. When we think about poverty, we must first isolate its causes. In doing that, we are forced to consider our culture and the way in which "we" do things. Debates about our policies to solve poverty tell us a great deal about how we perceive our world and the people in it. What do we owe our fellow citizens? Are people basically honest? What motivates people to try?

As we discussed, opinions about the poor tend to polarize the debate. The poor are poor because of their deficiencies (the more common view), or because the system made them that way (a less prevalent view). Thus, to discuss poverty is to fix blame, either on the poor or on the American system, the way we run our society.

This nation's attempts to deal with poverty have been guided by both views, which are usually described as "liberal" (often based on structural theories) or "conservative" (often based on flawed characteristics theories). Our thus far limited efforts to reduce poverty reflect the ongoing tension between these political views. In recent decades, we have seen programs aimed at breaking the poverty cycle in " deficient" cultures (for example, Head Start for poor children), removing obstacles to economic mobility through antidiscrimination laws, improving job skills, and providing jobs, either through subsidized private or public employment (sometimes called "workfare"). But with the general sense that poverty is primarily the fault of poor people themselves, public commitment to any of these efforts has been weak and often grudging at best.

These attitudes about poverty—and, more generally, inequality—are rooted in a general *ideology,* a set of beliefs that justify some social arrangement. Simply put, Americans believe that opportunity is plentiful, and that people should be personally responsible for their economic fates. What you achieve reflects your effort, skills, attitudes, and innate abilities. Americans believe that inequality motivates people: If everyone were equal, there would be no reason to try hard because everybody would receive the same regardless of effort.

This set of ideas, this ideology, legitimizes inequality, making it seem acceptable, perhaps even desirable. "Sure," most Americans will say, "some people never get out of the lower ranks, but that's because they didn't try hard enough, didn't get enough education perhaps." And what of those who have escaped the lower ranks of society, who have made it to college? Clearly, that reflects their hard work and ability. "Winners" want to believe that they deserve their success and that the "losers" deserve their fate—in short, that the system is fair.

Does everyone buy the dominant ideology? Almost everyone, including the poor. It is easy to understand why successful people would accept these ideas. After all, according to the ideology, their success results from their efforts. But what about the poor or near poor? In part, many such people accept responsibility for their fate because social institutions reinforce that idea. Schools teach that hard work leads to success. Religions teach that people receive their just reward. Employers in our capitalist economy, of course, stress the link between effort and reward, as does the law.

This ideology provides a ready explanation of poverty, justifying the current social reality and comforting its believers. But it does not necessarily provide an accurate view. "Common wisdom" can be either insightful or distorting. To think sociologically, one must be willing to challenge this wisdom systematically and thoroughly. As a first step, this means rigorously defining "poverty" and examining the characteristics of the poor.

## Defining Poverty

The existence of poor people makes clear the economic *stratification* of contemporary U.S. society. That is, amidst general affluence or at least modest material comfort, an *inequality of condition,* or differences in the way people actually live, remains highly pronounced. ("Equality of opportunity" refers to the chances of obtaining desirable things such as good jobs or education.) To have a sound sociological understanding of poverty in our stratified system, however, we must address two conceptual issues: How do we define poverty? and, Do the poor represent a socially distinct group; in particular, are they a class?

First, the definition of poverty is a social construction, and one that is subject to endless debate. Imagine that we are asked to create the official poverty line for the United States. Where do we draw the line so that all below this income level are considered poor? That is, what *operational indicator,* a measurable criterion, do we propose?

We might respond that individuals or their families should have adequate food, shelter, clothing, and perhaps health care. Thus, we might define the poor as people who do not have enough money to buy these goods. But before we can turn the matter over to statistical experts for final calculations (including adjustments for such matters as family size), we still have important decisions to make. For example, does "adequate shelter" mean indoor plumbing? What about heat? A certain amount of space per person? What about a telephone? Maybe a phone is not absolutely necessary for existence, but it connects most people in our society with one another. How much do people need to be truly part of our society?

This last question raises the issue of whether we want to consider poverty in absolute or relative terms. *Absolute poverty* indicates that income is insufficient to purchase specified necessities. We can compute a poverty line that reflects the current costs of these goods once we have decided what they are. The concept of *relative poverty* suggests that people are poor if they have far less than typical members of a society—for example, less than one-half the average standard of living. Obviously, even families whose income is one-half of the average (median family income in 1987, for example, was $30,850) can live much better than almost everyone in many other societies. Equally obvious, however, is the fact that these families will be deprived of many items that are hardly luxuries and which most Americans take for granted in the course of normal existence.

That is why we say that the definition of poverty is a social construction. There is no "right" way to define it. Any definition is bound to be arbitrary, subject to value judgments that have important political consequences. Indeed, the poverty problem could be solved by definition, simply by setting a very low line. Of course, a higher line increases the poverty problem.

In contemporary politics, conservatives and liberals debate these definitions in predictable ways. Conservatives favor a lower poverty line to support their view that society is fundamentally sound and that little government involvement is desirable. Liberals seek a higher line to dramatize their sense of social inequity and the need for government initiatives to reduce poverty. These debates are much more than philosophical disputes. Once people are officially defined as poor, they become eligible for a range of federal and state welfare-assistance programs.

In this light, consider the news report from *Newsweek* magazine. Conservatives want to include the cash value of government services and subsidies for which poor people are eligible as part of their actual income. As the news report indicates, this accounting scheme reduces the poverty "problem." Liberal critics, however, reply that poor people neither receive all benefits nor use all services. (Medicaid, for instance, does not provide income to a poor person who is not ill.) These critics believe that this procedure understates the prevalence of the problem.

# Poverty in America: On the Increase

Conservatives argue that the number of Americans officially classified as poor—34.4 million at last count—would decline if benefits like food stamps and Medicaid were included in their income. Last week, under orders from Congress, the U.S. Census Bureau unveiled the latest study of U.S. poverty that included the noncash payments. Sure enough, the number of poor Americans declined—to about 22.9 million.

But even the new measure showed poverty on the rise. Using cash-income figures, the bureau calculates that the proportion of Americans below the poverty level rose from 11.7 percent to 15 percent between 1979 and 1982; adding in noncash benefits, the proportion rose from 6.8 percent to 10 percent. Census officials attribute the increase to two recessions and inflation (noncash benefits are not indexed to the cost of living). The effect of budget cuts on welfare programs, they said, was hard to calculate.

Newsweek, March 5, 1984. Reprinted by permission.

Although still debated, the definition developed by government economist Mollie Orshansky in 1965 and now used by the Census Bureau is the most commonly accepted. This definition takes an absolute approach: The *poverty line* is set at three times the amount of money needed to purchase a nutritionally adequate diet; this assumes that low-income people spend about one-third of their money on food. Adjusted for such factors as family size, age, and location, this is the figure that is used to compute the number of poor people and their proportion in the general population. This proportion is the official poverty rate, the figure that is reported by the various media.

To judge how restrictive or generous this definition is, imagine raising a family of four in an urban area on a total income of $968 a month. This figure is the official poverty line for such a family in 1987 ($11,611).

## Who Are the Poor?

Using this definition and Census Bureau survey data, we can outline a quick portrait of the poor (see Table 5.2). These data reveal the following facts.

■ Slightly more than one-half (51%) of the poor are younger than the working age or older than the standard retirement age of 65.

**Table 5.2**  The Poor in the United States, 1987
Total Number of Persons Below the Poverty
Line = 32,546,000

| Characteristics | Percentage of the Poor |
| --- | --- |
| Age | |
| under 18 | 40 |
| 18–64 | 49 |
| 65 and over | 11 |
| Race | |
| white | 69 |
| black | 28 |
| spanish* | 16 |
| Sex | |
| male | 49 |
| female | 51 |
| Region | |
| northeast | 17 |
| midwest | 23 |
| south | 41 |
| west | 19 |
| Education | |
| 0–11 years | 54 |
| 12 years | 31 |
| 13 or more | 15 |
| Work Experience | |
| work full-time | 24 |
| work part-time | 17 |
| not working: ill/disabled | 13 |
| not working: housekeeping | 18 |
| not working: in school | 10 |
| not working: cannot find work | 6 |
| not working: retired | 10 |
| not working: other reasons | 2 |
| Family Status | |
| head of family | 22 |
| children in families | 38 |
| other family members | 17 |
| not in families | 23 |

*Spanish origin may be any race; thus percentages do not
add up to 100%.

Source: U.S. Bureau of the Census. *Money Income and Poverty
Status in the United States: 1987.* Current Population Reports,
Series P–60, No. 161. 1988. Washington, DC: U.S. Government Printing Office; and Current Population Reports, Series P–60, No. 160, *Poverty in the United States: 1986.*

- More than two-thirds of all people below the poverty line are white. Poverty is not confined to racial minorities, although they *are* more likely to be poor. One-tenth of whites, slightly more than one-quarter (27%) of Hispanics, and one-third (33%) of blacks are poor.

- The poor are almost evenly split between males and females.

- More than 40 percent of poor people aged 15 and older work, and almost one-quarter of this group works full-time. Work is no salvation from poverty—many jobs pay poverty wages. Having one full-time minimum-wage worker does not lift a family of three above the poverty line.

- Most of the nonworking poor are unable to work. Eighteen percent of poor people keep house, 6 percent are unable to find work, and the rest cannot work because of illness, age, or school.

- The poor are spread throughout the country, although poverty is worst in the South. Approximately 60 percent of the poor live in urban areas; most of the rest live in rural areas far removed from city ghettos.

- Thirty-eight percent of poor people are children in families. Twenty-three percent live alone or in nonfamily arrangements.

- Twenty-five percent of adult poor have less than eight years of schooling. Almost one-half (46%) have at least a high school education.

This is a snapshot of the poor in one recent year, revealing a varied group, greatly divided by age, race, family structure, location, and work experience. If we reported the snapshots for the immediately preceding years, the picture would be similar. In a slightly longer perspective, perhaps the most notable change is the increasing proportion of female-headed families among the poor. This is the so-called feminization of poverty.

That these snapshots have similar features year after year (for example, the proportion of poor who are black remains about the same) has led to a widely held belief that the poor population is largely stable, and that once poor, always poor.

This conclusion is widely accepted in national debates about poverty. We hear it as politicians and others discuss the plight of an "underclass," a large group that is thought to be forever outside the economic mainstream and unable to function within it. If true, the challenges of overcoming poverty in the United States may seem massive, even overwhelming. Does the evidence of these successive snapshots truly establish that this class exists?

# Another Perspective

To use the terms of sociological researchers, we need *longitudinal data,* information about the same individuals over time. Census Bureau snapshots (cross-sectional data) reveal, for example, that the proportion of blacks within the total poor population remains constant from year to year—approximately 27%. That does not mean, however, that the same black individuals remain poor. From year to year, some blacks may enter poverty, while others leave it. Only by using longitudinal data and studying the same people year after year is it possible to determine whether there is a permanent underclass and what proportion of poor people it includes.

The best available evidence—a longitudinal national survey of 5,000 families from 1968 to 1978—strongly contradicts the notion that many people are poor throughout their lives. A team of social science researchers at the University of Michigan found that only 2.6 percent of the population had been poor (that is, below the official poverty line) for at least eight years in this decade. Fewer than 1 percent were poor throughout the entire decade.

Although few people are chronically poor, short-term poverty is a common experience. Slightly less than one-quarter of all Americans were poor for at least one year in this period. The main reasons for falling into poverty were illnesses or deaths within families, the breakup of marriages, and the birth of children — all common events in the lives of many of us.

In the same way, the size of the population that depends on welfare is small. Two percent of the population depended on welfare for more than one-half of family income throughout the decade, and only 3.5 percent depended on it for at least five years in 1968–1978. During the same time, one-quarter of all Americans received some welfare, mostly for a short time to help with specific situations such as an illness.

Indeed, many people change economic positions, for better and worse over time. Of all families in the lowest one-fifth of incomes in 1971, only one-half remained at this level in 1978. Conversely, of all families in the highest one-fifth of incomes in 1971, fewer than one-half were doing as well seven years later. In short, there is considerable economic mobility among American families, for both those at the top and those at the bottom of the economic ladder.

Do the poor, then, represent a true class in our society? The concept of *class* implies a distinct social group that has a relatively permanent, broadly similar occupational standing. This position in the economic hierarchy marks an individual's lifetime, shapes important features of life, and is transferred to children. If an underclass of poor truly exists, we should see evidence of an impoverished group that exists outside the economic system—*under*neath the occupational structure—throughout their lives.

In this light, the class-like characteristics of the American poor are slight, or are perhaps more accurately confined to a small segment of those in poverty. Certainly, not all share a lack of occupation. Large numbers work, often full-time. Others are simply unable to work because of age or health. Their lack of employment reflects neither their rejection of the economic system nor their rejection by it. Most significantly, perhaps, the overwhelming number of poor people are so only temporarily. And because periods of poverty are generally brief, poor people are unlikely to develop a *class consciousness*, a sense of identification with each other, a feeling of belonging to the same group.

This is not to minimize the hardships of the persistently poor. We must recognize, however, that this group is not typical of the poor population. It has distinctive characteristics. The long-term poor are disproportionate among black families, particularly those without an adult man in the house. Nearly one-third of the persistently poor live in families that are headed by a black woman under age 65. They are also disproportionately rural and Southern. More live in rural areas (33%) than in large cities (24%), a fact that runs counter to the stereotype of the long-term poor as an urban underclass. Many cannot be expected to "earn" their way out of poverty because of the constraints of age or disability. And most healthy women have child-care responsibilities. Only one-sixth of these families have a healthy man aged 21 to 65 in the household.

If there is an underclass, then, it represents some part of this small group of the persistently poor. This practical point must be recognized as more than a conclusion about an academic debate. Undoubtedly, it will be expensive and difficult to deal with the problems of those who have been trapped in poverty throughout their lives. If we recognize, however, that few Americans are permanently poor, the challenges of improving their lives may seem more manageable and affordable.

# Evaluating the Sociological Theories

With these findings in mind, how convincing are the "flawed character" and "flawed system" theories of poverty? Are policies based on these theories likely to be effective?

The statistical portrait of the poor presented above shows clearly that these theories are limited in scope at best. Many of the poor cannot be expected to work, and many others already have jobs. Aversions to work or other deficient values do not explain their fates.

Furthermore, these perspectives are hard to reconcile with the fact that many Americans are poor at some time in their life, although rarely for long. Cultural values presumably reflect deeply held, persistent orientations to life. But a constant (such as cultural values) cannot be used to explain a variable condition—movement in and out of poverty. Is it reasonable to believe that people fall into poverty in one year because they suddenly acquired flawed attitudes and then move out of poverty in the next year because they regained the "right" attitudes?

Because the poor are a socially diverse and ever-changing group, there is also little reason to believe in a pervasive subculture of poverty. When sociologists speak of culture, they mean learned patterns of feeling, thinking, and acting that are transmitted across generations. Subcultures are specific groups within a society that have distinctive variations from the predominant patterns. Such subcultural variations generally emerge among people who are socially alike and frequently meet each other. These conditions describe only the persistent poor who live in urban ghettos and pockets of rural poverty—again, a small minority of the population and even a small minority of those who are ever poor.

This is not to deny that some of the persistently poor may have self-defeating attitudes and values, although the extent of this has not been reliably documented. Newspaper articles and television documentaries portray such people, but these vivid anecdotes do not establish the extent of these defeatist attitudes.

We might also question whether the Culture of Poverty theory has properly identified cause and effect. Did "bad" values cause poverty, as this theory presumes, or did the experience of poverty cause these values to emerge? One can imagine that the experience of extremely limited opportunities leads to fatalism, low self-esteem, and a desire to take small gratifications as they come. Perhaps there is an element of the chicken-and-the-egg paradox here, but surely this perspective neglects the influence of the social structure on the lives of poor people.

The obvious strength of the structural perspective is that it recognizes that many of the poor work. Their poverty is not the result of a lack of work but of low pay. But this explanation, too, fails to account for the most common patterns of poverty. Many of the poor are unable to work, making job opportunities irrelevant. Furthermore, most descents into poverty result from the loss of family income caused by a worker's illness, a marital breakup, or the arrival of a baby, not by some long-term exclusion from at least modestly paying employment.

Because cultural and structural explanations only apply to certain small segments of the poor population, situational factors—common occurrences of family life—must be the crucial component of an adequate sociological account. That poverty is rarely persistent indicates that most families can overcome these trying situations in a fairly short time. Unfortunately, our antipoverty programs have been guided more by limited theories about the poor than by an accurate sense of their condition.

## Poverty and Government Policy

Ever since the Great Depression of the 1930s, the federal government has sponsored numerous antipoverty programs. These programs have inherent views about the causes of poverty. Politicians who subscribe to the flawed character explanations have proposed policies that sought to correct individual flaws. Politicians who subscribe to structural theories about poverty have proposed policies that were designed to correct the system.

Antipoverty programs thus reflect the ebb and flow of political moods in this country. Political conservatives tend to emphasize individual characteristics as a cause of poverty, so their policies generally aim at correcting individual traits. Political liberals more often look to the social environment as a cause of poverty, and so tend to support programs that are designed to correct the flaws in the economic or social environment.

Before the Great Depression, the federal government had no programs to combat poverty. But with millions of people out of work, the pressures on government to take an active role were intense. Among other initiatives during the New Deal, President Franklin D. Roosevelt created many public sector jobs through the Works Progress Administration (WPA), the first major federal antipoverty program. Workers employed through the WPA built roads, schools, stadiums, and other public facilities. With the end of the Depression, however, public employment lost its popularity as a method of combatting poverty. Since then, even federal efforts to subsidize the creation of private-sector jobs for the poor have been minor.

President Lyndon Johnson launched his War on Poverty in the mid-1960s, the second massive federal effort to eliminate poverty. Johnson's antipoverty programs reflected both liberal and conservative viewpoints.

Individualistic theory was reflected in attempts to remake poor people, who were obliged to attend federally funded job training programs such as the Job Corps to learn good work habits and skills; children in poor families were to receive early education through the Head Start program to overcome the cultural deficiencies of their home lives.

At the same time, many federal efforts to change the system focused on removing obstacles to economic mobility. Antidiscrimination legislation addressed the disproportionate poverty of racial minorities. Much of this legislation applied to schools and places of employment. School busing was instituted in an attempt to correct problems of segregation, which was identified as one social problem that led to poverty. And federal block grants to cities were provided to clear away urban ghettos and undesirable housing.

Critics have long argued that the money spent in these programs was wasted. The continued existence of poverty, they say, is proof that poverty won the war on poverty. But others point out that the war on poverty was more a skirmish, and although not much was spent, what was spent accomplished a great deal. They correctly point out that the number of poor people declined in this period, particularly the number of elderly poor, a special target for many programs. Which side is right?

Actually, it is difficult to determine whether these programs worked because the debate about antipoverty programs has really been a debate about general views of the world, not about specific programs and governmental policies. When liberals and conservatives argue about welfare, they assert differing views and preferences about the desirable role of government. Those who believe that personal flaws determine the poor will almost inevitably find fault with government programs that seek to correct the system. In turn, those who see poverty as a product of flaws in the social system are strongly predisposed to find fault with government programs that seek to correct the individual. Consequently, the same results—the actual number of people who are poor—are interpreted by some as evidence of gains in the war on poverty and by others as evidence of failure.

In 1980, the country elected Ronald Reagan, a conservative president who was committed to minimal government and believed that self-initiative alone is enough to move people ahead. His election triggered a new debate about antipoverty programs, much of it involving workfare programs. In these programs, people who receive welfare checks must, with some exceptions, work or accept job training in return for their checks. This program is popular among those who believe that people are poor because they do not know how to find work or lack the skills and attitudes required to be employed. Both Republicans and Democrats have endorsed the general concept of workfare.

Although workfare programs differ in their implementation, a majority of states have programs with similar objectives. First, work is seen as the answer to poverty. Second, poor people must be required to work or at least be strongly encouraged to do so. Finally, many of them must be made "employable." In some states, workfare recipients are required to attend job-hunting classes. They are then expected to land a job within a specified period, perhaps with some assistance. In other states, job training often stresses counseling to build self-esteem and discipline. These programs attempt to reinforce the behaviors and attitudes that are demanded in most jobs. The general intent has been to correct the flaws of poor people.

As noted in the accompanying news reports, workfare is viewed as welfare reform. For the last three decades, assistance in the form of cash

# Workfare Bandwagon Gets a Push

## U.S. Governors Support $1 Billion Plan— at Federal Expense

By Timothy J. McNulty
and Tim Franklin
CHICAGO TRIBUNE

WASHINGTON—The nation's governors, reflecting a wide eagerness to reshape the welfare system to encourage recipients to find jobs, endorsed Tuesday a $1 billion reform package that is long on enthusiasm but still short on cash.

Although prospects for their plan were bleak, the desire for significant change in welfare rules was evident throughout the nation's capitol: The Reagan administration planned to detail its own welfare program this week and many individual congressmen have begun to jump on a fast-rolling welfare bandwagon.

"We are about to do welfare reform," Rep. Thomas Downey [D., N.Y.] declared to a half-dozen governors who appeared before a House subcommittee to promote their public assistance proposal.

"This seems to be an issue whose time has come," said Delaware Gov. Michael Castle, a Republican.

Others insisted widespread dissatisfaction with the current state of welfare had made change inevitable.

The governors, meeting here in a semiannual conference, voted 30–1 to back a proposal to require welfare recipients, including mothers with children older than three years, to get remedial education and job training in order to qualify for public assistance.

They recommended that welfare be put on a "contractual" basis with the recipients signing a pledge to take specified steps in finding a job.

The only vote against the plan was from Wisconsin's new Republican gov-

grants through the Aid to Families with Dependent Children (AFDC) program have been the primary solution to poverty. When people talk about welfare, they usually are referring to AFDC. The push for workfare stems from dissatisfaction with the current state of welfare. If widely adopted, does workfare promise success?

As the report by the General Accounting Office (GAO) notes, the minimum level of services that the poor receive does not prepare them well for decent long-term employment. Most studies of workfare programs indicate that participants who are placed in jobs would have found work anyway. Workfare, at its best, also has reduced AFDC outlays by less than 10 percent, which is hardly a fundamental improvement but not surprising because so many recipients cannot work because of age ernor, Tommy Thompson, who said his state's welfare program is already ahead of the nation.

Rep. Charles Rangel [D., N.Y.] also was skeptical, especially about comments that the White House had "embraced" the governors' proposals.

"In the difference between 'embracing' and making love, without paying for it, there is a wide gap," Rangel said, meaning that the Reagan administration is not willing to increase the cost of federal welfare programs.

The governors want the federal government to pay start-up costs of about $850 million in the first full year. The states' contribution would be an estimated $150 million.

That money would be in addition to the estimated $18 billion in federal and state money now spent for Aid to Families with Dependent Children.

The bipartisan governors' plan also called for eventually setting a national minimum level of welfare and for changing eligibility rules to allow unemployed fathers in the home to collect welfare. The governors were quick to add that the improvements could be paid for with the savings from getting people back to work.

Illinois' Republican Gov. James Thompson said he sensed a euphoria among the governors who met with President Reagan Monday, but he cautioned "some of the problems are seemingly intractable," including the notion of "training and educating large numbers of persons and finding them jobs in a time of a slowly growing economy."

In the current push for reform welfare, advocates are careful to avoid calling it "workfare," a term associated with punishing welfare recipients and forcing them to work at public service jobs. Their plan encourages private employment, they said.

Objections to the current welfare system include complaints that it encourages economic dependency by those who receive public money.

Some also complain the programs allow too many people to qualify for welfare.

Democratic Gov. Bill Clinton of Arkansas said that whatever specifics are eventually approved from their plan and from federal proposals to encourage work as a condition of welfare, the governors were "sending a signal to the country that we're coming together again around the fundamental values."

or health.[1] In short, despite widespread support, workfare offers no significant solution to poverty.

This conclusion should not surprise anyone. As we have shown, most poverty results from situational factors: births, deaths, and divorces—events that happen to everyone. Indeed, if we recognize the significance of situational factors for most of poverty, the best and simplest solution might be to give money or subsidized services directly to the poor. Most poor people need short-term help until they can straighten out their lives. Granting money for the short term is cheaper than running a

---

[1]  Williams, Marci Jo. "Is Workfare the Answer?": *Fortune* (114): p. 109, 27 Oct. 1986.

# Work-Program Effects 'Modest' for Enrollees

## GAO Says Effort Won't Slash Welfare Rolls

By Spencer Rich
THE WASHINGTON POST

Work programs for welfare recipients have "modest" effects on the job prospects of participants and therefore should not be expected to slash welfare rolls, according to a study by the General Accounting Office released yesterday.

The GAO, an investigative arm of Congress, studied 61 work programs—including "workfare"—for welfare clients in 38 states.

The study, requested by Rep. Ted Weiss (D–N.Y.), chairman of the House Government Operations subcommittee on intergovernmental relations, found that the programs often spent only a few

hundred dollars per participant, focusing on low-cost job-search assistance rather than on education or training.

"The minimal services these people received cannot be expected to prepare them for productive, well-paid, lasting jobs," Weiss said in releasing the report.

Because of laws banning mandatory work programs for women with children under age 6, the programs generally failed to enroll young mothers with small children, GAO reported, even though there is some evidence that such welfare recipients benefit most from work experience and training programs.

The study found that states and localities involved in the projects put com-

Monday, February 2, 1987, p. A7. Reprinted by permission.

whole host of often unnecessary training programs. In fact, given the extremely small numbers of people who suffer long-term poverty, existing programs have had unrecognized success. The goal of any antipoverty program, after all, is to get poor people back on their feet. The evidence suggests that for most poor people this does happen in relatively short order. Although abuses certainly exist, few people have made careers of welfare.

Despite the evidence of AFDC's success, most Americans are suspicious and distrustful of welfare. Most have no idea of how much and what types of welfare that the poor can get, what is required to receive it, or how many poor get it. Even so, Americans hold strong opinions about welfare and its recipients.

When asked, six in ten Americans believe that the United States spends too much money on welfare; eight in ten think that welfare paratively little money into them. It reported that in 1985, 72 percent of the $272 million spent on the projects came from the federal government, mainly from the Work Incentive (WIN) Program, which the Reagan administration seeks to phase out.

The study also found that while about 5 million adults—many of them young mothers—were in the welfare (Aid to Families with Dependent Children) program for at least part of 1985, only 714,448 participated in the work programs.

And while some welfare participants refused to participate, "the programs do not seem to make extensive use of sanctions," such as loss or suspension of benefits, the GAO said.

Three-fourths of the WIN demonstration programs "spent an average of less than $600 per person in 1985," the report said.

The GAO said that while "on paper" 70 percent of the WIN demonstration programs offered such services as remedial education, on-the-job training and postsecondary education, "in practice most participants engage in activities that send them directly into the job market without skill or work-habit enhancement." Only 3.2 percent of program recipients received remedial education; 2.3 percent, vocational training; and 4.5 percent, work experience. However, about two-thirds of the participants did job-search activities.

The study reported that almost one-third of the program participants later found unsubsidized jobs, but said many would have found jobs anyway.

Based on control group studies conducted by the Manpower Demonstration Research Corp. in San Diego, Baltimore and Arkansas, the GAO estimated that program participants' success rate in finding jobs is probably 5 to 7 percentage points higher than that of nonparticipants. (In San Diego, 61 percent of participants got jobs later, while 55 percent of nonparticipants did.) And GAO estimated that participants' earnings are boosted a few hundred dollars per year as a result of the programs.

The study said many people earned such meager salaries in their jobs that they remained poor and still needed government assistance.

recipients are not honest about their needs.[2] Our grudging expenditures on welfare reflect this fact. When combined, all forms of welfare, including retirement and disability benefits, represent only 8 percent of all federal government expenditures. AFDC alone accounts for only 2 percent.[3]

At the same time, a majority of people (60%) believe that government should guarantee jobs to all who want to work. Obviously, workfare more closely reflects popular attitudes than does welfare because recipients earn support through their personal efforts. Because of the domi-

---

[2]   Kluegel, James R., and Eliot R. Smith. *Beliefs About Inequality.* 1986. Hawthorne, NY: Aldine de Gruyter.

[3]   *Statistical Abstract of the United States,* 1987, Table 493. Washington, DC: U.S. Government Printing Office.

nant American ideology, workfare is acceptable while welfare is not. By its existence, welfare implies that the system may not be fair, that opportunity may not be abundant. By giving to the poor, welfare also is seen as rewarding the undeserving. Those who must work hard for their money feel cheated by those who do not work at all. But if the poor are required to work in order to receive welfare, there is no implication that things are unfair.

## A Sociological Prediction

Given this widely shared belief, programs such as workfare that focus on the individual rather than on social reform probably will receive popular support—even if they do not reduce poverty. If they prove costly, however, current enthusiasm is likely to turn. Historically, the poor have commanded moral judgments, advice, and some sympathy, but not much money. They still lack the political power to make their plight much different.

Discussions about the poor are as much about how nonpoor Americans want to view themselves as they are about the poor. Our solutions to poverty affirm our collective ideology. None will receive widespread acceptance if it refutes this ideology. But programs that are guided by this ideology make fundamental errors in their assumptions about the poor. In part, this tension between what Americans want to believe and what actually exists explains why we have been unable to solve our poverty problem.

That is our assessment as sociologists of what is likely to happen. What you believe should happen may be another matter.

## Suggested Readings

Danziger, Sheldon H., and Daniel H. Weinberg, Eds. *Fighting Poverty: What Works and What Doesn't*, 1987. Cambridge, MA: Harvard University Press. This collection contains up-to-date essays on the programs that were designed to combat poverty.

Duncan, Greg. *Years of Poverty, Years of Plenty*. 1984. Ann Arbor, MI: The University of Michigan, Institute for Social Research. The findings reported here explode myths about poverty. This is our primary source for longitudinal data about the poor population. Although the book mainly presents statistical findings, it is readily accessible to the college student who has no technical training.

Kaus, Mickey. "The Work Ethic State." *The New Republic* (195): 22–33, 7 July 1987; and "Welfare and Work: A Symposium." *The New Republic* (195): 18–23, 27 Oct. 1986. Kaus espouses a mandatory public jobs program to combat poverty and what he believes are the debilitating effects of the current welfare system. In the symposium seven prominent scholars evaluate his position. This debate illustrates how sociological interpretation, ideological preferences, and policy analysis are complexly intertwined on the issue of poverty.

Kluegel, James R., and Eliot R. Smith. *Beliefs About Inequality: Americans' Views of What Is and What Ought to Be.* 1986. Hawthorne, NY: Aldine de Gruyter. This sophisticated analysis uses survey questionnaires to explore Americans' ideology as it relates to inequality. The authors valuably consider both general orientations and views on specific types of policies.

CHAPTER 6

# Gender

## Women in Politics: Why So Few?

**P**owerful female politicians are so rare that they stand out anywhere in the United States. Even in 1990, seventy years after the passage of the 19th Amendment, which guaranteed women the right to vote, it is still quite newsworthy when a woman is elected to a state or national office. Even nomination for political office is newsworthy when the nominee is female. Banner headlines proclaim the official's sex before discussing anything else about her ("VIRGINIA ELECTS FIRST FEMALE ATTORNEY GENERAL"). Her sex, more than anything else, makes her unusual in the world of politics, which is, more than any other social arrangement in the world—including the economy, religion, education, and even the military—dominated by males.

Females are a majority of Americans (slightly more than 51 percent). Women constitute the majority of voters in the United States; in every presidential election since 1964, the number of female voters has exceeded the number of male voters. And a greater proportion of eligible females vote than do eligible males; in the 1984 presidential election, 61 percent of eligible females voted, but only 59 percent of eligible males. In short, women now outnumber men, vote more than men, and participate in elections more than men. But women do not rule. This leads to the central question of this chapter: "How can a large group of people learn to feel that it is more appropriate to allow others to govern for them rather than to participate in governing themselves?" (Sapiro, 1988).

UPI/Bettmann Newsphotos

Senator Barbara Mikulski (Democrat—Maryland)
recently became one of only two female U.S. senators.
In American politics, women vote, not govern.

Why are there so few powerful women holding national or state offices? Why is politics "a man's game"? In this chapter, we answer these questions by relying on sociological theories of political participation and power. We show how women participate in their own exclusion from the political process—often without knowing it. Indeed, we will show that women's participation in and acceptance of their own subjection to male governance is a prerequisite condition for that exclusion.

## Women in Politics: How Many?

In 1988, only two women held the office of U.S. senator (out of 100 senators). Twenty-three members (5 percent) of the House of Representatives were women. At the state level, only 12 percent of elected officials are women. Sixteen percent of state legislators are women, and that figure represents a high point. At no level of political office in the United States do women hold more than 16 percent of available positions, and never before in our history has the percentage been higher (Center for the American Woman and Politics, 1988). In the past two decades women have entered many previously all-male domains, but politics has seen virtually no change in the participation of women as leaders in most areas. Figure 6.1 shows the percentage of female elected officials since 1975.

Women are gaining in representation only in state legislatures and county governing boards, where they are a small minority, even though present at all-time highs. As Virginia Sapiro stated, the rule that applies to women in politics is, "The higher, the fewer" (Sapiro, 1988, p. 21); that is, the higher the level of political office, the fewer the women who are present.

Women are rarely even appointed, much less elected, to powerful political positions. At the national level, there has never been a female secretary of state or defense, or attorney general, the most powerful cabinet positions, although women have held the positions of secretary of transportation (Elizabeth Dole resigned in 1987 to help her husband, Senator Robert Dole of Kansas, in his unsuccessful bid for the Republican nomination for president) and secretary of health and human services (Margaret Heckler). The same is true at the state level. Table 6.1 shows the percentages of women in state cabinets by area of appointment.

Women in state cabinets are concentrated in the so-called "people" areas of social services (welfare and health), administration, employment security (unemployment programs), finance (tax collection), education, planning, and environmental issues. Few women hold cabinet positions in financial areas: banking, licensing, utilities, and highways.(transpor-

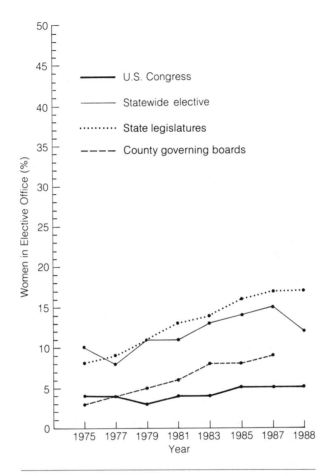

**Figure 6.1**   Women in Elective Offices by Year (%)
*Source:   Center for the American Woman and Politics.*
*"Factsheet." 1988. Rutgers University.*

tation), what Sapiro meant by "the higher, the fewer." "Higher" political positions are understood to be those that control the *distribution of resources.* The holders of such offices influence or decide who gets what and how much. "Lower" political positions have little to do with resource distribution, instead dealing with issues of administration (how programs *are* run) or planning (how programs *should* be run). Women politicians tend to occupy these lower positions, and very few occupy more powerful political offices.

---

**Table 6.1** Women in Cabinet Positions by Area

| Area of Appointment | Women Cabinet Members (%) |
|---|---|
| Health/social services | 17.2 |
| Government services/administration | 7.9 |
| Labor/employment security | 7.3 |
| Finance/budget/taxation/revenue | 7.3 |
| Community affairs/planning/housing | 5.3 |
| Environmental protection/natural resources | 5.3 |
| Education | 4.6 |
| Aging | 4.6 |
| Human rights/civil rights/women's rights | 4.6 |
| State personnel | 4.6 |
| Governor's staff | 4.0 |
| Tourism/recreation/culture | 3.3 |
| Licensing/regulation | 2.6 |
| Banking/financial institutions | 2.6 |
| Economic development/commerce | 2.6 |
| Energy/utility regulation | 2.6 |
| State | 2.0 |
| Transportation | 2.0 |
| Other | 8.6 |
| Total | 100.0 |

# Explaining Women's Political Participation

Differences between male and female political participation have been studied by sociologists and political scientists for many years. Three conventional explanations have been dominant. First, some have argued that women's "nature," or their attitudes and interests, interfere with their political participation; women simply are not interested in politics, lack a sense of civic duty, do not understand politics, and feel their participation would not make a difference. Second, it has been suggested that women's personal lives interfere with their political participation, that their involvement with home and family is a barrier to their involvement in politics. Third, it has been argued that women are socialized into a more politically passive role than are men. None of these explanations is adequate by itself, but together they suggest a more general answer to the question raised in this chapter. After briefly considering the three theories, we will suggest that they point to a set of American values and beliefs that relegate men and women to separate spheres of life—men to the public sphere, and women to the private. And politics is indisputably a public issue.

## Women's Attitudes and Interests

Political scientist Virginia Sapiro asks that we imagine a political system in which there is perfect opportunity for everyone to participate, where everyone is allowed but not required to participate in politics (Sapiro, 1988, p. 5). In this type of political system, what might determine how active individuals will be?

Clearly, one factor is political interest. How concerned is an individual with particular issues or with politics in general? Research on this point reveals clearly that education is the primary determinant of political interest. Thus, it is not surprising to find no evidence of significant differences between men and women in their respective political interest when their educational levels are so similar. Only very minor differences exist in the issues that interest males and females. In short, political interest does not account for the observed male–female differences in participation.

A second factor that can motivate people to political participation is their sense of civic duty or responsibility. Although males and females are equally likely to agree that citizens should vote or take active roles in their community, there is no agreement about the proper political roles for women. One-quarter of adults believes that "Women should take care of running their homes and leave running the country to men" (National Opinion Research Center, 1985). Thus, although males and females may have similar levels of civic duty, a sizable minority of Americans believes that women should not become involved in politics. It is not surprising that women who believe in male–female equality disagree with such sentiments (Sapiro, 1983).

A third attitude factor in individual participation in politics is whether people believe they are knowledgeable, competent, or skilled enough to make a difference, a trait that has been called "political efficacy." Differences between men and women in political efficacy are related to women's gender roles and attitudes. Traditional women (those who are less accepting of the concept of male–female equality) have less political knowledge and sophistication than men or less traditional women. Furthermore, mothers and homemakers feel less competent at politics than childless or employed women. In short, the acceptance of a traditional definition of gender and participation in traditional female gender roles (homemaker and mother) appear to foster lower political efficacy among women.

In sum, the findings summarized above indicate few large differences between men and women that would explain why so few women hold powerful political positions. Instead, the acceptance of a traditional definition of gender, a belief that males and females are not and should not attempt to be equal, is an important factor in political participation.

# Situational and Structural Barriers to Participation

Women's responsibilities for tending homes, husbands, and children may prevent them from becoming involved in politics; women do not have the time for politics, according to this argument. Further, if a woman is not working, she is not exposed to political issues and discussions about them. A test of the "situational barriers" explanation by political scientist Susan Welch (1977) reveals that marriage and children do affect political participation—but equally so for men and women. Other researchers have noted that married persons are more likely to vote than are unmarried persons, but the differences between married and single individuals are the same regardless of their sex (Kingston and Finkel, 1987).

Unlike the effects of marriage or parenthood, working outside the home has dramatic and large effects on all types of political participation—but only for females. In sum, marriage and children do not depress women's political participation any more than they do men's. Women who work, however, have much higher rates of political activity. This suggests that definitions of gender, rather than situational factors, are what matter. Perhaps working women hold less traditional ideas about the "proper" role of women in politics. Both men and women in the United States tend to see females as the keepers of children and the makers of homes. The few women who are in high political office (that is, at the national level) are almost always unmarried or beyond child-rearing age. American voters do not see politics and child rearing as being compatible for women, even though more traditional jobs and politics apparently are for men. Working women are less likely to accept this very traditional view of women (see chapter 12 on abortion).

Beyond such attitudes, why would working per se have such an influence on women's political lives? The answer is easier to see if we turn the question around: What about not working would keep women out of politics? There are three obvious parts to the answer. First, most political issues deal with business and occupations. The central issues of state and national politics—indeed, the definition of politics itself—involve the distribution and redistribution of collective goods and services; that is, issues of the economy, trade, tariffs, taxes, industrial policy, subsidies, and employment. Women who do not work are less likely to become involved in these issues.

Second, those who work typically have more education than those who do not. Education, we know, is critical in fostering political participation.

Third, a typical "status sequence" leads to the higher echelons of political office (Epstein, 1981). High political office depends on being *selected* as a candidate. Party officials, influential politicians, and financial backers must nominate a candidate to run, and to be known as a potential candidate one must be part of the political "network," knowing party officials on both informal and formal bases. Women are often excluded from the informal networks of men who make up the network, men who see one another at men's clubs, on tennis courts, or in locker rooms. The political "gatekeepers" are those who decide *who* will run as based on their beliefs that a candidate can both lead and win. Research shows that women are generally less likely to be perceived as either leaders or winners—especially women who are not employed (Sapiro, 1988).

To summarize, the situational and structural barriers to women's political participation are largely subtle. By virtue of being wives or mothers, women are viewed by others and perhaps themselves as being ineligible for political office. They may have less experience in the work force, particularly in such fields as law, which often leads to political office. They are excluded from the informal "old boy networks," and their lives are often focused on issues that are defined as being outside the main arena (the economy and jobs) of politics. In short, a host of situational factors lead men and women to define politics as a man's game, applying notions of gender to the world of power.

## Socialization

The third conventional explanation for women's political participation focuses on the consequences of socialization. Briefly, the argument suggests that women are brought up to think of politics as something in which they do not participate. From early childhood, some argue, girls and boys are taught different things about power and politics. According to this view, women are not so much prevented from assuming powerful political office as much as they have limited desires and expectations of political power—that is, women simply do not define themselves as potential leaders.

Research shows, however, that young children do have similar knowledge and interest in politics, regardless of their sex. Although children are aware of sex differences in the world of politics (the message is transmitted to them), "there is little evidence that children *learn* from these messages, and even less that children *act* upon what they have learned" (Sapiro, 1983, p. 39). But as we know, boys and girls develop different ways of looking at the world and clear notions of gender, what it means to be a man or a woman (see chapter 2 on socialization).

Although childhood socialization has no direct effect, it does lead men and women to assume different social roles as adults. As one political analyst has noted, "A woman does not simply give birth to a child, she becomes a *mother*. She does not simply participate in a ceremony . . . with a man, she becomes a *wife*. Each of these roles institutionalizes particular aspects of gender norms" (Sapiro, 1983, p. 52). Gender roles influence how other roles in life are experienced, affecting how men and women see the world and those activities and beliefs that fit with their definitions of themselves as women or men.

From considering the three explanations, one can conclude that few differences between men and women account for most of what we call "political participation"—becoming informed about issues, having a sense of civic duty, understanding the political process, or voting. Still, women rarely participate in political leadership. The explanation is found more in a set of values and beliefs about gender, beliefs that define power as a male prerogative. In other words, *gender*, not *sex*, is the real issue. Whenever such a set of beliefs justifies an unequal distribution of power, it is called an *ideology*.

## The Ideology of Separate Spheres

We have been discussing politics as if it were a form of behavior such as reading or public speaking. In actuality, however, political leadership is the exercise of *power*, the ability to direct and influence others, sometimes against their will. Seen in this way, the question becomes, " Why don't women exercise power in America?"

The answer is that many Americans view the world as divided into two separate spheres—the public and the private.

> Men are the masters of the public domain; they control social institutions, design social policy, wage war, create culture and support and protect women and children through their labors in the public arena. Authority, autonomy, obedience, love, and personal services are the

thanks they expect in return from women, children, and less powerful men. Women have their own sphere of control: the private domain, the internal world. Women bear and raise children, and nurture them, men, and other women. They organize and administer social and interpersonal activities, nurse the sick, tend the old, and provide round-the-clock personal and domestic service. They expect to be thanked in the coinage of love and respect and economic support (Lipman–Blumen, 1984, p. 23).

Because politics pertains to the public sphere, it has been considered a male domain. Furthermore, because politics is power, men are defined as powerful. What accounts for this particular division of the world? Why do men, but not women, exercise political power? To answer this question, we must consider briefly the nature of power itself. What is it and how is it exercised?

## Politics as Power

Sociologists define power as the process whereby individuals or groups gain or maintain the ability to impose their will on others, despite implicit or explicit opposition, to repeatedly have their way by invoking or threatening punishment as well as offering or withholding rewards.

Sociologist Jean Lipman–Blumen explains how power relations develop (Lipman–Blumen, 1984, p. 6). The basis for the need for power is the uncertainty of life. Humans, unable to predict the future, experience a sense of helplessness and anxiety that makes them seek ways to reduce these feelings of uncertainty. Several ways of dealing with uncertainty are common. First, people may entrust themselves to an all-powerful but unseen force, such as a god. Second, they may seek security in powerful institutions such as the police, the military, or large organizations. Third, people may submit to a powerful ruler, someone who they believe has their best interests at heart. Finally, people may seek control over others, thereby creating the illusion of power over one's *own* destiny. Traditionally, women have relied on the first and third ways, while men have relied on the second and fourth. The first and second solutions are not directly at issue here because they do not relate to politics, although it is a common observation that women are more religious than men and that men are more hierarchical and bureaucratic (the characteristics of large institutions) in their world views.

Consider the third approach, putting oneself under the protection of a more powerful individual who is believed to have one's best interests at heart. Such a strategy is sometimes a matter of choice, but often it is not. Children do not choose their parents, for example. Furthermore, the definition of *who* is the more powerful and capable of giving protection is often beyond one's control. For generations, men and women have assumed that males are more powerful and thus more capable of giving protection.

The fourth solution, controlling others, is the corollary of the third; there must be one who offers protection to those who seek it. The protector decides what is good and bad, what should and should not be done, and who should do what. In short, the protector becomes powerful as the protected become powerless. Thus, the third and fourth solutions to the uncertainties of life complement one another; one group finds security in trusting others to watch out for them, while the other finds security in the power derived from providing protection.

This arrangement continues as long as the powerless believe the powerful are more capable or knowledgeable and have their best interests at heart. Because controlling others provides a source of immense security and comfort, the powerful have little reason to alter such an arrangement, especially when it seems right and natural. All of world history seems to justify such an arrangement between men (the protectors) and women (the protected). The relationship is so "natural" that it is prescribed in the works of all major religious faiths—the Bible, Talmud, and Koran.

Power is not something forced on people, however; it depends on the continual renegotiation of affairs. Only with the consent of the ruled can the powerful sustain their position. In other words, men and women must both accept the arrangement for it to continue. And both accept it because a powerful ideology or belief system justifies it. Once in place, this ideology justifies and sustains the males' power over females.

Women, of course, are not passive recipients of men's decisions. In the public domain, men engage in what Lipman–Blumen calls "macro-manipulation," making most major *societal decisions* that have profound and sometimes drastic effects on people's lives. Relegated to the private domain, women respond with "micromanipulation," making *decisions about personal and interpersonal affairs*. After generations of subordination, women have developed methods of influencing men through the use of interpersonal behaviors. Women become expert at relationships, understanding and controlling them, reading and understanding verbal and nonverbal cues. "They learn to anticipate behavior, to evoke as well as smother pleasure, anger, joy and bafflement, to charm, to outsmart, even to dangle the powerful over the abyss of desire and anguish" (Lipman–Blumen, 1984, p. 30). For example, when men passed antiabortion legislation, women effectively neutralized the legal ban on abortions by using interpersonal influence to obtain illegal abortions (see chapter 12).

# The Ideology of Gender

Ideologies are not necessarily malicious. The system of beliefs that relegates females to less powerful status is accepted by men and women alike, and has become part of our culture. These beliefs are learned by children and reinforced daily throughout life. They are internalized and guide our behaviors, becoming part of who we are and experienced as part of our personalities. In short, they are almost taken for granted. To question such beliefs strikes people as unnatural, sacrilegious, or simply stupid.

What are the components of the ideology of gender? Following Lipman–Blumen, we present a series of ideas that form the core of American gender ideology. They may appear to be little more than stereotypes—that is, exaggerated statements about the differences between men and women that have little basis in fact. In large measure, these beliefs are exactly that—stereotypes. But what people believe to be facts often conflicts with the truth (see chapter 4 on drug use). Regardless of their factual basis, these beliefs form the core of our understanding of gender. Lipman–Blumen refers to these ideas as "control myths" because they justify the protection and control of women by men.

## Control Myths

1. *Women are weak, passive, dependent, and fearful; men are strong, aggressive, independent, and fearless.* In chapter 2 (socialization), we showed how powerful such labels as "sissy" and "tomboy" are in controlling behavior. Boys who appear dependent, weak, passive, or fearful are chastised, as are girls who appear aggressive. The history of our culture includes many examples of strong, powerful, and fearless individuals, warriors and heroes—Teddy Roosevelt, Daniel Boone, and Davey Crockett, for example. Almost without exception, these individuals are males. Legendary males are remembered for such traits, while legendary females are remembered for such things as their great sacrifices or moral crusades they may have led—Joan of Arc and Eleanor Roosevelt, for example.

2. *Women are intuitive, holistic, and contextual; men are analytical, abstract, field independent, and therefore smarter than women.* Men have traditionally been the intellectuals, the scientists, the inventors. Their skills are abstract and removed from the context of other individuals. Men fix things, and often for women. Female intuition is a trait that is attributed to individuals who possess great skills in interpersonal relationships—abilities to anticipate others' reactions and responses. Analytical and abstract skills, however, are valued more than intuition.

3. *Women are more altruistic, more nurturing, and thus more moral than men.* Young girls are taught to put others' needs before their own, to sacrifice and care for others. Self-denial is especially worthy. As a result of these orientations, women are seen as more moral than men. Females crusade for causes, especially those that benefit others. So central is sacrifice to the female identity that women have traditionally volun-

teered their efforts to help religious causes, moral crusades, and social reform. Even today, women are expected to perform household work without monetary compensation—that is, as volunteers. Any suggestion that homemaking should be paid is rewarded only by laughter; the idea is not taken seriously.

4. *Women are contaminating and contaminated.* Women are seen as dirty, or capable of polluting men, both socially and physically. Many people view gay men, for example, as having been influenced too much by women—that is, they have been contaminated socially. Adult women often are portrayed as illogical and overly emotional, as well as smelly and dirty, especially during menstruation. Male body odor is regarded as less of a problem than is a female's. The variety of deodorants and hygienic products that women are taught they need vastly exceeds that for men. Women's behavior is often excused by reference to their menstrual periods, which are portrayed as diminishing women's mental and physical abilities. Women are thought to be distracting to men at both work and war. These notions suggest that women must be restricted or confined to prevent the contamination of men.

5. *Beauty and sexuality are women's most valuable assets.* Even the most casual observation reveals the vast disparities in the varieties and costs of cosmetics and clothing for women and for men. The emphasis on female beauty has kept women from dirty and dangerous jobs. Instead, beauty can be exchanged for a man, preferably a rich or powerful one. Conversely, rich and powerful men can acquire beautiful women. If one believes that only beauty and not intelligence or capability can be traded for a rich or powerful man, it is obvious that "only the most stubborn, ugly, sexless, or idealistic women will persist in trying to demonstrate that they are as intelligent and able as the men" (Lipman–Blumen, 1984, p. 90), a charge that is often leveled at feminists and female politicians.

6. *Women talk too much.* The common wisdom is that women talk more than men—on the telephone, on television, in meetings, everywhere. Significant research shows, however, that men talk more than women, initiating more conversations and more interruptions. Usually, this is obvious in any college classroom. But that is not the social perception. Cognizant of this negative stereotype, women often restrict their talking in front of men; they do not attempt to control conversations or interrupt others as often—they are "polite." But by not talking, women appear less intelligent and less informed than men.

7. *Women are manipulative; men are straightforward.* Relegated to the private, less powerful sphere, women resort to interpersonal influence—persuasion, charm, seduction, and suggestion. Such influence, of course, is antithetical to the exercise of public power, where direction and purpose are necessarily overt.

8. *Men have women's best interests at heart; women can trust men to protect their welfare.* Given all other control myths, it seems only "natural" that men should be the ones who provide protection—that is, be more powerful. After all, men are stronger, more intelligent, and straightforward. Obviously, everyone's best interest is served if men rule. And because men and women must live with one another, such a belief is absolutely essential, or protection will be experienced as unfair subjection and domination. This last control myth is clearly most central to the ideology of gender in our culture.

## Gender Ideology and Politics

We began this chapter with the question, "How can a large group of people learn to feel that it is more appropriate to allow others to govern for them rather than to participate in governing themselves?" We now have an answer. The ideology of gender relegates women to the private sphere and men to the public. Unquestionably, politics is in the public sphere. As long as men and women accept these control myths, politics is likely to remain a male domain. Let us briefly consider how control myths influence women in politics.

During his time in office, President Ronald Reagan was known as the Great Communicator. His greatest personal asset was his ability to communicate effectively, especially to convince people that his ideas and programs were the only right ones. As a professional actor in Hollywood movies, Reagan had developed extraordinary skills in oral communication. Such communication is basic to all politics—how the messages are sent and received and what is communicated. Every politician understands this and pays speech writers and consultants to manage the politician's messages. The differences between male and female communication styles, however, work against women in politics.

Traditionally, female speech has shown more uncertainty. Women often preface their statements with such caveats as "It's only my opinion . . . ," or , "You may not agree, but. . . ." In mixed groups, women often turn statements into questions. And in debate, rather than declaring "so-and-so is true!," they often use the interrogative form: "But isn't it true that . . . ?" These differing styles are products of the seventh control myth—that is, females are manipulative, but males are direct. Indeed, studies have shown that men are viewed more positively when they speak directly, while women are viewed more positively when they do not. People often find "feminine speech" less convincing than "masculine speech," even when the same thing is said (Sapiro, 1988, p. 8). Uncertainty is hardly an asset for a political candidate.

Women's verbal styles also reflect the sixth control myth—that women talk too much. As noted many women refrain from talking, interrupting, or controlling conversations in mixed groups, which results in the appearance of being unknowledgeable and uninformed. Again, such an impression is fatal in politics.

The third control myth—that women are altruistic and more moral than men—has equally devastating consequences for women in politics. Imagine two women working for the same goals within an organization that is concerned with their neighborhood's safety. One claims to be fighting for safer streets for her children. The other says that she is fighting for safer streets for women or because she wants to become police commissioner. Would people's reactions to these women differ? The first woman probably would gain much greater acceptance and approval. In general, political activity by and for women is accepted as long as it is not viewed as political—that is, when it is altruistic, not selfish. When women appear to be motivated by a concern for their families or for others, their actions are seen as acceptable (Sapiro, 1988). But concern for families is hardly the stuff of powerful politics. Few important political issues lend themselves successfully to an interpretation of altruism, and yet the history of women in U.S. politics has seen altruistic concerns at the heart of almost every political issue in which they have been involved (suffrage is an obvious exception). Women were among the leading crusaders for the abolition of slavery. They organized for prohibition of drinking. Women were the first social workers (as volunteers), and women are the core of both the prochoice and prolife (that is, antiabortion) movements. All of the major anti–drunk driving crusades such as Mothers Against Drunk Driving (MADD) are dominated by women (see chapter 13 on social movements).

Attempts to promote social policies that directly benefit women as a group, however, have met stiff resistance. The defeat of a proposed equal rights amendment to the U.S. Constitution (which would have made discrimination on the basis of sex illegal) and comparable worth legislation (which would have required that women be paid comparable salaries as those paid men for work requiring comparable preparation, skills, and education) attest to the resentment of apparently "selfish" political efforts by and for women.

The corollary of this myth—that women are more moral—means that women are excluded from positions that routinely confront corruption and immorality. Because such temptations are likely in positions that control powerful resources, women tend to be in less powerful positions. In state and national cabinet positions, for example, we saw earlier that women are concentrated in less important areas such as welfare and social services, which are usually absent of fraud and corruption.

Because beauty and sexual appeal are so central to the cultural image of women, it is female politicians who have an extremely difficult time breaking through the old boy network and soliciting and receiving the sponsorship of powerful male politicians. Almost any connection between a powerful male politician and a female candidate has a taint of impropriety, the implication of a sexual relationship. As a result, male politicians resist sponsoring female candidates lest they be suspected of improper behavior—or stated differently, lest they be contaminated, the fourth myth. Because beauty and sexual appeal are assumed to be commodities that women exchange for powerful men, women who ask for male sponsorship may send the wrong message to voters or potential sponsors—that they are willing to exchange sexual favors for sponsorship. Where such sponsorship has been obtained, voters may dismiss a woman's candidacy because they suspect she received her endorsement "on her back."

Little need be said here about the first and second control myths—that women are weak, men are strong; and men are analytical, abstract, and smarter. The implications of these two myths for political candidates are obvious. But it is interesting that politics is viewed as analytical and abstract. One can easily imagine a political system in which the leaders are intuitive, holistic, and field dependent—that is, where "female" traits are valued. This leads to our final question: "Would politics in the United States be different if women had a significant share of political power?"

## Conclusion: Female Leadership—Would It Matter?

We are tempted to answer this question affirmatively. Given the differences between men and women, it seems obvious that a large number of female politicians would change the way affairs are conducted in the United States. Or would they? Several considerations suggest that they would not.

First, the similarities between men and women are much greater than their differences. We have seen that political knowledge and concern are similar for the two sexes. Thus, it is unlikely that a "female" political agenda would materialize, primarily because of the vast array of differences that exist among women on almost every issue. Sex per se does not unify individuals on any major political issue, and neither sex is united on important issues. Even women who press for women's issues are frustrated to find as much opposition from other women as from men; one of the most famous "antifeminists" is a woman, Phyllis Schlafly.

This is not to deny that certain issues not presently considered politically legitimate might emerge as such if women were equally represented in office. To believe they would, however, is to believe in common "women's issues" on which women agree, a debatable proposition.

Second, the records of women who are in state and national politics indicate that there are few differences between them and their male colleagues. Although female politicians are marginally more "liberal" in their voting patterns and somewhat more sensitive to women's rights issues, the differences are slight (Darcy, Welch, and Clark, 1987, p. 154).

Finally, and most important, political power in our system is institutionalized. This means that power resides largely in positions rather than in specific individuals. Political power becomes *authority*—that is, institutionalized power that is viewed as legitimate. The power that politicians have resides more in their offices and less in their personalities. Presidents, senators, and representatives, of course, have their own special interests and concerns, but their actual power is constrained by legal limits on their authority. As a result, the exercise of authority often differs more in style than in substance.

So, is there anything wrong with a political system that excludes women from leadership roles? A great deal! As political scientists Darcy, Welch, and Clark conclude:

> Having a more proportional representation of important societal groups such as women accords government greater legitimacy, allows us to fulfill more closely the requirements of the democratic form of government we claim to prize, provides a previously excluded group with an indication that its interests are now likely to be more thoroughly considered, and makes better use of the talents available in society (1987, p. 153).

# References

Center for the American Woman and Politics, Egleton Institute of Politics. "Fact Sheet." 1988. New Brunswick, NJ: Rutgers University.

Darcy, Robert, Susan Welch, and Janet Clark. *Women, Elections, and Representation.* 1987. New York: Longman.

Epstein, Cynthia F. "Women and Power: The Roles of Women in Politics in the United States," in *Access to Power: Cross National Studies of Women and Elites,* C. F. Epstein and R. L. Coser (Eds.). 1981. London: Allen and Unwin.

Kingston, Paul W., and Steven E. Finkel. "Is There a Marriage Gap in Politics?" *Journal of Marriage and the Family* 49: 57–64, Feb. 1987.

Lipman–Blumen, Jean. *Gender Roles and Power.* 1984. Englewood Cliffs, NJ: Prentice–Hall.

National Opinion Research Center. *General Social Survey.* 1985. Chicago: National Opinion Research Center.

Sapiro, Virginia. *The Political Integration of Women.* 1983. Chicago: University of Illinois Press.

Sapiro, Virginia. *Women, Political Action, and Political Participation.* 1988. Washington, DC: American Political Science Association.

Welch, Susan. "Women as Political Animals: A Test of Some Explanations for Male–Female Political Participation Differences." *American Journal of Political Science* 21: 711–731, 21 Nov. 1977.

## Suggested Readings

Lipman-Blumen, Jean. *Gender Roles and Power.* A sociologist presents the control myths that are used to justify the near-exclusion of women from political power in the United States.

Sapiro, Virginia. *Women, Political Action, and Political Participation.* This text reviews the major findings concerning women in politics in the United States.

# CHAPTER 7

# Race

## From the Playing Field to the Office Suite: Blacks in Sports Management

**B**aseball remains America's game, our peculiar athletic invention absorbing the attention of millions. Great players have mythic stature, the game's lore is recounted in countless conversations, and the fates of teams are dissected with intense emotion.

Life inside the ballpark has its separate reality, almost "unmodern" with its irregular fields, leisurely pace, and untimed length. In pure form, it dramatizes the "joy of victory and the agony of defeat" (to use the television cliche), as well as the virtues of physical ability and strategic decisions, individual talent, and team play. If it is an escape from a complex, often frustrating reality, it is one that transports Americans to a noble, uncorrupt realm.

Baseball is located in Sports World, a place that sportswriter Robert Lipsyte has called "a sweaty Oz you'll never find in a geography book." Lipsyte (1975, p. x) further describes the role of Sports World in our culture:

> . . . [S]ince the end of the Civil War it has been promoted and sold to us like Rancho real estate, an ultimate sanctuary, a university for the body, a community for the spirit, a place to hide that glows with that time of innocence when we believed that rules and boundaries were honored, that good triumphed over evil, and that the loose ends of experience could be caught and bound and delivered in an explanation as final and as comforting as a goodnight kiss.

Bill White (on the right), the new National League President, poses with Dr. Bobby Brown and George Steinbrenner (center), the owner of the New York Yankees. White is a "racial pioneer"—blacks have excelled on the playing field but have been almost totally excluded from management positions in baseball and other sports.

Of course, the reality of the larger society has inevitably intruded into this Oz, but Americans seem prepared to overlook its unflattering sides and celebrate its uplifting spirit.

This myopia is certainly the case with the issue of race. Jackie Robinson's inclusion on the 1947 Brooklyn Dodgers has been widely heralded as a milestone in black civil rights, spurring on the advance of blacks in other walks of life. Highly paid black superstars followed the Robinson breakthrough, allowing baseball to bask in the glow of a racially progressive image.

This progressive image, however, showed its flaws as a troubling question was increasingly raised: Why were there so few black managers, especially when so many blacks had distinguished themselves as players? Black progress in sports has had obvious limits: Blacks were "good enough" to be on teams, but not to run them—play, but not think.

The illusions of Sports World were not greatly threatened, however, until the racist comments of a baseball executive were aired on national television in early 1987. Ironically, while appearing on a program honoring the fortieth anniversary of Jackie Robinson's breaking of baseball's color barrier ("Nightline," an ABC network news show), Al Campanis, an executive with the Los Angeles Dodgers, was asked why so few blacks had leadership positions in baseball.

Campanis's answer: "They [blacks] may not have some of the necessities to be field managers or general managers."

He continued, "How many [black] quarterbacks are there? How many pitchers?" His implication, clearly, was that these "necessities" involved intelligence, a quality that blacks lacked.

These comments set off a storm of reaction. Prominent blacks such as Frank Robinson, a former superstar and manager, denounced the remarks as indicative of a racism that permeated baseball. Others, especially those within the black community, raised a broader indictment: Campanis's views reflected a racism that continues to infect all of American society.

The California state assembly was moved by the public outcry both to censure Campanis and urge Commissioner of Baseball Peter Ueberroth to address the virtual absence of blacks in baseball management. Ueberroth pledged his office's commitment to increasing the number of blacks. As part of this effort, he chose Harry Edwards, a black sociologist at the University of California at Berkeley, as his special advisor on minorities in baseball.

## Larger Implications

The details of this story certainly have their own intrigues and ironies. For example, Harry Edwards, having a fine appreciation of the dramatic gesture, appointed Campanis as his consultant. But the incident is sociologically compelling because of the larger questions it raises:

- Do Campanis's remarks reflect a more general white racism in just baseball or in the larger society?
- Does white prejudice alone account for the low numbers of black managers?

That is, Campanis's comments have sparked soul-searching about the general state of race relations in American society that goes well beyond what he said. Surely the public attention given to these brief remarks attests to how prominently baseball figures in our national consciousness. Note that Americans have recently focused on the fact that there are no black baseball managers — not the fact that there are no black governors or senators, black chief executive officers of a Fortune 500 company, black Nobel prize winners in scientific fields, or black presidents of Ivy League universities.

In a way, this focus may seem trivial. After all, baseball is only a game. But sports can dramatize important emotions, bringing them into sharp relief. It is probably too simplistic to say that baseball or any other sport is a microcosm of society, but larger social issues are played out in sport. Sport both reflects the larger social environment, including its racial problems, and offers a valuable prism through which we can view and understand this environment.

Some apologists, of course, have denied that the Campanis incident holds any general lesson. He has been portrayed as an unfortunate, confused man who spoke for no one but himself. Baseball as a whole is not racist, they say, and more blacks will be accepted into management when they get the necessary experience.

These apologists are hard-pressed to explain, however, why so few blacks have been allowed to gain this experience. One might also ask whether all this talk about being qualified through long experience is not unduly inflated, a defense of the old boy network. Sparky Anderson, an acknowledged "super" manager, once said, "My biggest job as a manger is that I don't trip the players going down the runway."

Suspicions that Campanis voiced general sentiments within the baseball establishment have surely not been quieted. How else can the black exclusion from managerial positions be explained if not by racism, many ask? Indeed, black spokespersons and others have charged that Campanis voiced the sentiments of the real white America often hidden behind a veneer of polite racial tolerance. These charges have an extra force given the many recent incidents of racial harassment on college campuses and greatly reduced governmental action to address racial inequalities. Thus, in this view, there is a simple, direct way to explain why blacks have so little decision-making power *throughout* society: white prejudice.

In our judgment, neither the baseball apologists nor those who have alleged Campanis speaks for white America are right. Baseball has racist practices and some members of the baseball establishment surely have prejudiced attitudes toward blacks. At the same time, most white Americans do not accept Campanis's racist vision, even if subtler racist attitudes remain. Moreover, it is much too simplistic to view white racist *attitudes* as the problem. To understand why blacks do not have managerial power in baseball and elsewhere, it is also essential to see how everyday institutional practices have discriminatory consequences, even without discriminatory intent.

In a nutshell, that is the thesis that we will develop in this chapter. First, it is worth documenting the black exclusion from managerial positions in both the dugout and the office suite.

# The Managerial Scoreboard

There is no disputing the critics' charge: Whites run baseball. Frank Robinson and a handful of other blacks have broken the managerial color line, but in 1988 there was only one black manager and no black general managers or owners. At the time, about a third of all major leaguers were black.

Now under the public microscope, baseball has made some progress in promoting blacks in a short time. One year after Campanis's interview on "Nightline," Commissioner Ueberroth released a report detailing that 102 minority workers had been hired in front office positions since April 1987—36 percent of total hirings, a higher percentage than that for the new players. During this same time, however, thirteen managerial and general managerial vacancies were filled: not one of these positions went to a black.

Major league baseball's management hardly stands alone as a white preserve in Sports World. Richard Lapchick and Joe Panepinto of Northeastern University's Center for the Study of Sport in Society have documented the barrier to blacks in all major sports at the collegiate and professional levels (see Table 7.1).

The color line in the managerial ranks of professional football and basketball is perhaps even more flagrantly drawn than in baseball because so many of the players are black and have been so for many years. As long ago as the mid-1970s, almost one-half of professional football players and approximately 70 percent of professional basketball players were black. These players have constituted a potential managerial recruitment pool that has been overlooked. Currently, there are no black

**Table 7.1**  Blacks in Sports Management

|                                      | College (%)* | Professional (%)† |
|--------------------------------------|:------------:|:-----------------:|
| Head Coach                           | 4.2          | 5.0               |
| Assistant Coach                      | 3.1          | 10.0              |
| Athletic Director/<br>General Manager | .7          | 3.0               |
| Athletic Department/<br>Front Office | 1.2          | 4.0               |

*Football, men's and women's basketball, and men's track and baseball

†National Basketball Association, National Football League, and Major League Baseball

Source: Lapchick and Panepinto, 1987

head coaches in the National Football League and only three black head coaches in the National Basketball Association.

It is hard to say, however, that the situation in Sports World is worse than in the rest of society. Consider the percentages of blacks in the following occupations:

- 1.56 percent of university faculty members;
- 1.8 percent of the senior officers in the U.S. Department of State;
- 3.3 percent of all physicians;
- approximately 1.5 percent of all elected officials; and
- less than 0.5 percent of senior executives of Fortune 1000 companies.

(Putting these figures in perspective, approximately 12 percent of the total U.S. population is black.)

The obvious point is that blacks are barely represented in decision-making positions throughout society. To the extent that blacks have made gains in the professional–managerial world, it has been largely in the public sector, where hiring decisions are scrutinized closely and minority groups have been able to wield political influence. Even there, however, the gains have been limited. Blacks have filled public relations jobs (high visibility, but little clout) and positions that involve dealing with a minority clientele (for example, welfare departments) in disproportionate numbers.

# White Attitudes

Defenders of Campanis such as Tommy Lasorda, the manager of the Dodgers, have attested to his basic decency. "Look at the man's track record," Lasorda has said. "He got caught in a trap of words."

Campanis's track record, however, does not really get him off the hook. In his nineteen years as Dodger vice president in charge of personnel, no black held a position higher than first base coach. Of course, we cannot know why particular hiring decisions were made, but Campanis's recent remarks suggest that potential black candidates had at least two strikes against them.

Before concluding that this incident "says something" about the basic causes of racial stratification in the United States, however, we should first look systematically at the racial attitudes of white Americans. No doubt many share Campanis's sentiments. Probably all of us have seen blatant racism at some time, but such views are no longer part of the white mainstream.

How can we make such a generalization? We look to the record of public opinion surveys, which have tracked racial attitudes over many years. Because these surveys include many of the same questions each year and are answered by a nationally representative sample of Americans, we have strong evidence of considerable change.[1]

For example, the National Opinion Research Center has asked survey respondents, "Do you think Negroes should have as good a chance as white people to get any kind of job, or do you think white people should have the first chance at any kind of job?" One would probably think, "Of course, as good a chance," and, in fact, virtually all Americans now say this. A little more than thirty years ago, however, less than one-half of white Americans said that.

Obviously, we should not rely too much on the responses to this question, but when the answers to a series of related questions go the "same way," we have greater confidence in our conclusion.

Consider, then, how white Americans responded to the question, "There's always much discussion about the qualifications of presidential candidates — their education, age, race, religion, and the like; if your party nominated a generally well-qualified man for president and he happened to be a black, would you vote for him?" In 1957, 37 percent said yes; in 1967, 52 percent; and in 1983, 81 percent said yes—an increase of 44 percentage points.

---

[1]   All the public opinion data presented below are reported in Howard Schuman, Charlotte Steeh, and Lawrence Bobo, *Racial Attitudes in America* (Cambridge, MA: Harvard University Press, 1985).

Like most sociologists, we do not interpret these results as referring only to the presidential vote. Questions such as these are intended to "tap" broader orientations. They give respondents a concrete focus as researchers explore dimensions of racial tolerance. The reasoning is that people who are willing to accept a black person as president are also accepting of blacks in less responsible positions, and thus are more racially tolerant overall.

We can multiply examples to show, on matters of basic principle, that most white Americans accept integration. Let us simply note that about 90 percent believe in integrated schools and open housing, and two-thirds believe there should be no laws against intermarriage (although only 40 percent "approve" of such marriages). These questions do not directly get at whites' feelings about blacks, but it is a reasonable inference that if whites accept interaction with blacks in many settings, they generally do not harbor deep prejudices about blacks.

Moreover, we have direct evidence that Campanis's characterization of blacks is no longer widely shared. In 1942, a slight majority of white Americans thought that blacks were less intelligent than whites, but by 1964 only some 20 percent of whites believed blacks to be their intellectual inferiors. (The question about intelligence was not included on the more recent national surveys.)

Of course, no one can say that responses to a questionnaire reflect what people believe deep in their hearts. Undoubtedly, whites who claimed support for, say, open housing have varying degrees of enthusiasm. It is also easy to imagine that many survey respondents now are pulled in a prointegration direction because they sense it is the "right thing" to say. The possibility that many whites feel this pressure, however, is significant in itself, pointing to the reality of a normative shift for white Americans. Whites feel that prointegration attitudes are "right" because they are so common among their fellow whites.

We do not need to accept survey responses at face value to see clear signs of a significant decrease in the levels of white racial prejudice. Indeed, the public reaction to Campanis's remarks is very telling about this normative change. Thirty years ago, his comments would have barely caused a stir, but now they provoke public outrage. The comments are "news" because they offend public sensibilities.

None of this is to say that white America has purged itself of racism, or has even come close. It should be recognized, however, that real progress has occurred, that white racism generally no longer involves a fundamental aversion to blacks or a denigration of their abilities. Contemporary white racism is less encompassing and surely less overt than the attitudes revealed by Campanis's remarks.

For these reasons, white racism is harder to document. But we can see the reality of continuing antiblack prejudice in the fact that whites seem reluctant to support governmental initiatives to implement nondiscriminatory practices. In recent years, only the minority of whites has favored specific efforts to promote black entry into schools, housing, and jobs.

Many social psychological experiments also point to a gap between the increasing progressive principles of whites and their behavior in dealing with blacks.[2] Experimenters had a black woman and a white woman separately drop groceries in the path of white customers as they left a supermarket. About the same proportion of white customers stopped to give some help to each woman. In 63 percent of the incidents with the white woman, however, the white customers helped her pick up all the groceries, while in 70 percent of the cases with the black woman, customers helped to pick up only a few items. Numerous other "helping studies" show similar discrimination. (Black subjects were generally as likely to favor their own race as were whites.)

Researchers have also systematically studied conversational patterns. In several experiments, white college students were found to sit further away, use less friendly tones, make less eye contact, and speak for a shorter time when talking with blacks than with whites. Clearly race mattered, even for those students who espoused progressive racial attitudes.

Before Jackie Robinson's breakthrough, the exclusion of blacks from major league baseball could be easily explained by direct, overt racism. Now it is essential to understand how both subtle forms of racist attitudes and everyday practices hold back the progress of blacks.

## Institutional Discrimination

Let us imagine that as a group, high-level baseball executives do, in fact, hold relatively progressive racial views. That is, in principle they do not object to hiring blacks for responsible positions and are willing to do so even if they believe that others might object to this decision. Their only concern is to hire the best qualified person.

In making this judgment about potential managers, baseball owners and executives stress the importance of experience, which usually means a long stint of managing in the minor leagues and perhaps some time as a coach at the major league level. Typically, these executives say they want to hire someone with a proven track record.

---

[2]  This brief review of social psychological research draws directly on the extensively documented summary in Thomas Pettigrew and Joanne Martin, "Shaping the Organizational Context for Black American Inclusion," *Journal of Social Issues* (43):41–78, 1987.

So why are there so few black managers? The baseball executives can point to the fact that virtually no blacks have the "necessary" experience. They may genuinely regret this situation but still believe in the proposition, "There's no substitute for experience."

If they remain committed to this practice, however, the outcome is no different than if they were blatantly racist. Acting on nonracist motives, they still systematically exclude blacks. The fact that few blacks have acquired the desired experience undoubtedly reflects previous racist attitudes, but their continued exclusion from managerial positions can be maintained without discriminatory intent.

Baseball hiring practices illustrate the phenomenon of *institutional racial discrimination*. This involves the usual, customary practices of institutions that systematically advance the racial majority ahead of the racial minority, even though these practices are not necessarily intended to have this effect. Institutional discrimination involves organizational practices (for example, an emphasis on experience in hiring decisions), not the attitudes and behaviors of individuals. It is recognized by its effects (that is, few blacks in positions of responsibility), not by its intentions.

The concept of institutional discrimination illuminates many aspects of contemporary American racial problems. In previous generations, for example, residential segregation of the races could be readily explained by overt discrimination by whites. Now whites apparently have more tolerant attitudes and federal and state laws prohibit discrimination, and yet residential segregation remains a pervasive reality. This segregation continues in part because zoning laws restrict the types of housing that can be built in many areas. Residents in a suburb that prohibits multiple or public housing may stress that they only seek to "protect" property values. They may say, "*Anyone* who can afford to live here is fine with me." But such statements make our point. It is entirely predictable that blacks will be less able to afford a home in this type of suburb than will whites. Thus, zoning laws become the usual customary practice, perpetuating segregation even more than the overt actions of bigots.

Of course, the defenders of such "nondiscriminatory" practices are not blind to their racial impact and may even support them because of this impact. "Standard policy" is much easier to justify to others and oneself than is racial prejudice.

Indeed, the stoutest defenders of such usual practices as insisting on "experience" often overlook its violation. For example, owners have justified not hiring former black players because they lack managerial experience in the minor leagues, but few questioned the decision to hire Pete Rose, a white former player who had no managerial experience. Rose, an extraordinarily fiery player, is an exception, people might say. True, but why have there not been black exceptions?

## Segregated Networks

Perhaps deep-seated racial prejudice remains in the hearts of baseball team owners and executives, but actively negative attitudes do not need to be involved. All people, black and white, are inclined to favor others like themselves. They are familiar, comfortable, and because they do things the same way, they do them the "right" way.

Baseball owners live in a white world in which personal contacts fundamentally shape hiring decisions. A son might handle marketing; a college buddy may be the team's lawyer. The knowledgeable "baseball man" (usually the general manager) hires former teammates as scouts and assistants. Little bureaucratic procedure ensures that the best qualified are actually hired.

In short, these gatekeepers draw upon their own social networks to find job candidates, and they often make their decisions without clear evidence of merit. There is no active discrimination against blacks here so much as positive discrimination in favor of personal contacts, almost all of whom are white.

The significance of social networks in hiring decisions extends far beyond baseball. For example, sociologists Jomills Braddock and James McPartland (1987) examined employment practices at a large sample of firms and found that for college-degree jobs, "the chances are significantly greater that an opening will be filled by whites when social networks are used as a major employer recruitment method." The reason is obvious: Blacks are not tied into the networks that help to get a person's foot in the door.

People often state that the race problem is an "attitude problem," and that by changing enough hearts, society will change. But given the impact of both institutional discrimination and the widespread reliance on social networks in hiring decisions, such changes in the hearts of whites are not enough to bring blacks into positions of responsibility in baseball or in other fields. The subordination of blacks is maintained through the normal social processes of organizations. To bring blacks into the mainstream, changes must be made in how institutions operate, not just in how individuals think.

## Being a Pioneer

Against the great odds set by these barriers, blacks have succeeded in breaking into formerly all-white worlds, but usually only a few at a time. Baseball had Jackie Robinson and Larry Doby, and other sports and walks of life have had their pioneers as well. Inevitably, the pressures on all of them were enormous, a fact to keep in mind as we consider the difficulties of integrating baseball management and other segregated worlds.

If a white player on the 1947 Brooklyn Dodgers struck out with men on base, he might have heard some scattered boos for his *personal* failure. Robinson's performance in the same situation was a test case for a *black's* ability to come through under pressure. Similarly, Robinson's hard slide into second brought up issues of black competitiveness, sportsmanship, and feelings toward whites. White players never endured such scrutiny. Moreover, this burden was one that would have fallen on any black pioneer, whatever his characteristics as a player or person.

To understand this sociological point in a more general light, look quickly at the nine letters below:[3]

xxXXXXOXxX

What do you "see"?

Maybe you overlooked the "O," but if you saw it, you also probably gave it more attention than any "X." Also, the X's may seem more alike than different because of their contrast and dissimilarity with the O. At the same time, it is easier to fit O's to generalizations ("all O's are like that") than to do so for X's. Because there are more X's, there are more examples to possibly disconfirm a generalization. An O may not fit the generalization, but it is easier to explain away or ignore a few discrepancies rather than many.

In short, the simple fact of being rare and different (an O, a black baseball manager, a male nursery school teacher) is linked to the following important tendencies in the ways that people see the social world:

*Unusual attention:* Pioneers get more attention than the usual group members.

*Contrast,* or polarization or exaggeration of differences: The presence of an O within a uniform group increases the group's sense of " we-ness," of its internal similarities and differences from others.

*Assimilation:* The characteristics of pioneers are misperceived to fit existing generalizations; that is, they are more subject to stereotyped thinking than are the dominant types within the group.

Thus, pioneers in any setting are distinctly visible as being different, and yet they are denied their own individuality, especially in ways that

---

[3] We draw this example and the following discussion of the impact of numerical skews on social interaction from Rosabeth Kanter, *Men and Women of the Corporation* (New York: Basic Books, 1977), especially chapter 8. She focuses on women in business (and uses the term "token" where we use "pioneer"), but her general points are readily extended to race relations.

counter existing stereotypes. These perceptual tendencies make it difficult for pioneers to perform well—and, perhaps more important, to have good performance recognized.

Consider the implications for a black's life as a baseball manager. His visibility means that he lives in a fishbowl. All decisions are interpreted as being done the "black way"; all of his mistakes are readily noticed. Faced with this reaction, he may become unduly self-conscious, thus denying himself the personal comfort and benefits of acting decisively on his natural inclinations. What receives notice is his blackness, not his ability, a fact that he may well resent. This reaction will surely add little to his self-confidence.

Maybe the whites in the baseball establishment will willingly rethink their operating assumptions because a few blacks intrude into their midst, but it is hard to be optimistic. In other social settings, the intrusion of an outsider often makes the insiders anxious. They do not like the fact that the "usual way" may be challenged ("What are *they* going to want next?"). Insiders also resent the need to think about what is "acceptable" behavior and what can be tacitly understood. Where everyone is alike, people can unreflectively behave. They know that their peers accept their ways and share the understandings (a distinctive sense of humor, for example) that make interaction comfortable and efficient.

Reacting to the self-consciousness and uncertainties that are created by the pioneer's presence, insiders often exaggerate their group's characteristics. Male business executives are given to conspicuous displays of "male talk" in the presence of female executives ("Scored big last night!"), or they interrupt conversations in ways that remind women of their outsider status ("Is it okay to swear?"). This kind of behavior shores up the solidarity of the insider group and, of course, keeps the outsider apart.

Any pioneer such as a black baseball manager will sense the insiders' unease and the resulting isolation. It is therefore difficult to develop the intimacy that is necessary for good working relationships (and the loyalty of colleagues that will help him keep his job). He is caught in a dilemma: If he acts himself, he risks continued isolation ("They're too difficult to deal with"); if he passes the various "loyalty tests" and becomes like the insiders, he bears the cost of self-denial.

Furthermore, pioneers must often battle the burdens of negative *stereotypes.* Stereotypes can be either positive or negative but always involve associations between types of people and clusters of characteristics—for example, all sociology professors are [fill in the blank]. We all have stereotypes; they arrange our understanding of the world in manageable patterns. But they can be very wrong; they deny real differences among people, and they are hard to erase. Even in the face of obvious contradictory evidence, people often tenaciously hold on to their stereotypes.

If little is expected of a black pioneer simply because he is black, it will be hard for him to demonstrate that his individual performance really is "good." Although a win-loss record might seem an indisputable indicator of job performance, the true performance yardstick in baseball management and other fields is quite elastic, subject to the impressionistic preferences of those who hire and fire. Some white managers with mediocre win-loss records still are defined as "good" and retain their jobs. Given negative stereotypes about blacks, however, it is hard for those whose impressions matter to subtly evaluate the pioneer's talent and the particular circumstances of his performance.

Indeed, social psychologists Thomas Pettigrew and Joanne Martin (1987) argue that blacks are often subject to the *ultimate attribution error,* especially when they are pioneers. If a black does something "bad," it is because of his blackness ("Wouldn't you know it; that's how they are"), and that fact cannot be changed. If a black does something "good," however, it is seen as the "exception that proves the rule," or as the outcome of unusually favorable circumstances.

In either case, the black pioneer might well ask: How can I win? The web of a negative stereotype can disguise individual merit and frustrate those who are caught within it, hardly the conditions to build a successful career in baseball or elsewhere.

## Conclusion

The general sociological point here is that, in itself, a social skew in the population of a particular setting (for example, many whites, few blacks) predictably disadvantages minority group members. The black manager is not likely to escape these disadvantages by sheer force of personality. Nor are white executives likely to remove these consequences simply by expressing their individual good will. These disadvantages are built into the *social* situation—the fact of numerical inequality in group representation. The burden of being a pioneer will remain until the skew is balanced, when the O is no longer isolated in the midst of the X's.

## References

Braddock, Jomills, and James McPartland. "How Minorities Continue to Be Excluded from Equal Employment Opportunities: Research on Labor Market and Institutional Barriers." *Journal of Social Issues* (43): 5–39, 1987.

Kanter, Rosabeth. *Men and Women of the Corporation.* 1977. New York: Basic Books.

Lapchick, Richard, and Joe Panepinto. "The White World of College Sports." *New York Times,* 15 Nov. 1987, S12.

Lipsyte, Robert. *Sports World: An American Dreamland.* 1975. New York: Quadrangle/New York Times Book Co.

Pettigrew, Thomas, and Joanne Martin. "Shaping the Organizational Context for Black American Inclusion." *Journal of Social Issues* (43): 41–78, 1987.

Schuman, Howard, Charlotte Steeh, and Lawrence Bobo. *Racial Attitudes in America.* 1985. Cambridge, MA: Harvard University Press.

## Suggested Readings

Farley, Reynolds. *Blacks and Whites: Narrowing the Gap?* 1984. Cambridge, MA: Harvard University Press. This book thoroughly details the economic position of black and white Americans. It shows that we have taken forward and backward steps in the quest for racial equality.

Lapchick, Richard. *Broken Promises: Racism in American Sports.* 1984. New York: St. Martin's Press. This passionate indictment of American sports effectively mixes personal experiences and more general sociological insights.

Pettigrew, Thomas, and Joanne Martin. "Shaping the Organizational Context for Black American Inclusion." This article effectively summarizes research about the problems blacks face in the labor market and proposes sensible remedies.

Schuman, Howard, Charlotte Steeh, and Lawrence Bobo. *Racial Attitudes in America.* The authors subtly analyze the best available evidence about racial attitudes from public opinion surveys. They document considerable change.

# CHAPTER 8

# The Family

## Life in the Two-Job Family

## A Day in the Life

6:45 AM Husband and wife awake and start to mobilize their three children. They fix breakfast, pack several lunches, and remind the older two children to go to the after-school program.

7:45 AM Husband and wife separately drive to their jobs. Husband drops the youngest child at the babysitter's house on the way.

2:30 PM Wife picks up youngest child from the babysitter on way home. She then vacuums the house and starts the laundry.

4:30 PM Wife picks up the other two children at school and drives all three to soccer practice. She meets her husband there at 5:15. While the oldest child practices with his team, the father looks after the other two. In the meantime, the wife drives back to her school to teach a night class.

6:15 PM Father and children eat dinner at a fast-food restaurant.

7 PM Father bathes the youngest child and checks the homework that his daughter did at the after-school program. Children watch television for one hour.

9 PM All children are in bed. Father reads.

10 PM Wife returns home from teaching. She tells her husband where the children will be the next day and re-

Jane Scherr/Jeroboam, Inc.

Juggling two jobs and children is part of many contemporary marriages. Many solutions exist, although most result in one of the spouses working unusual hours or part-time.

minds him to call about the plumbing repair. She folds laundry. Then she takes a quick shower and goes to bed. He reads a while longer before also going to bed.

This is a real day in a real family, with nothing unusual or dramatic. Like most couples with young children, this one faces the challenges of simultaneously managing two jobs, a range of domestic responsibilities, and relationships as husband and wife, mother and father. With the great surge of women into the labor force, the "traditional" family—husband as sole breadwinner, wife as full-time homemaker—is now a minority, including those families with young children.

Of course, this family has its own distinctive joys and problems, and its members generally view the "management" of their work and domestic lives as private concerns. They must negotiate who does what in the home, arrange for child care, decide how much priority to give their jobs and their family, and find time to be alone and together. Their solutions do not satisfy all of their desires, and they do not always work smoothly. But because working wives have become so common, this couple's *private life* represents a *public concern*.

As with millions of other parents, they have worried that sending their youngest child to a babysitter is not good for him. Can another person help him develop, intellectually and morally, as well as a parent? Few parents, especially mothers, entrust their children to others without misgivings or feelings of guilt.

Like most couples, they also wonder if their marriage can withstand the tensions of coordinating the schedules of two jobs. Have the demands made them just ships passing in the night, an economic unit with little chance to develop emotional warmth and support?

Also, as do most couples, they question who is now supposed to handle various parts of domestic life—washing the laundry, arranging the children's dental appointments, taking time off from work to pick up a sick child from school, and deciding how to spend the family's money. In the "old days," matters were simple: The husband brought home the money and had final control over its spending; the wife was responsible for most domestic chores and their children. Does the wife's monetary contribution now give her greater say on financial matters? Do her work commitments mean that her husband is expected to help more around the house and with the children?

Setting aside thoughts about what constitutes a fair division of labor in the home and outside it, this couple and millions of others face the concrete challenge of getting lots of things done. After all, the day is only so long, and time in one activity is unavailable for another. What loses out in the competition for time?

Many critics have argued that such new family arrangements point to a social decline, even disaster. They see a neglect of children that results in poor school performances, drug use, and other delinquencies as women "selfishly" pursue their careers. These critics see a deterioration of the marital bond because couples lack time for intimacy or evaluating their marriages in terms of economic costs and benefits. They also point to the instabilities and tensions of relationships that are built on undefined or "unnatural" roles. In this view, then, the *private* decisions of individual married women to work have resulted in *public* problems.

Not all social observers agree. Looking at these new arrangements, some see the emergence of more appealing family lives, especially for women. They see wives' employment as essential for more egalitarian relations between the sexes—that is, grounds for intimate relationships that are built on mutual respect, not dependence. More than that, these observers believe that it has resulted in a more involved family role for fathers, an involvement that ultimately benefits children.

In this chapter, we examine the effects of married women's employment on family life in light of the best available social science evidence. Because the impact has been alleged to be so great, we range widely across such issues as the effects of work schedules on family life, the financial benefits of two wage earners, marital happiness, divorce, the division of labor, and the implications for children. On a matter so often clouded by personal anxieties, ideological preferences, and unfounded speculation, objective research on general patterns can place personal situations in a larger and more useful perspective.

Our first order of business is to document the prevalence of the employed wife in American families.

## Measuring the Change

Traditionally, wives worked at home, doing most of the household chores, caring for children, and supporting their husbands. Since the end of World War II in 1945, however, this pattern has gradually become the exception rather than the rule. Of the approximately 50 million married couples in America today, almost 70 percent have working wives, and 60 percent have both working husbands and working wives (U.S. Bureau of the Census, 1986).

More significantly, married mothers of young children have entered the labor force in unprecedented numbers. In 1950, only 10 percent of mothers of preschoolers (under age 6) worked, but now one-half do. About one-quarter of mothers of school-aged children (7 to 17) worked in 1950, but more than 60 percent do today (U.S. Department of Labor, 1984). In short, married women, whether or not they have children, are more likely to be working. But this has only been true for about two decades; before the late 1960s, working wives were the exception rather than the rule.

Lest we leave the impression that most Americans live in two-job families, however, we must note that although such arrangements are typical of married couples, they are not so typical of all living arrangements. Indeed, Americans live in a wider range of situations today than at any time in our history. To appreciate the importance of wives' employment, we must put this in perspective. How many Americans live with spouses? How many of these couples have two wage-earners? In how many of these two-earner couples do both spouses work full-time year round? And, finally, how many two-earner couples are "dual-career" couples?

The variety of living arrangements in the United States today reflects the growing prevalence of independent living (more Americans live alone or are unmarried and without children), separation, and divorce (more Americans today live without a spouse but with children). So many people live alone or without a spouse that only 60 percent of living arrangements are of married couples. And because only one-half of married couples are two-job households, a little arithmetic shows that only one-third of all Americans have employed spouses.

Moreover, while at any one time approximately 60 percent of married couples have two earners, many employed wives move in and out of the labor market or work only part-time. In actuality, in only one-quarter of all marriages do both husbands and wives work full-time year-round.

The meaning of two jobs also can be easily misinterpreted. Often the press, television, and movies show families in which both the husband and wife have careers, the so-called dual-career couple. In such families, both work long hours to meet important deadlines in high-powered, high-paid positions. But many employed spouses, especially wives, do not have careers in the sense that they consistently commit themselves to acquiring experience and expertise within a particular field so as to advance within it. Given all the attention that dual-career families receive, it is astonishing that fewer than 7 percent of married couples, even by the most generous definitions, fit this description (U.S. Bureau of the Census, 1987, Table 6).

In our own research, we have found it useful to think of the work commitments of two-job families in terms of the "family work day"—that is, the pattern of husbands' and wives' combined work schedules in two-earner families (Nock and Kingston, 1984). For example, a particular family commits 16 hours of each day to work as a unit (both husband and wife working 8 hours). But the husband starts work at 8 AM, and the wife ends work at 8 PM. Such a couple has a 12-hour family work day. Another couple also commits 16 hours to work, but both the husband and wife work the same hours; theirs is an 8-hour family work day. For two-earner American couples, the typical family work day is approximately 11 hours.

Together, two-earner couples commit an average of 17 hours a day to work (husbands average 9 hours, wives 8). This means that about one-half of two-earner couples have something less than two full-time jobs. More important, fewer than 10 percent of two-earner couples work exactly the same hours. For at least some portion of the family work day for the vast majority of working couples, one spouse works while the other does not.

Given that so many working couples have wives (or perhaps husbands) who work something less than a typical 8-hour day, it might be more appropriate to discuss a "one-and-some-fraction-job family" rather than the two-job family. Admittedly, such a description is awkward, but it points to the reality of how Americans tend to accommodate two jobs and their family lives.

# The Financial Benefit

Two-earner couples do not have twice the income of those with only one, but the monetary advantage is still considerable. In 1984, the average (median) income for families in which only the husband worked was $23,582, while that for two-earner families was $34,668. The wife's employment typically increases family income by approximately 30 percent (U.S. Department of Labor, 1984, Table A). But the income difference between one- and two-earner couples is significant and would make a big difference in life-styles for most people. A difference of $10,000 or more per year could mean the difference between being able or unable to send children to college, purchase adequate health care, or buy a home.

For many, perhaps most, couples, whether the wife works is not an option. Indeed, the primary reason for large increases in two-income families is economic necessity. Many years ago, a family could often purchase a house and a car and maintain a decent standard of living with one income. This is no longer possible for large numbers of families today; most couples *need* the additional income. Beyond economic necessity, however, married women have embraced paid work for many other reasons. For one, the types of jobs that are available today are more open to women, especially the clerical and service occupations. In addition, increasing numbers of women complete college and expect to have careers. The high divorce rate also forces many women to enter the labor force or develop paid skills so that they will be employable should their marriages fail. Finally, many of the attitudes about male–female equality have changed. Wives are no longer assumed to be completely dependent on their husbands; to avoid such dependence, women must have their own independent sources of income.

Later we will consider why employed wives earn so much less than employed husbands, a matter that involves thinking about wives' unpaid work in the home.

# Marital Happiness

Although the financial benefits of wives' employment are readily measurable, there is the question of whether this new type of family produces as much happiness. We all know the adage "Money cannot buy happiness," but there is more to working than the money it provides. Maybe money cannot buy happiness, but the lack of it surely can lead to unhappiness. In addition, the contacts that people make through their jobs are a source of stimulation and enjoyment in themselves, as much as the sense of purpose that a job provides. All the same, jobs take time, interfering with other things that a person might wish to do, especially raising children. In short, working has both negative and positive consequences for families.

A sociological analysis of two-income families reveals that working wives are not the same as working husbands. The demands on them are as fundamentally different as the rewards of working. In many ways, a wife's occupation has significantly different consequences for her and her family than a husband's work has for him and his family.

Two theoretical considerations highlight the problems faced by working women but not working men. The first problem is *role conflict*. Most Americans hold different values about the appropriate family roles of women. Most Americans believe that women are entitled to decide whether they will work. But even if they work, they are expected to care for their children. Thus, a wife's job may appear to interfere with her other responsibilities in a household. She may not be able to cook, clean, and care for her children in the way that her husband believes she should. In short, a working woman may not be able to conform to what men and women in the United States define as her proper role as wife. A wife who is also a librarian, for example, must balance the demands of her occupational role with those of her family, "failing" in one or the other at various times.

The second problem is *role overload*. When women take jobs, they do not exchange one set of tasks (paid work) for another (housework). Instead, they assume additional responsibilities. Both men and women in the United States expect wives to care for children even if they work. Husbands' contributions to child care and homemaking are almost always defined as "helping," as though such tasks are not expected of them.

Despite the possibility of disagreements and the problems that are associated with role conflict and role overload, most research indicates that employed wives report happier marriages than do traditional wives. For example, in a national survey of Americans in 1987, 65 percent of employed wives reported their marriages to be "very happy," while only 55 percent of those who did not work responded in kind. More telling, perhaps, is the fact that 7 percent of nonemployed wives reported their marriages to be "not too happy," while less than 1 percent of employed wives gave that response.

An interesting point is that whether a wife works out of the home or is a traditional homemaker does not influence her husband's marital satisfaction. Identical percentages (69 percent) of husbands married to employed wives and those married to nonemployed wives report their marriages to be "very happy" (1987 General Social Survey).

Whether the wife works is less important than how the couple feels about her work. When husband and wife agree that she should work, the quality of the marriage does not appear to suffer. But when there is disagreement or when her employment is solely out of economic necessity, some tension is likely to result. Some husbands believe that their wives' employment reflects badly on them, indicating their inability to provide for their families. For some men, a working wife signals a loss of masculinity: "Real men" earn enough to provide for their wives and children. Some wives also believe that they should be able to stay at home to raise their children, so they may resent being forced to leave their children with a babysitter. These results do not point to any one particular recipe for a happy marriage.

At the same time, unusually long work hours can pose a real challenge to developing intimacy. In our own research, we used highly detailed time diaries in which individuals recorded their daily activities, noting their time and place and with whom. For a national sample of working couples, we found that long work days cut sharply into a couple's time together, especially the time reserved for fun; this effect was compounded when a couple worked out of "synch" with one another. Time together *is* linked to marital happiness. Couples with less time together express less satisfaction with their marriages. Thus, to the extent that work prevents individuals from seeing each other, marriages may be strained. Indeed, women's employment has been a factor in the increased numbers of divorces over the past two decades.

## Divorce

As divorce rates soared through the 1970s and early 1980s, one popular suspect for this trend was the increasing female employment rate. Women who worked could afford to divorce, it was argued, or work itself undermined the family by taking wives away from their children and traditional domestic responsibilities.

Underlying such popular speculations is a serious sociological insight. The wife's traditional domestic responsibilities are not compensated by the labor force. Work in the home is viewed as less valuable than employment because it is unpaid. Indeed, when people speak about "working women," they usually are referring to women who hold paid jobs, as if housework does not qualify as "work."

A basic sociological principle is that control over resources leads to greater power. To the extent that people have a desired commodity that cannot be obtained elsewhere, they have power over others. Specifically, they are able to extract payment for what is desired. That payment may be not only money, but also honor, esteem, labor, or virtually anything.

Marriages may not appear to involve issues of power because husbands and wives do not typically order one another around. But issues of power can be found in many aspects of a relationship. A marriage is a social structure, and thus social processes that govern power apply as much to domestic life as they do to any social arrangement. Studies show that consistent differences exist in marriages in terms of who does the "dirty work" and who makes the most important decisions and concessions. These are the ways in which power is manifest in a marriage.

To the extent that a wife does not possess resources that are valued by society, while her husband does, he has power over her. He may demand things from her in return for his support. If she has few marketable skills, her options are limited; she is more or less forced to accept this situation. This situation may not appear obvious, but it is nonetheless real. A husband may expect, for example, that his wife do certain things because his job demands them, such as moving when he is offered a new position in another location or entertaining his business associates on short notice. Such expectations may appear to him to be the consequences of his job. But to his wife, they are demands made by her husband. He is able to expect her to do these things even if she is not happy about them.

Wives who do not work have less power than their employed husbands. And if wives do not possess marketable skills, they are less able to leave abusive, loveless, or intolerable marriages. This observation helps to explain the low divorce rates seen with wives who are not employed; divorce is less of an option for these women because they have few alternatives to depending on their husbands.

When wives enter the paid labor force, however, this situation changes significantly. With her own resources, a wife is able to negotiate a more even balance with her husband. If need be, she can leave the relationship and support herself. The basic principle here is that *economic independence leads to social independence*. To the extent that individuals are economically independent of others, they have greater social independence. They have greater power in relationships and greater freedom in what they must do, as well as more options in general.

Given the above, one would expect that wives in two-income families would have much greater independence and power. Studies have indeed shown that women who work for pay have more power than do housewives. Employed wives also report that they contemplate divorce more frequently than wives who do not work for pay. And, not surprisingly, employed wives avail themselves of the social independence that employ-ment provides. Wives with their own income are more likely to divorce than those without them. We stress, however, that such findings emerge even after many other factors that are linked to divorce are "held con-stant"—that is, are controlled. Working wives are more likely to under-take divorce regardless of social class, religion, presence of children, or length of marriage.

Sociological research strongly suggests that the dramatic increase in divorce over the past two decades is attributable to the equally dramatic simultaneous increase in the participation of married women in the labor force. Not only does employment provide women an escape hatch from intolerable, loveless, or abusive marriages, but also it fosters a self-con-cept that goes beyond the traditional wife and mother role. Employed women see themselves, and are seen by others, as more independent, powerful, resourceful, and interesting.

Employment is not the only reason for the dramatic increase in the divorce rate, but it is a major factor. In chapter 14 on population, we show how demographic factors are another prime factor in divorce rates (the age structure of the population, in particular).

To this point, the results may seem paradoxical: Employed wives report happier marriages than do traditional wives but are more inclined to divorce. By the usual reckoning, this seems to be a gain and a loss. How happy could these women really be if they are more likely to seek divorce?

This paradox is partially resolved if divorce is viewed as other than a pathological or personal disaster. American couples increasingly expect that marriages should involve emotional warmth, open communication, and mutual respect. Women, especially, seem increasingly determined that they not be "second-class citizens" in their marriages, and that they share equally with their husbands in decision making and other impor-tant domestic concerns. Intact marriages that involve two employed spouses are happier because the couples are bound by choice, not only by financial dependence. In a real sense, marriages so based *are* more fragile than those based on dependence, because there is less to compel spouses to remain together during those inevitable times in all marriages when love falters, whether momentarily or for extended periods. Eco-nomically dependent wives were once forced to "ride out" such periods. Some marriages undoubtedly rebounded to their earlier happy state, but others did not. The wives in these unhappy relationships were trapped.

A divorce might be viewed as representing a person's insistence that marriage be founded on love, mutuality, and equality. A job provides the necessary freedom to realize this commitment. Without denying the hardships of divorce, we recognize that wives' employment seems to tip the balance of marriage toward the quality of the relationship between two spouses. In this light, the connection between employment and di-vorce may signify something other than a loss.

# Who Does What at Home?

Managing and running a home, especially one that includes children, is a full-time job. When husbands and wives are both employed, however, the question arises as to how they divide domestic tasks. Does the employed wife bear the burden of two jobs, one paid and one unpaid, while her husband keeps a single job? Or does her employment mean a new, more equitable division with the husband running the vacuum cleaner, ironing clothes, cleaning up the children, and packing lunches?

As already noted, wives' greater economic independence has given them greater social independence. Have financial resources allowed women to "escape" the drudgery of housework? Out of necessity or choice have fathers taken more active roles in the rearing of their children?

The short answer to these questions is that husbands have added little to their traditional domestic responsibilities. Wives continue to be almost completely responsible for both housework and child care. Husbands do less than one-quarter of the total work done by all household members. Results from our own research convincingly demonstrate this conclusion (see Table 8.1).

Clearly, working women continue to do most of the work around the house. In fact, working wives differ little from nonworking wives in the share of housework performed. Several studies have shown that among two-earner couples, less housework is done overall, but what is done is overwhelmingly the wife's responsibility.

One final consideration highlights these conclusions. Not only is the husband's contribution typically small, but also his efforts are viewed as "helping" or "assisting," not as sharing. Wives assume responsibility for organizing the tasks of the household—deciding what must be done, when, and how. To the extent that husbands participate at all, they typically help their wives. In short, women are responsible for domestic jobs.

# Time with Children

Housework is only a small part of what must be done at home. Much more crucial is the care of children. This responsibility has traditionally fallen almost exclusively on mothers. Have fathers assumed greater responsibility for such tasks now that their wives are working? Is there a "new" father today, one who is closely involved in child care and child rearing? The answer seems to be "no."

Research clearly reveals that a wife's employment does not significantly alter the balance of responsibility for child care between husband and wife; both employed and nonemployed mothers assume major re-

**Table 8.1** Two-Earner Couples: Time Spent in Activities on a Work Day

| Activity | Average Time (Minutes) | | |
| --- | --- | --- | --- |
| | Couples | Husbands | Wives |
| Paid work | 942 | 529 | 413 |
| All housework | | | |
| • Cooking | 97 | 21 | 77 |
| • Cleaning | 53 | 6 | 46 |
| • Home maintenance | 20 | 13 | 7 |
| • Household management | 38 | 15 | 23 |
| • Shopping | 26 | 7 | 19 |
| Total | 234 | 62 | 172 |
| Activities with children | 74 | 21 | 53 |
| Child care | 49 | 12 | 37 |
| All work (paid and unpaid) | 1176 | 591 | 585 |
| Leisure | 363 | 188 | 175 |

sponsibility for their children (Nock and Kingston, 1988). On a typical workday, employed wives spend an average of approximately four hours (230 minutes) with their children, while husbands spend only two (137 minutes). Wives, both employed and otherwise, perform more than four times as much child care (bathing, dressing, and changing diapers) and five times as much child-related homemaking tasks (cleaning up after their children) as do husbands.

Working couples must arrange for someone to care for their children while they are at work. Such arrangements, of course, are of great concern to parents. But more generally, there is widespread concern that children reared for large portions of the day by babysitters or day-care personnel will suffer in some way. Few people, however, have questioned whether a *father's* absence from his children because of his work might be detrimental. But many people hold traditional notions about the importance of a mother's care. As you may have guessed, whether children benefit or suffer from surrogate care while their parents work is an issue about which there is little agreement.

On one side of the argument are psychologists and sociologists whose research demonstrates that a mother's employment has few, if any, negative consequences for her children. Indeed, on balance, the gains in a mother's self-esteem, income, and escape from routine may actually lead to better outcomes for her children. On the other side of the argument are a few researchers whose studies indicate that very young children (those under age 2) who spend their days with babysitters are less mature intellectually and emotionally.

Taken together, the accumulated evidence thus far tends to support the conclusion that a mother's employment per se has few, if any, profoundly negative consequences for her children. The only agreement reached thus far in the debate is seen in the following statement by a panel of experts on infant and child development.

> When parents have choices about selection and utilization of supplementary care for their infants and toddlers, and have access to stable child-care arrangements featuring skilled, sensitive and motivated caregivers, there is every reason to believe that both children and families can thrive (*Family Circle*, Sept. 20, 1988, p. 108).

Obviously, few among us would quibble about leaving children with motivated, skilled, sensitive, and stable caregivers. But few parents have much choice about the selection and use of such caregivers, and fewer still are able to locate such ideal arrangements as described above. The only honest answer to the question of whether children benefit or lose from being cared for by others is that we do not know. That is why the problem is so perplexing to working parents.

When the responsibility for children is added to the responsibility for homemaking, it becomes clear that mothers have considerably more to do than fathers. In an effort to do all that they must, wives often work fewer hours for pay than do their husbands. The net result, as shown in Table 8.1, is that husbands and wives have almost identical amounts of "work" each day; hers as a combination of paid and unpaid, and his primarily paid. This partly explains why wives do not earn as much as their husbands.

# Explaining the Wife's Fraction

We described working couples earlier as "one-and-some-fraction-job" couples rather than two-job couples because so many wives work only a portion of any day, week, or year. How do we explain this finding? Why do wives, but not husbands, curtail their paid work to care for their homes and children?

One explanation is offered by economists and sociologists who propose the theory of the New Home Economics. The basic proposition is that a woman's potential contribution to the economic success of the family is less than a husband's. She will simply earn less for her time in the labor force. Given this fact, husbands and wives decide that she, not he, should care for the home and children because her efforts at such tasks are less costly—that is, she loses less than he would by not working. In short, if someone has to care for the home and children, it is better for the spouse who earns less to do so.

The problem with this theory is that it assumes that husbands and wives mainly seek to maximize *income*. The theory does not account for the importance of those values and norms of society that govern human behavior. In fact, sociologist Sara Berk (1985) argues that shared notions about gender are part of what is *produced* in a household. Not only do husbands and wives produce income, but also they produce *gender* by the way they arrange their household tasks.

Irving Goffman, the great social psychologist, argued that we must all continually display our gender by specific ways of appearing, acting, and feeling. Such gender displays establish each of us as a member of the appropriate sex in the eyes of others. Many of these displays are part of the sex roles that we learn as children, but many are not. Indeed, gender is continually redefined throughout life, and all people must demonstrate that they conform to the appropriate norms. As we all realize, people who fail to appear appropriately masculine or feminine often are shunned or ridiculed. Thus, the demonstration of appropriate gender behavior must be viewed as an ongoing requirement for all members of society. So, how do people demonstrate—that is, "display"—their gender?

Berk believes that the household is where gender is displayed, calling the home a "gender factory" because men and women establish their relationships to one another there. It is in the home that masculinity and femininity are most central to peoples' lives: They enact their roles as husband or wife, father or mother, son or daughter, social roles that are most strongly defined by their own sex.

Couples do more than attempt to maximize their combined incomes. They also define themselves as males and females as they divide household tasks. They define their relationships to each other in accord with social norms of masculinity and femininity. As Berk argues, "When the time comes to allocate the household members' labor, there are available a host of good reasons that husbands, *regardless* of other considerations, should be market specialists, and wives either household specialists or modern-day generalists, devoting time to both work sites" (1985, pp. 205-206).

Here, once again, we see the operation of the most basic of sociological principles: Individual behavior is caused in part by the social environment in which one lives. Life in a two-income household reflects the operation of strong social forces from the larger society, particularly the social definitions of masculine and feminine traits. We also see the operation of another basic principle: Social norms are experienced as personal preferences. The rules of our society are so taken for granted that when we conform to them we believe we are doing so out of individual choice or free will. Through this process, social control becomes self-control.

Nothing makes this point more clearly than the reports of spouses themselves in two-income families. Despite the fact that wives appear to make the greater sacrifices, perform the greater amount of dirty work, and earn lower incomes, 80 percent of the wives and 90 percent of the husbands feel that these arrangements are fair (Berk, 1985, p. 193).

We should not be surprised to learn that relationships within the household reflect the norms of the society in which they exist. Indeed, to find otherwise would be astonishing and would refute the most basic of sociological principles.

## Solutions?

Most two-job families do not face unsolvable problems on a regular basis. As does the couple whose diary opened this chapter, they make personal accommodations that work reasonably well. But the combination of work and family life often involves difficult and delicate balancing acts that require all the ingenuity and initiative that families can muster, and without much formal support.

For example, how do working parents handle child care? One solution is to stagger work hours so that at least one parent is at home to care for young children. Indeed, our own research has found that couples with very young children are most likely to have such staggered hours. On average, these couples have six hours of unsynchronized work (one spouse at work, the other at home) per day compared to five hours per day for parents of school-aged children and only four hours for couples without children. In this way, they can save at least some of the costs of child care and have the satisfactions of providing direct parental care.

This option, however, is severely constrained. Most jobs do not allow workers to decide how many hours to work or when to work. Typically, jobs that provide a full range of benefits such as health insurance and retirement plans come with the standard work schedule—40 hours spread over 5 days, 8 AM to 5 PM, take it or leave it.

Some firms have instituted "flextime" arrangements that allow employees to choose when to work, although there are specified limits. Usually, employees are required to work certain hours so that tasks involving meeting other employees can be done. But these workers have discretion over when they begin and end their workdays as long as they put in their full time.

Recent estimates indicate that only 12 percent of American workers have flextime even though it is popular with workers and either increases or has no effect on productivity. In Western European countries, more than one-half the work force has flextime, a fact that suggests it is suited to a wide variety of work settings and does not present insurmountable technical problems.

Part-time work is appealing to many workers, especially women with children. But the economic drawbacks are considerable: lower pay and few if any benefits such as health insurance or retirement. In addition, most part-time work has low status, often a dead-end job with little opportunity for moving up a career ladder.

To improve the quality of these jobs and help people to reconcile work and family responsibilities, businesses have been urged to institute both permanent part-time work and job sharing. With permanent part-time work, part-timers are not shunted into irregular, low-status positions, but have access to responsible positions with prorated benefits and potential for upward mobility; in short, these are "careerlike" jobs. Such a policy makes economic sense, because part-time workers are generally more productive than their full-time counterparts. Most businesses, however, have been unreceptive.

The related idea of job sharing also has not taken hold. Under this arrangement, two workers split a single job, perhaps alternating days or dividing each day. Advocates point to successful examples of organizations that have gotten more than a "half job" out of each "sharer," but only a minor fraction of American workers actually have such jobs.

In general, the rhythms of the work place and other institutions remain stubbornly out of synch with the time demands of many families. Schools are out in the summer, but most jobs continue. School ends at 3 PM or so each afternoon, but most jobs do not. After-school programs fill the gaps for some parents, but most communities do not make these provisions. On-the-job day-care facilities could ease the pressures on working parents with young children, but relatively few of these programs exist.

The family is a reactive institution, accommodating the demands of work and school. Our workplaces and schools are organized on the model of the traditional family, one with a single breadwinner. Thus, social tension grows as working couples and single parents seek to balance their work and family lives.

The record to date suggests that market forces have done little to induce changes in employment practices. Some critics have argued that businesses will need to be more responsive if they want to attract and retain productive employees. In other words, enlightened self-interest will bring about institutional changes that reduce the strains of balancing work and family lives. But even easy-to-institute changes such as flextime are gaining little ground, while more fundamental and expensive policies such as paid maternity leave with job protection have met active resistance. Today, new mothers receive a paid maternity leave (usually, six weeks) only if they have disability insurance, which makes birth the equivalent of an automobile accident. The one-half of women workers that does not have even this coverage is out of luck. Even this limited maternity "policy" only emerged from legislation, not from the voluntary efforts of businesses. As a point in comparison, note that for every other industrialized country in the world, the *minimum* paid maternity leave is twelve weeks, and this covers all working women. The United States is unique.

To be sure, one can find magazine and newspaper articles about the corporate lawyer who works part-time so that she can be with her child or celebrities such as Jane Pauley, who takes her child to work. But these people are news only because they are unusual. They also illustrate the proposition that those who need help the least get the most.

In conclusion, the public issues that surround the emergence of the two-job family have been addressed mainly by private solutions. For the first time in history, the 1988 presidential campaign made "family issues" such as day care more than incidental, but it is a long road between campaign rhetoric and substantial, concrete change.

## References

Berk, Sara F. *The Gender Factory.* 1985. New York: Plenum Press.

Duncan, Greg. *Years of Poverty, Years of Plenty.* 1984. Ann Arbor: University of Michigan Press.

1987 General Social Survey, National Opinion Research Center, University of Chicago.

Nock, Steven L., and Paul W. Kingston. "The Family Work Day." *Journal of Marriage and the Family:* 333–343, May 1984.

Nock, Steven L., and Paul W. Kingston. "Time with Children: The Impact of Couples' Work-Time Commitments." *Social Forces* (67), September 1988.

U.S. Bureau of the Census. "Earnings in 1983 of Married-Couple Families, by Characteristics of Husbands and Wives." CPR, series P-60, no. 153. 1986. Washington, DC: U.S. Government Printing Office.

U.S. Bureau of the Census. "Household and Family Characteristics: March 1986." CPR, series P-20, no. 419. 1987. Washington, DC: U.S. Government Printing Office.

U.S. Department of Labor. "Families at Work: The Jobs and the Pay." Bulletin 2209, Special labor force report. 1984. Washington, DC: U.S. Government Printing Office.

Voydanoff, Patricia. *Work and Family Life.* 1987. Beverly Hills, CA: Sage Publications.

## Suggested Readings

Voydanoff, Patricia. *Work and Family Life.* This text thoroughly reviews research on the linkages between family life and work.

Duncan, Greg. *Years of Poverty, Years of Plenty.* Economists at the Institute for Social Research, University of Michigan, describe the tremendous importance of the family in explaining the economic situation of individuals.

# CHAPTER 9

# Education

## The "Excellence Movement" in High Schools

In 1983, a commission appointed by U.S. Secretary of Education T. H. Bell published a short report titled *A Nation at Risk*. The report raised a sharp alarm: The poor quality of the U.S. educational system, especially that of its high schools, imperiled our economic existence and our claim to greatness as a society.

The introduction read:

> [T]he educational foundations of our society are presently being eroded by a rising tide of mediocrity that threatens our very future as a nation and a people. What was unimaginable a generation ago has begun to occur—others are matching and surpassing our educational attainments.
>
> We have, in effect, been committing an act of unthinking, unilateral educational disarmament.

Government reports, of course, are issued all the time, and some commentator is always pronouncing the educational system to be in some crisis. These warnings are usually ignored, but not so *A Nation at Risk*. Its release crystallized a growing, widespread sense that U.S. schools should teach better and students should learn more, that we needed what the report called a "commitment to excellence."

Within a few months of its publication, 400,000 copies had been sold. In a national survey, of those who had heard of the report, 87 percent agreed with its conclusion. This call for reform, however, was hardly limited to one publication.

Elizabeth Crews/Stock, Boston

America has been called a "nation at risk" because students learn so little in school. In response, educators have promoted more rigorous standards and a greater emphasis on traditional academic subjects. However, perceptions of an "educational crisis" reflect anxieties about the American way of life more than any new concern about lack of learning.

Among educators, 1983 became known as the Year of the Report. In a flurry, seven major private reports were also issued, all calling for urgent action to improve the academic capabilities of American students.

In many ways, these reports did not discover a crisis as much as reflect popular sentiment. Throughout the country, parents demanded a return to "basics"—the traditional academic emphases on reading, writing, and computation. They also demanded "standards"—high expectations of academic achievement and disciplined, orderly behavior. At the same time, at local and state levels, school boards, superintendents, "good citizen" groups, business groups, legislators, and governors all organized task forces to propose reforms.

The rallying cry for all these efforts is "excellence," and the proposed reforms have come to be called the Excellence Movement. All together, the initiatives to impose tighter graduation requirements, stricter assessment of student performance, teacher competency tests, and the like represent the emergence of a *social movement*. By this, sociologists mean a relatively persistent organized effort by a large number of people to bring about (or resist) social change.

In this chapter, we try to explain why the Excellence Movement emerged—that is, why is there currently an effort to bring "rigor," "standards," and a "core curriculum" to high schools?

To answer this question, we must consider how the educational system relates to the larger society. As a fundamental *institution* in our society, education influences people's lives—their outlooks and opportunities, as well as their collective beliefs and ways of doing things.[1] At the same time, what takes place in schools and how they are organized also are inevitably shaped by a variety of social forces—political, economic, and cultural. In fact, that is the underlying assumption in the sociology of education. As with every other educational development, the Excellence Movement does not exist in a social vacuum.

General theories about education can help us locate relevant factors to consider. To structure our discussion, we will assess the main competing theoretical interpretations of the link between society and schools—*functionalism* and *neo-marxism*. (You will probably recognize these general interpretations from any introductory textbook, although the text may have discussed conflict theory, a general approach that incorporates the specific points of neo-marxism.)

---

[1]  In a sociological perspective, *institutions* are large complexes of enduring social patterns within important realms of human life. In effect, they are society's standardized solutions to a set of problems—for example, how to socialize the young. Institutions create expected behaviors, or roles, for the people who have particular positions (statuses) in these broad realms of life. Thus, within the institution of education, the activities of administrators, teachers, and students follow regular patterns. Their activities are all constrained by the role expectations of others.

We will argue, however, that neither perspective accurately characterizes the school–society connection. Both theories imply that the organization of schools reflects the "needs" of our economy, an argument that misses the fact that some features of our schools are economically irrational.

As an alternative, we will interpret the Excellence Movement as the outcome of a struggle for privilege. Education is a valued resource, creating many opportunities for those who have it. In our society, middle-class groups have long dominated this resource and have used it to advance their children's lives. Recently, however, they have seen education move beyond their control. In response to school policies that promised more equality and cultural diversity, they have tried to reassert their dominance, and through it, their economic and cultural position. The Excellence Movement largely reflects their political efforts. This interpretation is consistent with *status conflict theory*, a view that we develop at the end of the chapter.

Before turning to these arguments, we briefly indicate the major thrust of the contemporary reform movement.

## Diagnosis and Prescription

Although not every member of this movement sees the "crisis" in exactly the same way, the various reports and task forces diagnose the problem in strikingly similar terms and prescribe largely similar solutions.

Above all, the crisis is defined as poor cognitive achievement. Perhaps the most noted barometer of academic performance has been students' Scholastic Aptitude Test (SAT) scores. Since the mid-1960s, these scores have declined; only recently has this slide ended. Scores on other standardized tests also have dropped, even to the point that American students lag behind students in many other countries. Poor test scores thus have come to be equated with poor education.

These critics further charge that our schools are burdened with a vague, confused sense of mission. They believe that academic concerns have been overlaid with too many social goals—for example, a concern for promoting healthy psychological development or racial equality. In their view, schools have weakened their commitment to teaching as they sought to serve these other goals. In short, schools have not stuck to their business.

These critics therefore believe that our nation is not producing enough productive workers who will be able to handle the demands of modern jobs. The failures of the U.S. economy, especially where they involve international competitiveness, are thus attributed to the failures of American schools. A faltering sense of common purpose also is alleged. Critics see students drifting through a series of trendy, unrelated courses and failing to appreciate our cultural traditions.

This prescription follows: A more intellectually demanding common curriculum is needed, one that focuses on developing general cognitive abilities through the study of the traditional academic subjects. "Rigor" and "standards" are commonly used terms in all these proposals, meaning that more academic coursework should be required and with demonstrated levels of achievement met. Mathematics courses, not "life adjustment" courses; diplomas linked to mastery, not "social passes," the practice of simply passing students to the next grade because they have reached a certain age.

These suggestions quickly led to significant changes in American schools. Just two years after the publication of *A Nation at Risk,* the following reforms had been initiated:

- 48 states had increased their graduation requirements with a definite emphasis on basic academic courses;
- 43 states were installing statewide student assessment tests;
- 29 states had mandated teacher competency tests, and another 10 were evaluating similar policies.

State and local education budgets also had increased, and local school districts were mandated to develop policies on homework, attendance, and discipline.

Now, in the late 1980s, this renewed commitment to a traditional academic emphasis continues to shape school policies. These reformers continue to prescribe a heavy dose of old-time educational medicine, not a new vision.

The traditionalist goals of the Excellence Movement, however, set it apart from the ideas and practices of the recent past. Reform reports in the late 1960s and early 1970s indicted schools for their authoritarianism and lack of relevance to the individual developmental needs of students. Influential educators said there was too much emphasis on order and too much attention to traditional definitions of what was educationally important—the opposite of today's sentiments.

Also during that time, educational policy makers had focused on inequalities of opportunity, especially the problems that minority students encountered in their schools. In contrast, the current primary concern is to identify the "winners," and with much less concern for the "losers." Although many reformers assert the compatibility of "equity" and "excellence," the primary purpose of their proposals aims toward the latter.

Looking at American education in a longer historical perspective, we can see that the educational goals of the current reformers are much like those that prevailed in the first few decades of this century, and which also surfaced in the late 1950s. How can we explain this reassertion of traditional education?

# Theoretical Perspectives

Historical events such as the Excellence Movement do not arise from a single and simple cause, and no theory can reasonably expect to account for all of their complexities. Inevitably, specific social changes reflect distinctive historical circumstances, even though they are shaped by more general social forces. But the test of good theory is whether it helps us understand the primary features of specific events. Does a theory suggest the *types* of factors that we should consider? Does it also allow us to see specific events as part of larger patterns of social life?

Specifically, the most prominent theories of education suggest that we assess whether the Excellence Movement was caused by 1) the technical demands of the economy—that is, a functional interpretation, or 2) the political efforts of capitalist elites—a neo-marxian interpretation.

## Functionalism

As a perspective about education, functionalism is a wide-ranging mixture of empirical and normative statements about the contributions of schools to modern society. That is, it attempts to analyze the actual consequences of schools (a matter for empirical scientific testing). And, at least implicitly, these consequences are generally approved (a normative view that reflects personal values). We focus on the empirical aspects of this theory.

This perspective reflects the conventional wisdom about schools, and one that has been seriously questioned only in the last fifteen years or so. Thus, when we criticize functionalist theory, we also disagree with widespread popular opinion about the consequences of education. Without knowing it, most politicians and other commentators on education speak like functional theorists.

When functionalists analyze education, they base their arguments on several general assumptions about modern society.

- Modern society's dominant value is rationality. This means that disciplined thought guides action and promotes progress, especially in the economic realm.

- People in modern society are committed to "meritocracy," the belief that individual achievement should and largely does affect personal rewards.

- People in modern society are committed to democracy, a broad sense of equal individual rights.

- The main institutions of society are organized and work together to promote these commitments.

With education in particular, functionalists argue that schools serve the "needs" of this modern social order. Thus, schools are believed to be responsible for teaching individuals the necessary cognitive skills and cultural outlooks that are required of successful workers and good citizens. Because education also makes individuals more productive, the spread of schooling throughout the population improves overall economic performance.

Functionalists also believe that mass education provides an efficient, fair way of sorting talents so that the most capable person can assume the most responsible positions. That is, people can develop and demonstrate their merit in schools. They then acquire occupational positions in line with their abilities, an arrangement that presumably benefits society as a whole and one which society's members can accept as just.

The organization of schools and what they teach is thus portrayed as being functional—that is, an economically and socially effective way of responding to the requirements of our society. Why, then, changes in educational policy? Because society has new demands that must be met. By this reasoning, the Excellence Movement may be explained as the educational institution's adaptive response to changing social conditions.

We should cautiously examine this explanation, however, first for basic logic. Can we assume that the existence of certain social needs (technically sophisticated workers, for example) automatically *causes* the emergence of school programs that will satisfy these ends? Just because something may be desirable does not mean that it will occur.

The problem with this functionalist argument is the danger of circular reasoning. Why do we have the Excellence Movement? Because it fulfills societal needs—that is, it has functional consequences such as creating better workers. How do we know what these needs are? We infer them from the existence of the Excellence Movement: If it exists, it must be responding to some need and thus be functionally necessary.

But we can use the *consequences* of a social arrangement such as a new curriculum to explain why it emerged only if we can specify the *processes* by which requirements produce the called-for means. Functional theories of education, however, do not detail the "feedback" mechanism that induces particular practices in schools. They simply imply the existence of some self-correcting tendency in social organization, much as nature selects adaptive traits in evolutionary development.

Even so, the functionalist perspective suggests a valuable starting point for a plausible general explanation of educational change, including the Excellence Movement. We might image that social changes that have implications for general economic well-being (such as a new shortage of technically sophisticated workers) generate a strong force for related changes in education (the increased production of such people in schools).

The recent educational reports themselves allege the significance of particular changes. They argue that global survival depends on the ability to compete in a world economy that is increasingly driven by technical sophistication and innovation. In *A Nation at Risk*, we read that "knowledge, learning, information and skilled intelligence are the new raw materials of international commerce. . . . Learning is the indispensible investment required for success in the 'information' age we are now entering."

But *America's Competitive Challenge* (1983), published by the Business–Higher Education Forum, also argues that our nation is deficient in this learning:

> [T]he American work force may not be prepared for the new competitive challenges. Shortages are developing in critical skills, such as computer science and engineering . . . and one in five American workers is functionally illiterate, unable to participate in even entry-level training.

The declining intellectual ability of the American worker is thus at least partially blamed for recent economic troubles. Educational programs that equip many students with sophisticated skills could therefore be viewed as a necessary and effective societal response to the increasing demands of a more complex and competitive society.

We all read that we now live in an "information age." High technology industries such as computers, robotics, bioengineering, fiber optics, and the like also are heralded as the emerging dominant forces in our economy. They demand more intelligent workers, or so it is alleged. This is standard fare in both the popular media and political speeches.

In short, functional theory suggests that we look to the deficiencies of American workers as the cause of the Excellence Movement. But are workers really incapable of handling jobs in the contemporary economy?

**New labor demands?**   Claims of fundamental shortages of skilled labor are difficult to accept because many analyses have shown that large numbers of Americans are overqualified for their jobs. Sociologists have assessed the typical capacities of workers with a particular number of years of schooling (the mathematical abilities of high school graduates, for example) and the technical requirements of jobs as they are currently performed (say, the skills that a key punch operator needs to perform the job adequately). Every study shows tremendous underuse of talent. Our work force has more education than is technically necessary, and the expansion of our educational system has far exceeded the changes in the technical demands of jobs. (Of course, education can be viewed as a benefit for many other reasons.)

Government estimates of the types of workers who will be needed in the future also do not indicate that there are or will be any great new demands for highly skilled workers. In fact, managers and professionals will account for a lower proportion of the work force in 1990 than in 1980. Although some technically sophisticated occupations will grow rapidly, they will provide few jobs in absolute numbers. From 1978 to 1990, more growth is projected in the number of janitors (672,000) than in the combined number of computer operators, computer systems analysts, and computer programmers (497,000). Low-level clerical and service positions will account for most new jobs.

Moreover, a recent large-scale study of U.S. employers (Crain, 1984) directly contradicts the assertion that the low ability of high school graduates contributes to declining productivity in business. Personnel officers in a cross section of U.S. businesses were asked, "How difficult is it to find the kinds of new employees you need?" Only some 5 percent reported having problems with graduates who were deficient in basic skills or with locating qualified graduates for available jobs. Employers also showed little interest in graduates' grades or the quality of their schools. One would expect employers to be interested in these matters if they value the academic skills promoted by the Excellence Movement. These researchers concluded that "there is little evidence that employers need high school graduates with trigonometry, calculus, physics, chemistry, foreign languages, or the skilled ability to comprehend literature."

Of course, many people believe that education plays a central role in modern society and that it is a critical factor affecting the United States' strengths and weaknesses. But it is difficult to portray the current reform movement as a technological necessity. There does not seem to be much economically "broken" that needs to be educationally "fixed."

## Neo-marxist Explanations

Inspired by Karl Marx's interpretation and critique of capitalism, neo-marxist theories of education also proceed from certain premises about society. The most significant are the following:

- The capitalist organization of our economy—private ownership—defines the class structure. This is marked by a fundamental divide between owners (capitalists) and workers. This organization of the economy critically shapes all social institutions and beliefs.

- The capitalist class holds dominant power by virtue of its control of the economy, and the working class is alienated and relatively powerless.

- The interests of capitalists and workers are inevitably antagonistic, and their struggles define the course of society.

Not only do neo-marxists seek to analyze the inequalities of this system, but also they believe that these inequalities should be overcome. They condemn a system that functionalists largely praise.

As applied to education, neo-marxist theory's main point is that the organization of schools primarily reflects the interests of the corporate capitalist economy. Education must therefore fulfill needs or interests of the capitalists. These interests are alleged to include the creation of a compliant work force that accepts capitalist power and is sufficiently skilled to generate profits for capitalists, and the reproduction of the class system by efficient training and allocation of people to their "appropriate" slots in the corporate hierarchy. This means having working-class students learn to be workers and channeling them into working-class positions. Relatedly, affluent students learn what is suitable for their own eventual positions of command and control.

Why, then, are American schools organized as they are? The neo-marxists answer that this advances capitalist interests.

Note the striking similarities between the neo-marxists and the functionalists, even though they evaluate contemporary society in such fundamentally different ways. First, they both see a close fit between what goes on in schools and the organization of work. Education is a *reactive* institution, largely shaped by economic forces. Second, they both use the same type of causal argument.

Rather than looking to the needs of society as a whole, however, the neo-marxists invoke the needs of the capitalist order as the starting point for an explanation of educational change. For this reason, the neo-marxists are subject to similar criticisms. One obvious difficulty is that the analyst must be able to specify capitalist interests in concrete detail before saying that these caused educational change. Otherwise, virtually any educational reform can be "explained" after the fact as advancing one capitalist interest or another.

For example, some neo-marxists argue that the educational reforms of the 1960s, especially the "open" and "free" school movements, reflected an evolving need in capitalism for self-directed, cooperatively oriented workers. Presumably, alternative schools were better suited to producing such students than were traditional schools. This is certainly plausible. But if so, can the neo-marxists account for the very different thrust of contemporary reforms—the imposition of measurable standards, the identification of individual success and failure, and the return of authority to educators? All seem incompatible with the new "need" as they have posited it. To explain such a reversal of educational policy, neo-marxists must claim that some fundamentally different capitalist need has emerged within the course of a decade, hardly a convincing argument.

Another difficulty that most neo-marxist accounts of educational change face is that they do not indicate how capitalist needs actually create specific policies. It is one thing to say that schools "reflect" or "correspond to" capitalist interests, but it is quite another to say that these interests caused schools to be a particular way.

In response to this criticism, neo-marxists sometimes point to the direct political activities of capitalist elites. Undoubtedly, such elites have more resources for political struggles than do other groups, and their assertion of power has clearly shaped some of our educational history. But little evidence suggests that the change in educational policy from the 1960s and early 1970s to the present was caused by the political activity of the corporate elite. The liberal policies of the earlier era were promoted with business on the political sidelines. Now, business people are more visible in educational debates, but they have neither pushed for changes over and against opposing views nor assumed a leading role in the Excellence Movement.

Several of the reports have received corporate support and advanced business-oriented positions. The Excellence Movement, however, was already well under way before their publication, and one key recommendation was for business to *become* interested in educational policy. Business is viewed as a desirable ally by educators who hope to sell their reforms and by state politicians who seek to strengthen their own positions. Many states have been wooing business with promises of educational reform without any strong pressure from business for such changes.

## Power and Institutional Autonomy

Although the Excellence Movement cannot be attributed to the direct exercise of corporate power, business interests still have indirect but significant influence on all educational policy. Business interests constrain what others can do.

Because they control the economic fates of many people, business interests are inevitably and systematically given favorable treatment. This point is accepted by marxists and many non-marxists. Almost everyone in our society tends to think that we are better off if business is healthy; if the economy fails, society as a whole suffers. Thus, business confidence becomes a prime concern for politicians. Business people will invest, and thereby create jobs, only if they feel that their money is safe and they can anticipate good returns. As political scientist Charles Lindblom writes, "Businessmen consequently do not need to strain or conspire to win privileges already thrust on them by anxious legislators and administrators" (1978, p. A19).

In a capitalist economy, everyone who influences educational policy is constrained by this reality. It is inconceivable that educational practices will fundamentally challenge capitalist interests. No group could successfully push for such change because so many others other than the capitalist elites closely identify the national interest with business interests. Indeed, educational reformers can usually strengthen their position by citing the economic benefits of their proposals.

Nevertheless, the constraints of the system typically allow for a considerable range of educational policies. Except in the most general ways, the capitalist organization of society does not dictate the organization and practices of schools. American capitalism has accommodated to significant swings in educational policy and has often been largely indifferent to them.

The critical point to recognize is the considerable *institutional autonomy* of the educational system from the economic order. This is not to argue that schools are isolated from their social environment. As we will discuss, they are often caught in the middle of social conflicts and anxieties. These social influences, however, cannot always be reduced to the imperatives of capitalist organization.

In sum, business interests limit the range of possibilities, but the room for maneuver remains wide. To appreciate the more specific causes of the Excellence Movement, it is necessary to look to factors that have varied in recent years: the political mobilization of middle-class groups, the organizational activities of factions within the educational system, and changes in general attitudes.

## Status Politics

At a theoretical level, our main purpose is to suggest the value of a *status conflict* approach in understanding contemporary educational change. This perspective emphasizes how social groups use education to win and maintain privilege; for example, by controlling access to well-rewarded credentials. The evolving structure of the educational system reflects the outcome of these ongoing struggles.

Perhaps the most notable feature of the Excellence Movement is that it first emerged at the grass-roots level. Public opinion polls throughout the late 1970s showed strong support for more emphasis on basics, a willingness to enroll children in traditional schools, and a desire for competency testing.

By 1978, some 70 percent of all local school districts had openly and formally discussed the state of basic skills. By this time, too, one-quarter had changed their curricula to increase time on basic subjects, and another 30 percent were considering such changes. Local pressures on state legislators also resulted in a great surge of legislation that enacted minimum competency testing for students and teachers, often against the opposition of professional educators and without any clear mandate from business groups.

These grass-roots efforts initially drew in many school districts except for the wealthy "showcase" districts, which featured some of the nontraditional reforms of the 1960s; these were among the last to join the movement. The poorest urban districts, beset by the most troubling academic and social problems, were also not in the lead. Middle-class groups, which are generally outside the professional world of education, appear to have played a central role.

In the past, educational policies had largely reflected middle-class concerns and interests. Public schools espoused their values, and their children got ahead because they got more education. The middle classes could maintain their advantage over lower-status groups in the "credential market" simply by acquiring more education.

This strategy had its successes, and education became cherished as the avenue for mobility and the guarantor of at least modest privilege. The economic downturn of the late 1970s, however, seemed to dim the economic prospects of middle-class children. Because greater numbers had access to schools, education became an investment of declining value. The educational reforms of the 1960s and early 1970s were therefore threatening to the middle class's position. As Robert Hampel observes in *The Last Little Citadel* (1986), a history of high schools since 1940:

> The vigorous pursuit of egalitarian reforms promised to clarify, expand, and protect the claims of the disadvantaged. Disparate groups— ethnic and racial minorities, the learning disabled, the poor, the physically and emotionally impaired, and teenagers in need of social services—previously served in niggardly fashion now found a more comfortable place in secondary schools. Before, their place had been marginal; in the 1970s, their once tenuous hold on school resources and respect grew firmer (p. 137).

For the middle class, these egalitarian policies created anxieties. Policies that sought to increase equality, such as "social" promotions and affirmative action for honors programs, constituted a threat. They made middle-class academic achievement more commonplace and hence less economically valuable.

Furthermore, with the dilution of standards in schools (little required homework, many "life adjustment" courses, and "dumbed down" texts), the middle class also feared that education would provide its children with less ability to compete successfully in the occupational world. The reality of this threat may have been exaggerated, but the changes in schools signaled to the middle classes that schools were less "theirs" than ever before.

The middle class's desire to have schooling "mean something" has not been only an abstract concern for learning. It wants to reestablish the market value of schooling as well as control over it. The middle class concern is to distinguish itself from the disadvantaged and reimpose school policies that support its own position. Schooling that will better equip middle-class children to compete with elite groups also is desired.

But the recent politics of education cannot be neatly reduced to a struggle between specific social groups. Although the "liberal consensus" that prevailed in the decade before the end of the 1970s concerned itself with equality, its policies were advanced by activist government officials and such narrow interest groups as advocates of the handicapped and teachers' groups with little public involvement or enthusiasm.

After the broad middle strata of society, including relatively successful minority group members, came to resist these policies, no significant social force was around to defend the gains of the disadvantaged. Thus, as the Excellence Movement progressed, middle-class activists and their political representatives largely pressed their views against educational professionals who lacked a base of popular support.

A similar concern for academic standards followed previous efforts to broaden access to schools. After the turn of the century, for example, when working-class representation in high schools dramatically increased, middle-class groups sought to protect their competitive advantage by pressing for a "track" system that slotted students into different occupational paths. They did so with the cooperation of educational professionals.

Predictably enough, middle-class students disproportionately filled the more valued academic tracks. Later, in the 1950s, although the track system was firmly established, the expansion of the high school population caused further strains. The main "problem" that confronted high schools was defined as the fate of the advantaged students, the talented minority, which was supposedly slighted by the lack of rigor in education. Middle-class parents advocated this view and predictably, again, their children were the prime beneficiaries.

These parents also pushed hard for the expansion of public higher education as a way to maintain their advantage in economic competition. In each case, although the class conflict was not obvious, efforts to maintain privilege propelled changes in schools.

But now, as before, schools not only are the battleground for economic struggles, but also for cultural issues—that is, *whose* values and traditions will enjoy privileged status in schools? The middle-class sense of threat appears to have extended beyond a concern for the place of its children in the economic hierarchy.

Indeed, much of the recent discontentment with schools stems from worries about the larger society. As the Excellence Movement gathered force, public opinion polls registered declining confidence in most of our major institutions. In a general sense, *authority* had been undermined.[2] The "counterculture" of the 1960s had questioned the values of discipline and hierarchy. Government scandal and a lost war in Vietnam had undercut political trust. And poor economic performance, especially in the international marketplace, weakened our faith in a system that had long promised continued progress and national might.

The thrust of school policies seemed to undermine the values of merit, individual accomplishment, and self-discipline, all in the name of equality of condition, diversity, and self-expression. The prevailing social anchors had been cut, and the middle class seemed adrift. The system that provided middle-class comforts and a sense of security was faltering, and schools seemed an accomplice in this failure.

This largely conservative reaction has vilified education.[3] Americans fervently believe in education as the road to progress—in effect, it is our secular religion. We often see societal problems as educational problems, and by the same token, we think they can be solved by education. As a case in point, consider the widely held view—in the face of overwhelming counterevidence—that productivity problems in the economy arose because of a shortage of adequately educated workers.

Our *collective myths* about education hold that educational solutions are effective, fair, and progressive.[4] We have expressed our faith in education during other times of perceived crisis—for example, when the Soviets launched the Sputnik satellite in 1957, we soon launched crash programs in science education. Similarly, education was to solve our racial problems in the 1960s.

Reflecting the prevailing conservative sentiments, this faith in education now stresses traditional concerns. Breakdowns in school discipline and declining test scores have reinforced a sense of social decline, a sense that we have moved away from the commitments that had created our earlier success. The attempt to reimpose school authority and old-fashioned basics is part of a more general political effort to seek conservative solutions for social ills. Thus, in the late 1980s as the Reagan administration sought lesser government in social services, stricter control of crime,

---

[2]  By *authority*, sociologists mean the legitimate, or socially accepted, use of power. It implies relationships that involve a right to command and a duty to obey, all in the service of a moral order to which everyone in these relationships owes allegiance.

[3]  The labels "conservative" and "liberal" are thrown around so loosely in political discussions that they have only vague meanings. We use the term here in the very broad sense of an orientation *to conserve*, to maintain traditional social arrangements.

[4]  When sociologists and anthropologists talk of *myths*, they mean the widespread unchallenged assumptions of what is true. Myths are consequential not only because everyone believes in them (regardless of their truth), but also because everyone "knows" that everyone else believes in them. In effect, they *are* true.

and reduced regulation of business, it also promoted the Excellence Movement.

Middle-class groups have been particularly inclined to draw upon our educational myths to resolve their anxieties about their way of life. Their success, however, reflects the fact that these myths are widely held and readily activated. Indeed, popular sentiments about education have taken on a life of their own that constrains what any group can do. Thus any educational solution to a social problem must be consistent with the popularly accepted myths about what education can and should do.

At the same time, conservative educators have sharpened the focus of popular concerns about schools. Writing reports and promoting specific legislation, these professionals have given organizational force to grass-roots sentiment. When liberals had dominated educational policy in the early 1970s, these educators had been on the sidelines.

In short, the Excellence Movement was shaped by a variety of forces: the political efforts of nonelite and elite groups, the organizational activities of some educational professionals, the broadly conservative sense of social failure, and the belief that education promises progress.

We should not lose sight of the general point, however, that schools are often a battleground where status groups try to increase or defend their privileges. A threatened middle class, given support by business and educational groups, seems to have made the fight and carried the day in the most recent of education wars, and thus the Excellence Movement.

# References

Aronowitz, Stanley, and Henry Giroux. *Education Under Siege: The Conservative, Liberal and Radical Debate over Schooling.* 1985. South Hadley, MA: Bergin and Garvey.

*America's Competitive Challenge.* 1983. Washington, DC: Business–Higher Education Forum.

Boyer, Ernest. *High School: A Report on Secondary Education in America.* 1983. Princeton, NJ: Carnegie Foundation for the Advancement of Teaching.

Crain, Robert. *The Quality of American High School Graduates: What Personnel Officers Say and Do About It.* 1984. Report No. 354. Baltimore, MD: Center for Social Organization of Schools, Johns Hopkins University.

Hampel, Robert. *The Last Little Citadel: American High Schools Since 1940.* 1986. New York: McGraw-Hill.

Hurn, Christopher. *The Limits and Possibilities of Schooling.* 1985. Newton, MA: Allyn & Bacon.

Kingston, Paul W. "Theory at Risk: Accounting for the Excellence Movement." *Sociological Forum* 1(4): 632–656.

Lindblom, Charles. "The Business of America Is Still Business." *New York Times*, 4 Jan. 1978, p. A19.

National Commission on Excellence in Education. *A Nation at Risk: The Imperative for Educational Reform.* 1983. Washington, DC: U.S. Department of Education.

## Suggested Readings

Aronowitz, Stanley, and Henry Giroux. *Education Under Siege: The Conservative, Liberal and Radical Debate over Schooling.* This provocative collection of essays was written by two radicals who are committed to a more democratic, egalitarian society. These essays clearly show the inherently political aspect of educational issues.

Boyer, Ernest. *High School: A Report on Secondary Education in America.* This readable, widely noted indictment of the quality of our high schools includes "mainstream" proposals for reform.

Kingston, Paul W. "Theory at Risk: Accounting for the Excellence Movement." *Sociological Forum.* This article extends and documents the argument that we make in this chapter.

National Commission on Excellence in Education. *A Nation at Risk: The Imperative for Educational Reform.* This report dramatized the issue of our chapter.

CHAPTER 10

# Religion

## "Creation Science" Versus Evolution

**H**ow did life start and develop on this planet? More than any other seemingly "scientific" issue, that question has inflamed public debate for some two centuries. Back in 1925, John T. Scopes was put on trial for teaching evolution in a Tennessee high school. To fundamentalist Christians, Scopes symbolized the antireligious forces that were undermining God's will on earth. To his defenders, he symbolized the quest for a rational modern society.

Scopes's celebrated trial and conviction did not put this issue to rest as a general public issue. In the 1980s, the issue emerged again as certain fundamentalist Christians actively pushed for the mandated inclusion of "creation science" in high school curricula. Their legal challenges had sufficient force to take them to the U.S. Supreme Court.

This scientific question is a public issue, then, because it is simultaneously a religious question. Few passions are more intense than religious ones.

For many devout Christians, there is no need to look beyond the words in the biblical chapter of Genesis to know how life started. As does all biblical scripture, these passages represent revealed Truth, an account of divine action that cannot be doubted by fallible humans. To these Christians, other explanations of life's beginning are more than differences in intellectual judgment. Other explanations diminish or deny the role of God as Creator and are affronts to the Supreme Being and a challenge to their faith.

From *The King's Business*, July 1922. Permission granted by Biola University, Inc.

Conservative Christians have long viewed modern science, especially theories of evolution, as a threat to their moral order. This cartoon appeared a few years before the famous Scopes "Monkey Trial" in 1925. Recently, some fundamentalist Christians have attempted to require schools to teach "Creation Science" as a Biblical alternative to evolutionary science. Thus, schools have once again become the battleground in a cultural struggle for moral authority.

But if the children of these Christians attend a typical public high school, they are unlikely to hear the biblical explanation described as being true. The lessons of any biology class challenge this faith. This may not be their intent, but it is their effect.

Students learn evolutionary theory, which involves the accepted scientific explanation of the development of life. Even if the subtleties and limitations of evolutionary theory are inadequately analyzed in high school texts, students learn enough to see a great discrepancy between the scientific explanation and the religious explanation.

Most significantly, humans have evolved from simpler primates who themselves had evolved from still simpler forms of life. This complex, multilinked process was guided by the process of natural selection, which involves the survival and reproduction of those species that are best adapted to the environment. Thus, there was no Adam and Eve in the literal sense of two wholly created creatures who were the ancestors of all human beings.

Similarly challenging is the teaching that life emerged slowly, irregularly over millions of years, neither in the six days that the Bible describes, nor within the last 100,000 years as some have interpreted the scriptures.

The fundamentalist religious explanation, a *literal* reading of Genesis, and the scientific explanation—first elaborated in Charles Darwin's *The Origin of the Species*—cannot both be right.[1] The fact that these explanations are so irreconcilably different, however, does not make them sociologically significant. After all, bitter intellectual disputes abound with only the slightest ripple in public life.

This dispute about the origins of life has poured into our public life for more than the last fifty years because it crystalizes larger issues about belief and the scope of religious authority. That is, to what extent does religious faith shape how individuals think and how our public life is organized?

As the religiously committed have recognized throughout history, science is a potential enemy of faith. Science emphasizes skepticism ("Your data don't support that conclusion," the scientist says) and rationality ("I only accept statements that are based on verifiable, empirical observations," the scientist also says). By definition, however, faith involves unquestioning acceptance, not skepticism; and belief in a Supreme Being is irrational in the sense that this deity transcends the knowable world.

---

[1] Let us be clear: One can believe in a Supreme Being who created the universe *and* in evolution. In this case, the Supreme Being is the creator who began the evolutionary process. The literal biblical account and the evolutionary explanation, however, are truly incompatible.

Although religion and science have peacefully coexisted in the contemporary United States, recent impassioned struggles over creation science indicate that tensions have not been fully resolved. In this chapter, we look at the creation science controversy as part of the larger pattern of reconciliations and tensions between religion and science. We further consider the implications of this pattern for the fate of religion, particularly religious orthodoxy, the strict adherence to traditional religious beliefs, in the modern era.

## Historical Background

The controversy between creationists and evolutionists over the content of biology curriculum is rooted in Charles Darwin's *The Origins of the Species* published in 1859.[2] Up to this time, and actually for several decades afterward, the biblical account went unchallenged in high school texts. By the turn of the century, however, a new generation of scientific writers presented evolution as accepted scientific wisdom. The creationists' legal attack on evolutionary teaching began in the 1920s, and only after evolutionary instruction was well ingrained in U.S. high schools.

The antievolution campaign had its own cast of memorable characters, perhaps none more so than William Jennings Bryan, the Midwest populist and often-defeated presidential candidate, who led the prosecution at the famous "Scopes Monkey Trial" in 1925. But this campaign should be seen as part of a larger effort by fundamentalist Protestants to defend their hold on American culture. For example, the Eighteenth Amendment, which called for Prohibition, was ratified by the states in 1919. This antidrinking campaign was largely spurred by small-town Protestants who were fearful that their way of life and ethical codes were ever more threatened in an increasingly urban, multiethnic society. Drinking was not merely unhealthy; it was sinful, a blatant symbol of moral breakdown.

Encouraged by their recent success in the crusade against the use of alcohol, many conservative Protestants took on evolutionary teaching as another threat to their cultural authority. Their passions are revealed in the words of crusader T. T. Martin: "Ramming poison down the throats of our children is nothing compared with damning their souls with the teaching of evolution."

These crusaders had their first success in Oklahoma, where an antievolution law passed in 1923. But the most fateful action took place in Tennessee two years later. Governor Austin Peay signed into law a bill

---

[2]  Our account here, including all quotations, up to discussion of the 1987 U.S. Supreme Court ruling, draws directly from Edward Larson (see references).

that read, "It shall be unlawful for any teacher to teach any theory that denies the story of Divine Creation of man as taught in the Bible, and to teach instead that man has descended from a lower order of animal." Peay clearly justified his decision on *moral* grounds:

> Right or wrong, there is a deep and widespread belief that something is shaking the fundamentals of the country, both in religion and morals. It is the opinion of many that an abandonment of the old-fashioned faith and belief in the Bible is our trouble in a large degree. It is my belief.

This law set the stage for the 1925 trial, a test case in which small-town teacher John T. Scopes was tried for teaching evolution. He was defended by flamboyant lawyer Charles Darrow, who was sponsored by the American Civil Liberties Union. The prosecution was led by Bryan, who, like the defense, saw the case as part of a general struggle for cultural authority. From the outset, Bryan vowed that there would be "a battle royal between the Christian people of Tennessee and the so-called scientists."

Bryan won the legal battle. Scopes was convicted and fined $100, although the conviction was reversed because of an error in sentencing. (For Bryan, the victory was pyrrhic—he died shortly after from the stress of the trial.) The victory cleared the way for several other Southern states to enact their own antievolution laws. The decision in favor of the anti-evolutionists, however, came at great cost: The fundamentalists were subjected to harsh, widespread ridicule as being ignorant, "backward" people. In effect, they were shunted to the margins of the larger culture. Antievolution legislation never gained any support outside the so-called Southern Bible Belt.

On the legal front, the fundamentalists suffered their biggest defeat in 1968 when the U.S. Supreme Court overturned an Arkansas law that barred the teaching of evolution in the state's public schools. The Court held that the Arkansas law violated the "establishment clause" of the First Amendment: "Congress shall make no laws respecting an establishment of religion." That is, the Court held that the primary intent and effect of the law was to promote a particular religious position.

This ruling severely narrowed the creationists' maneuvering room. In reaction, they promoted "balanced treatment" laws, legislation that would require schools to give equal attention to both biblical accounts of creation and theories of evolution. By 1982, such laws had been enacted in three states.

In 1987, on a 7-2 vote, the U.S. Supreme Court ruled that a Louisiana law mandating this balance was unconstitutional. Justice William Brennan wrote that "the pre-eminent purpose of the Louisiana Legislature was clearly to advance the religious viewpoint that a supernatural being created humankind." This conclusion led to the ruling that the law violated the establishment clause. The law, Brennan added, "actually serves to diminish academic freedom by removing the flexibility to teach evolution without also teaching creation science."

As this brief historical review shows, the creationists' victories have been few, and their losses have steadily mounted. What is more, recent court rulings give scant promise of victories to come.

But the issues that are inherent in creationism versus evolution are hardly dead. For one matter, a nationally representative 1988 survey indicated that 69 percent of all American adults believe that schools should teach both the biblical account and evolution (Williamsburg, 1988). So do substantial majorities of business, government, and religious elites. Perhaps even more significant, the *general* discontentments about contemporary culture that motivate creationists have retained their social force. If reform of the biology curriculum has become a dead end, fundamentalist Christians have other targets in their quest to reassert cultural authority or, at least, acceptance.

We will develop this point as part of our general assessment of religion's role in the contemporary United States, but first let us address a general point that has been raised by the debates about creation science. What *is* science?

## Defining "Real" Science

The U.S. Supreme Court has never truly said whether creation science is "good" or "bad" science, or even whether it is science. Its rulings have hinged on perception of religious intent in the "balanced treatment" legislation. Setting aside legal reasoning, the obvious analytical question is, What distinguishes religion from science? Each claims to present truthful knowledge.

Ask a scientist, "What is science?" and you are likely to hear something about rigorous attempts to explain the natural world. The problem with this answer is that the dividing line between science and other intellectual endeavors still remains fuzzy. Are both astronomy and astrology science? The practitioners of each certainly would claim that their discipline fits this definition, but one would probably hesitate to see them as the same. The scientist might then say, "Science is knowledge based on the scientific method." But this answer just sidesteps the issue because the defining characteristics of this method are so ambiguous.

One should not conclude, however, that scientists are especially inarticulate or unaware of what they do. Their confusion reflects the fact that the meaning of science is not fixed. Indeed, most of the recent philosophers and sociologists of science have concluded that it is impossible to demarcate the unique and essential characteristics of science as an intellectual activity (Gieryn, 1983). The commitments that some have called distinctly scientific have been found in intellectual activities that are not usually associated with this endeavor. Moreover, as scientists go about their day-to-day routines, they do not always follow the prescribed scientific commitments.

As a practical matter, however, the demarcation between science and nonscience is made and has real consequences. As sociologist Thomas Gieryn writes, "education administrators set up curricula that include chemistry but exclude alchemy; the National Science Foundation adopts standards to assure that some physicists but no psychics get funded; journal editors reject some manuscripts as unscientific" (Gieryn, 1983, p. 781).

When a sociologist is asked, "What is science?" the answer probably will be something on the order of, "Science is what scientists do." Because scientists do different things at different times, the boundaries of science change and remain imprecise. It is not surprising that scientists try to establish boundaries that further their interests on matters such as intellectual authority, career opportunities, and freedom from political interference.

This view suggests that *intellectual authority*, the ability to be regarded as the only believable source, has been up for grabs throughout history. In this intellectual struggle, religion has often been pitted against science. In the prescientific era, religion had a virtually uncontested monopoly of intellectual authority, extending from matters of morals and political philosophy to explanations of the natural world. Science has not always emerged victorious as it challenged this monopoly, and religion retains a strong hold on some domains of intellectual activity. But the monopoly was surely lost long ago. Science has carved out its own domain: "[A]nyone who would be widely believed and trusted as an interpreter of nature needs a license from the scientific community" (Barnes and Edge, 1982, p. 2). So conclude two noted historians of science, and few others would disagree.

The scientific victory in this domain of knowledge seems so complete that we can easily forget that scientists had to work hard to win and defend their intellectual authority. Throughout history, a key strategy has been to publicly define science in ways that reflected favorably on their own activities and excluded competing authorities such as religion. In varying ways, scientists have said, "*We* know about these matters, and *they* are not like us."

The current struggle between creationists and evolutionists can be seen as such a boundary dispute. At issue is the definition of science. Recognizing that they could no longer assert religious authority in science curricula, fundamentalist Christians sought to label their explanation as science—creation science. If accepted, that label would give them legitimacy and a forum in which to promote their views.

An overwhelming number of conventional scientists have resisted this effort, fearing that any definition of science that included creationism might subject their research to unwanted religious influence. In its brief against the balanced treatment legislation, the National Academy of Sciences argued that "creationism is not based on scientific research." The Academy further argued that such legislation "would be contrary to the nation's need for a scientifically literate citizenry and for a large, well-informed pool of scientific and technical personnel."

Against the standard description of "science is what scientists do," creationism does not qualify as science. In a 1982 ruling against a balanced treatment law, an Arkansas judge noted that no creationist article had been published in a recognized scientific journal. Moreover, the state could not produce a single creationist who could claim that his or her science was not influenced by religious presuppositions.

Some observers may see this scientific victory as little more than the resolution of a "last gasp" struggle in a larger battle already won—just another nail in the religious coffin. The idea is that religious superstition has generally given way to reason, and religious authority has been undermined by the rationality of the modern world. But the significance of religion in contemporary society cannot be dismissed so simply. Religion's obvious loss of authority on matters relating to the natural world *is* important, but so, too, is its continuing effect on social life.

## Secularization

To place the meaning of the recent controversy over creationism in a larger context, let us briefly set out the *secularization thesis*. This is a general and long-accepted argument about the broad direction of modern society. Jeffrey Hadden, a colleague and thoughtful critic of the thesis, offers this useful summary:

> Once the world was filled with the sacred—in thought, practice and institutional form. After the Reformation and the Renaissance, the forces of modernization swept across the globe, and secularization, a corollary historical process, loosened the dominance of the sacred. In due course, the sacred shall disappear altogether except, possibly, in the private realm (1987, p. 590).

In other words, *modernization*—the complex process involving industrialization, urbanization, and increased use of science-based technology—has meant the slow death of religion. That is the thesis, but is it correct?

The loss of religious authority in explaining natural events is plainly consistent with this thesis. As the creation science controversy suggests, religious authority cannot even be invoked to decide biology curricula. Religious authority must argue its case by claiming scientific status.

In the contemporary United States, political leaders may be personally religious (and even use religious appeals to their political advantage), but they do not have political authority because of their religious authority. Votes, programs, appeals to such secular ideologies as patriotism may confer political authority, but not the sanction of God. So, again, we see the lesser hold of religion than in some medieval kingdom.

In the economic realm, religious authority also holds little sway. Business people in a capitalist society such as ours charge what the market will bear, not some religiously prescribed "just" price. When they hire and fire, their calculations are based on the quest for profits, not some sense of ethical obligation to others. Indeed, all workers and owners are presumed to be motivated by material incentives and are required to rationally calculate what is in their own best interest. We take this for granted in a developed capitalist economy, but in less secular societies, church authorities have had a decisive say on such economic matters as interest rates, the obligations of economic groups to one another (for example, peasants and landlords), and even what is produced.

Similarly, the formal separation of religiously defined morality (and related "church law") from public legality is an accomplished fact in all modern societies. The precepts of the Judeo-Christian tradition obviously influence the content of our law, but they do not define it, and church rulings do not have the force of state authority behind them. To put the matter baldly, one can sin and do so legally.

In the great historical sweep, then, the institutional authority of religion has been constricted in the industrially advanced countries of the world. The signs of secularization are undeniable and point to significant changes in social organization. The modern faith in rationality is institutionalized in science, politics, economy, and law.

But in assessing the status of religion in modern society, we are reminded of Mark Twain's comment on reading his own newspaper obituary. Twain wrote to the editor, "Reports on my death are vastly exaggerated." So, too, were all those prophecies of religion's eventual demise.

Indeed, the more extreme statements of the secularization thesis seem absurd in light of Americans' strong religious commitments, often to strongly orthodox beliefs. Nationally representative opinion polls conducted by the Gallup organization have shown ongoing religious vitality, as the following show.[3]

- In 1981, 95 percent of all Americans professed belief in God or in a Universal Spirit. Since World War II, that percentage has remained essentially constant.

- In 1983, 80 percent of Americans believed that Jesus Christ is divine and that he rose from the dead. Thus, Americans hold firm to the central tenet of Christianity: Jesus Christ is the son of God. Again, there is no sign of declining belief in recent decades.

---

[3] All of the poll data here are taken from *The Gallup Report* (see references).

■ In 1984, church membership stood at 68 percent. The highest rate in the post–World War II years was 76 percent in 1947, although there has been little decline since the mid-1970s.

■ In 1984, in a typical week, church attendance was 40 percent. This was somewhat lower than in the mid-1950s (49 percent), but higher than in 1940 and very similar to the church-going rates for the last decade.

■ In 1984, 86 percent of Americans claimed that religion was a significant influence in their lives: 56 percent said it was "very important," 30 percent said it was "fairly important," and only 13 percent thought it was "not very important." This represents a decline since 1952 when 75 percent said religion was "very important," but the figures have recently stabilized.

These survey responses indicate that, in behavior and belief, Americans remain a religious people (see the box, "Americans: The Most Religious People"). Not only has religion "survived" modernization, but also there are clear signs that orthodox, traditional forms of religion have retained their appeal, as the following show.

■ In a 1984 survey, 22 percent of Americans were identified as "evangelical" (that is, Protestants who believe in the literal truth of the Bible, claim "born again" experiences, and encourage others to believe in Jesus Christ).

■ Thirty-seven percent of all adults believe that the Bible is the actual word of God.

■ For the last few decades, membership in the "mainline," "liberal" Protestant churches such as Presbyterian and Episcopalian has declined, while membership in such "conservative" churches as Baptist has grown significantly.

Americans also support religious expression in our public life (Williamsburg, 1988):

■ 64 percent agree that "it's good for Congress to start sessions with a public prayer";

■ 77 percent say that "public schools should set aside a moment of silence each day for students to pray if they want to"; and

■ 80 percent agree that "it's okay for a city government to put up a manger scene on government property at Christmas."

So how do we assess the secularization thesis in light of this seemingly contradictory evidence? To answer this question, it is necessary to distinguish between religion at both the *institutional* and the *individual* levels of behavior and belief.

At the former level, the long-term decline of religion and the related secularization of society are profound. At the latter level, the signs of stability, even vitality, are equally profound. We do not want to conclude here, however, by suggesting that religion has merely "retreated" into the private sphere, a last bastion for unmodern thought. Modernization has been accompanied by religious transformation.

## The Modernization of Religion

Throughout history in all societies, humans have shown a strong desire to believe in something, especially to give their lives some larger purpose or meaning. More than any other system of meaning, religions are concerned with the meaning of the *whole* of life. They provide ready-to-adapt answers to questions such as, "What is the purpose of life?", "How should I live?", and "Where do I 'fit' within the vast universe?" These are the "big" questions, the transcendental issues that we all worry about in some way as we go about everyday life. By providing this larger meaning, religion functions as an influential source of psychological comfort.

Paradoxically, as religion lost its authority to interpret the facts of the natural world and to control our social lives, its distinctive ability to create the comforting sense of transcendental meaning may have come into sharper relief. Challenged by natural reason and institutional changes, contemporary religions have increasingly emphasized their capacity to address questions inherently "beyond the reach" of science. In short, as its intellectual authority narrowed and its social control function diminished, religions have become more oriented to providing psychological comfort.

By redefining itself in this way, religion secures its place in the modern age. Robert Wuthnow (1988), a sociologist of religion, makes the argument that

> the world of facts with which the empirical sciences deal must be seen ultimately in another context—a context given meaning by religious symbols. . . . As a result, religious symbols have been put beyond the reach of rational and empirical criticism by identifying them with a different type of reality construction (pp. 302–303).

This redefinition of religion to stress the "comfort function" has involved an increased concern for the self—the general sense that each person's life is distinctive and the personal feeling that what "I" do is the most important consideration. Many observers of religion have noted that God is increasingly portrayed as a personal friend, a source of solace who provides answers to individual problems. At the same time, the symbolic meaning of religion appears to have new significance. That is, the focus on the absolute truth of religious faith may have declined in favor of an appreciation of how religious liturgy and ritual help people "make sense" of life or "cope" with its pressures. This concern for both self and symbolic meaning reflects general modern tendencies and thus makes religion more adaptable to the complex demands of contemporary society.

As the data we cited above suggest, Christian religious orthodoxy has not simply withered away as this redefinition has taken place. Belief in the literal truth of the Bible, for example, has declined, but a significant minority still holds to this view. But orthodoxy itself is not an unchanging tradition.

James Davison Hunter (1987a), another colleague in the sociology of religion, systematically studied the beliefs of students in evangelical colleges and seminaries, what he termed "the coming generation" of evangelicals. He generally concluded that younger evangelicals have made theological and social "accommodations" to the modern world view. Although retaining their commitments to traditional beliefs, this coming generation of conservative Protestants has moved in line with the general modern redefinition of religion, although to a lesser extent than have the liberal religious traditions.

The effect of this trend, Hunter argues, is the loss of "binding address." By this, he means the power that a culture has to direct an individual's moral energies and compliance with inherited rules. For evangelical Protestants, belief remains but certainty is incomplete; religious prescriptions may be accepted, but they are examined and not automatically followed. Hunter boldly concludes that "for conservative Protestantism the confrontation with the modern world (particularly from the end of the nineteenth century) has meant the slow but decisive loss of its binding address" (1987a, p. 211).

# Contemporary Cultural Battles

At this point, the record of legal decisions does not provide much hope for the creationists in their attempts to get balanced treatment legislation for school curricula or to reassert religious authority over interpretations of the natural world. There may be further rounds of legal skirmishing, but this particular battle appears lost.

But the larger confrontation of religious orthodoxy and modern secular society is very likely to continue to generate political struggles. Instead of pitting religion against science, the battlegrounds for this cultural struggle are primarily defined by opposing views of morality and related social policies. Thus, the religiously orthodox take a leading role in pressing the antiabortion campaign (see chapter 12, "The Politics of Abortion"), opposing the Equal Rights Amendment (ERA) as part of their larger effort to reinforce the "traditional" family, and promoting traditional values and prayers in schools. This last effort involves rooting out the moral relativism and liberal ideology that allegedly permeates American textbooks.

Not evolution, but "secular humanism" is now the main educational enemy of the orthodox. In a ruling favorable to the conservative Christians who brought the case, an Alabama judge ruled that many school texts promoted secular humanism, which was defined as a religion.[4] Offending passages referred to such matters as the need for each person to decide what is right and the normalcy of single-parent families. Also criticized was the neglect of religion's role in our history. The judge thus ordered the books banned from Alabama schools, although the decision was later overturned.

Our point here is neither that this particular court ruling says anything decisive about American cultural struggles nor that creationists, ERA opponents, those with antiabortion (pro-life) sentiments, and those who oppose secular humanism are one and the same people. In varying ways, individual conservative Christians may or may not identify with each of these campaigns, but conservative religious beliefs, among Protestants and others, remain the primary roots of this cultural counterattack. A variety of Orthodox religious groups—Jewish, Catholic, and Protestant—are the primary recruiting grounds for the organizational activists in those movements. Indeed, there is some indication that, at least at the elite organizational level, the orthodox are forming alliances across religious lines.[5]

Perhaps, in the long run, the orthodox may make so many accommodations to the modern, secular impulse that their discontents fizzle out as a political force. Currently, however, their numbers remain considerable and their passions remain high. The social tensions revealed by the long-running creation versus evolution debate remain unresolved.

---

[4]  Secular humanism is a vaguely defined enemy. In part, it seems to be a general orientation that grows out of a commitment to the values of rationality and science and a sense that the good of humankind is the measure of morality. Critics also equate it with moral relativism, atheism, and an egalitarian, left-oriented political ideology.

[5]  For a fuller development of this argument, see James Davison Hunter (1987b) (see references).

# Americans: The Most Religious People

**A**s a general social process, modernization has fundamentally transformed all industrialized countries of the world. Their institutions and cultures have certain important common features. Modernization per se, however, has not had a universally negative effect on religiosity.

In fact, the United States stands out as the most religious society within the industrialized West, although it is generally regarded as the most "modern" society. This is clear in Table 10.1 below. Respondents were asked to rate, on a scale of 1 to 10, how important God is in their lives. National averages are reported.

Countries of predominantly Protestant heritage have both high scores (United States) and low scores (Sweden). The same is true for countries with predominantly Catholic heritage (Ireland and France). We therefore cannot explain Americans' distinctive religiosity in the modern age by their commitment to any particular type of theological belief.

**Table 10.1**   Importance of God in Life (10-point scale)

| | |
|---|---|
| United States | 8.21 |
| Republic of Ireland | 8.02 |
| Italy | 6.96 |
| Belgium | 5.94 |
| West Germany | 5.67 |
| France | 4.72 |
| Japan | 4.49 |
| Sweden | 3.99 |

Source: Religion in America. *The Gallup Report.* No. 236, May 1985

continued

How can we account for Americans' distinctive religiosity? One obvious factor is the nation's religious heritage. Many of our founders and early settlers came here to freely express their religious convictions. Another likely factor is that the United States has never had a state-sponsored religion, which has been the rule in other modernized countries. With state sponsorship, religious authorities can rest secure in their monopoly position. They do not have to win support. By contrast, in the United States, church leaders have had to support themselves and compete for believers and resources. Because religious freedom is legally protected, many religions and denominations can enter this competition. Religious competition therefore has spurred the organizational energies of churches, and these organized efforts have provided a social reinforcement to ongoing individual faith.

# References

Barnes, Barry, and David Edge (Eds). *Science in Context.* 1982. Cambridge, MA: MIT Press.

Gieryn, Thomas. "Boundary Work and the Demarcation of Science from Non-Science." *American Sociological Review* 48: 781–795, 1983.

Hadden, Jeffrey. "Toward Desacralizing Secularization Theory." *Social Forces* 65: 587–611, 1987.

Hunter, James Davison. 1987a. *Evangelicalism: The Coming Generation.* Chicago: University of Chicago Press.

———. 1987b. "American Protestantism: Sorting Out the Present, Looking to the Future." *This World* 17: 53–76, Spring 1987.

Larson, Edward. *Trial and Error: The American Controversy over Creation and Evolution.* 1985. New York: Oxford University Press.

Williamsburg Charter Foundation. *The Williamsburg Charter Survey on Religion and Public Life.* 1988. Washington, DC: Williamsburg Charter Foundation.

Wuthnow, Robert. *The Restructuring of American Religion.* 1988. Princeton, NJ: Princeton University Press.

Gallup, George. "Religion in America: 50 Years: 1935–1985." *The Gallup Report* no. 236, May 1985.

# Suggested Readings

Hunter, James Davison. *Evangelicalism: The Coming Generation*. This work is a vivid portrait of this changing religious group, based on survey data and a wealth of historical materials.

Wuthnow, Robert. *The Restructuring of American Religion*. This is a very detailed, comprehensive account of changes in the organization and content of religion as well as its role in American society.

Larson, Edward. *Trial and Error: The American Controversy over Creation and Evolution*. This interesting historical account details the legal struggles but locates them in the context of social struggles.

CHAPTER 11

# The Economy

## When the Plant Closes

# Fluvanna Industry to Close

By Kathy Hoke
THE PROGRESS STAFF

CARYSBROOK—Fluvanna County's largest private employer, a textile dyeing and finishing plant, will shut its doors by the first week in May, laying off 290 workers and dealing the rural county a serious economic blow.

Stehli Corp., located on the Rivanna River at Carysbrook near Fork Union, announced the closing after its parent company, Carisbrook Industries Inc., sold its sales and marketing divisions to Andrex, a New York-based textile firm that did not want the manufacturing division, plant manager Avery Currie said Wednesday.

The decision to close the manufacturing division was made "because the market projections were not favorable after two fairly bad quarters," Currie said.

"Fluvanna losing Stehli is something like Detroit losing a General Motors facility," said Jerome Booker, a Fluvanna supervisor who represents the Fork Union District.

"It's definitely going to have a pretty devastating effect on Fluvanna County," Booker said this morning. "Even though a lot of the 300 employees are not residents of Fluvanna County, quite a bit of revenue derived went to merchants and businesses from that plant being here."

The plant, which opened in 1971, has a $45,000-a-week payroll for its 290 employees, many of whom lived in nearby Buckingham County. It manufactures knit fabrics, and dyes and finishes fabrics for assembly elsewhere.

The closing will boost the unemployment rate in Buckingham and Fluvanna counties to 10 percent.

From *Daily Progress*, March 15, 1984, p. B1. Reprinted by permission of the publisher.

© Eugene Richards/Magnum Photos, Inc.

Conspicuous shutdowns of many large American manufacturing firms have led to laws requiring a thirty-day notice before closing a plant. Some people fear that the United States is becoming "deindustrialized." But a sociological analysis shows that most displaced workers find employment quickly, and often at higher wages. Manufacturing continues to be a large and vital part of our economy.

**W**hat happened in Fluvanna County may elicit sympathy from some. "What are those people going to do? Don't they deserve better treatment?" Others may read this news with a sense of economic inevitability, even desirability. "There's always change and no one can count on a job. Owners have to invest their money where they think they're going to make the most. That's free enterprise."

Few of us, however, would probably stop to think much about the Fluvanna economy or the lives of the people there except that plant closings have affected so many communities throughout the country. Many factories that long contributed to the industrial muscle of American society have been permanently closed.

Such was the fate of the South Works of U.S. Steel, which was located in South Chicago. At the turn of the century, this huge plant made rails. During World War II, it produced metal for ships and tanks and employed 16,000. In the mid-1970s, less than one-half that number turned out structural steel products.

On March 30, 1984, the day the plant finally closed, fired workers held a funeral for the South Works. A funeral cortege started in South Chicago at the local union hall and drove in procession to the plant. The cars had signs such as "MACHINE SHOP REST IN PEACE." Most of the drivers were men with twenty-five and thirty years' time in the South Works. Because of their seniority, they were the last survivors. Back at the union hall, a thousand workers and their families held a wake.

Does this wake symbolize the death of a way of life built on manufacturing prowess? Closed factory gates are a common feature of our industrial landscape, especially blighting Northeastern and Midwestern cities with concentrations of heavy industries such as steel, rubber, and cars—the so-called Rust Belt. In the face of increasing foreign competition, many workers in these industries have lost jobs, often highly paid, and the economic bases of whole communities have been hard hit. Many have claimed that we are witnessing the deindustrialization of the United States—that is, the decline of the manufacturing core of the economy.

On the other hand, there is some good economic news. During the 1982 recession, unemployment reached more than 12 percent, but in 1988 it dropped below 6 percent, its lowest level in the decade. The U.S. economy has been a job machine, producing 15.5 million new jobs between 1982 and 1988, a rate far exceeding our European and Japanese competitors. Many of these new jobs are in smaller establishments in the service sector—retail trade, restaurants, financial companies, information-processing firms, and so on.

In short, we are in the midst of an economic transformation leading to a lesser role for manufacturing, at least as a source of employment. At issue, however, is the overall extent of this transformation and its impact on individual lives. How widespread are the experiences of the displaced workers at the Stehli Corp. and the South Works? What "costs" do they bear other than the obvious loss of income?

Also at issue are the implications of this economic transformation for the larger society. Many analysts have raised fears that the rise of the service economy will increase inequalities in our society. They see a work force increasingly dominated by many low-paid, dead-end jobs at the bottom, fewer well-paid professionals at the top, and lesser numbers in between.

Journalist James Fallows depicts this emerging two-tier society: "If there is one widely accepted symbol of today's changing economy, the 1980s version of the allegorical Joad family hitting the road during the Depression, it is the proud steel worker who gets laid off in Youngstown and is reduced to flipping burgers for one-fifth his former wage."

There is reason for these fears because service jobs generally do pay less than manufacturing jobs, and increasing numbers of people work in the service sector. But before we write the obituary for the middle class— death caused by manufacturing decline—we should examine relevant data carefully for vital life signs.

Interesting enough, but what has this to do with sociology? Sounds like economics—unemployment, economic sector, costs, wages, and income distribution.

Of course, economists help us understand this transformation, but it is also important to tell other parts of the story. For example, a laid-off work force can be said to represent an "economic dislocation" as investors reallocate capital to improve their return. Perhaps the economy as a whole *does* benefit from all decisions to maximize profits, as many economists claim. But there is a human side to this dislocation that economists' vision typically obscures. The costs of a lost job cannot be measured in dollars and cents alone. They also may involve emotional and physical trauma and communal vitality.

Furthermore, the effects of the quality of jobs and the distribution of incomes are not confined to the economic realm. They shape family lives, political struggles, and general values. Just as the economy is socially embedded, economic and sociological analyses need to complement and draw on one another.

First, we must see the context of individual shutdowns—that is, the general trend of the economy.

# A Nation of Hamburger Stands?

The largest shutdowns throughout the country—in Detroit, Michigan; Akron and Youngstown, Ohio; and Buffalo, New York—represent the lost jobs in basic manufacturing industries. True, certain industries have been hit hard in the last two decades, and small service establishments such as McDonald's and its imitators have sprouted everywhere. But the view that the United States is fundamentally deindustrializing in a new service economy deserves careful scrutiny.

It is certainly hard to argue that manufacturing is an historical relic, as the following facts demonstrate.

- For the entire post–World War II era until 1980, the absolute number of workers in manufacturing increased. In the 1980s, the numbers declined, although in 1985 19.4 million workers worked in manufacturing; this is a greater number than in 1965.[1]

- The percentage of the labor force in manufacturing has decreased in recent years: 26 percent in 1970, 22 percent in 1980, and 20 percent in 1983. This proportional decrease, however, largely reflects the growth of service jobs, not any large drop-off in manufacturing work.[2] Moreover, Census Bureau projections indicate that manufacturing jobs will account for about the same proportion of employment in the decade ahead as they do now.

- Manufacturing continues to account for a large share of the total value of all goods and services produced in the economy—the gross national product (GNP). In 1960, 1973, and 1980, the ratio of goods output (that is, manufacturing production) to the GNP was virtually constant at about 45 percent.

- In the years after the 1973 oil embargo, manufacturing output increased at a rate higher than for our European competitors (although lower than Japan's). Investment in manufacturing plants and equipment also increased.

These national statistics undercut claims of a fundamental transformation. To the extent that we have undergone deindustrialization, it is a regional phenomenon. To use the economists' phrase, we have had extremely high capital mobility within and between regions, which means there have been many business closings and openings. The result is that some areas have been left behind and others have gained. In particular, the Great Lakes region has deindustrialized, resulting in lesser employment (absolutely and relatively) in manufacturing, lesser industrial output, and a lesser proportion of national industrial output.

The decline of the industrial Midwest, however, should not be viewed as an unprecedented historical change, an unfortunate and

---

[1]   U.S. Bureau of the Census projections through 1995 also indicate further absolute growth.

[2]   Here we exclude workers in construction and mining. Both categories are projected to employ more workers in the future. This is additional evidence against the argument that the future belongs to the service sector.

unique side effect of the modern economy. New England towns, for example, were home to the early American textile industry but were left as economic ghost towns when the manufacturers moved to low-wage locations in Southern cities. Similarly, cities and towns that grew rich because of their location along lines of river transportation fell into decline as other types of transportaiton became more economical. Moreover, the large-scale displacement of farmers from their lands throughout the early part of this century was far greater than the displacement associated with recent declines in some manufacturing industries.

New winners and losers emerge in the national economy as economic demands change and new methods of production develop. That is the inevitable consequence of capitalism, a system that says "go out and make as much money as you can—wherever you think you can make the most."

But for all the disruptions that have accompanied the recent hypermobility of capital, the current plight of certain industries such as household appliances, cars, and textiles does not signal a fundamental unraveling of the American economy. Both hamburger stands and computer-service consulting firms are a part of the U.S. economic future, just as are manufacturing plants. Rather than sounding a premature death knell for manufacturing, we should attempt to understand the consequences of the changes that have occurred.

## Defining the Scope

People become unemployed all the time for many reasons: They are fired for incompetence, they lose out as a company makes seasonal adjustments in its labor force, or they quit one job and have not yet found another. The closed plant gate, however, focuses attention on a particular type of unemployment, that of displaced workers. These men and women lost their jobs because of business shutdowns or severe cutbacks in operations.

Displaced workers represent a particularly troubling form of unemployment because their fates often seem rooted in permanent changes in the economy, not the normal ups and downs of the labor market. For example, employment opportunities in basic industries such as steel have plummeted and probably will remain bleak. The closed gate also puts both new and older workers on the street. Although the young may be relatively adaptable, many workers with long service at a particular firm in a declining industry have acquired specific skills that are no longer in demand.

Surveys conducted by the U.S. Bureau of Labor Statistics indicate that the experiences of workers at Stehli and South Works are common throughout the country. From January 1981 to January 1986, 10.8 million workers 20 years of age and older lost jobs because of plant closings, employers going out of business, or layoffs from which they had not been recalled. Some 5.1 million of these displaced workers had been at their jobs for at least three years.

Approximately one-half of the displaced workers with three years of employment had worked in the manufacturing sector, often in machinery, metal, and transportation-equipment plants. These workers appear to be the victims of the alleged deindustrialization of the United States. And yet, the fact that one-half of these displaced workers had been employed in other sectors indicates that the dislocations in our economy are not merely the products of faltering manufacturing operations.

How well has the economy reabsorbed these workers? This is what displaced workers who had previously had three years of employment were doing in January 1986: employed, 66.9 percent; unemployed, 17.8 percent; and out of the labor force, 15.3 percent. (This last group includes workers who retired as well as those who could work but who had stopped actively seeking a job.)

The employment world reabsorbed workers at much different rates. Older displaced workers were less able or inclined to land a new job than their younger counterparts. Less than one-half of workers 55 to 64 years old took other jobs; one-third retired or gave up looking. Furthermore, displaced men had higher employment rates than displaced women (71 percent to 60 percent), and displaced whites had higher employment rates than blacks (68 percent to 58 percent).

How this reabsorption is assessed depends on whether one sees the teacup as half-full or half-empty. True, a substantial majority did get other jobs, but it also is true that a substantial minority remained out of work. The reemployed were typically out of work for 12.5 weeks (the median), while the unemployed had been without work for an average of 20.5 weeks.

The standard of living for most workers who managed to get other jobs did not dramatically differ from their previous levels. Of those with full-time positions, 730,000 (30 percent) suffered a drop in income of 20 percent or more, but an almost equal number, 712,000 (29 percent), increased their incomes by 20 percent or more. Indeed, somewhat more of the displaced workers with new full-time jobs equaled or improved their previous income than took lower-paying jobs. Their good fortune, of course, greatly exceeds that of the millions who remained out of work entirely.

Almost one-half of reemployed workers took new jobs in the same general occupation they had left. And few of the displaced factory workers added to the swelling ranks of service-sector employees. For example, less than 20 percent of blue-collar manufacturing workers moved into service-sector jobs.

Most displaced workers also stayed put geographically. Only 14 percent moved out of their city or county, hardly an exodus such as that seen in the Great Depression of the 1930s.

All these figures on the typical events in the lives of displaced workers should not obscure the fact that many Americans, millions of them, suffered severe and sustained economic losses because of business shutdowns. Their pain cannot be minimized by saying that they are not typical.

At the same time, these figures should dispel certain images that seem current in popular discussion. First, displaced workers are not the by-products only of deindustrialization. Just as many are the victims of closed offices or stores as shutdown factories. Most displaced workers are not formerly high-paid factory workers who end up permanently unemployed or employed in some lousy service job far from their homes. Far more commonly, after a period of hardship (including the loss of health insurance), displaced workers land jobs near their homes much like those they lost.

## Assessing the Costs

> If you don't have a job, you don't have a purpose in life. I've worked all my life. I never collected a dime in compensation. So to be without a job! I had bottles of pills. I'm not kidding. I had pills under my pillow and would think that one night I was gonna get up and end it all.
> Dorothy Gomez, a laid-off worker (Bensman and Lynch, 1987, p. 97).

In thinking of the workers' costs after a shutdown, our first thought is monetary: making payments on a home, paying grocery and utility bills, and deferring dreams for more material comforts. These expenses must continue to be met without income until a new job is found, and even then they may continue to cut into a budget if the worker must accept lower pay. But because a job is much more than a source of income, the costs of unemployment may be more extensive.

A job provides a sense of identity, and even worth, as Dorothy Gomez's remarks suggest. When we ask an adult, "What do you *do*?", we typically mean, "What kind of job do you have?" Many Americans believe that a job is *the* defining mark of a person's life, or at least one of the most important. This is not surprising. At work, people have the chance to define themselves, to find out their strengths and weaknesses; they often make friends, and learn what others think of them; and their job experiences shape the rest of their lives. In many ways, a job makes a person.

What we must do, then, is see how displaced workers have responded to their job losses. How common is the trauma that Dorothy Gomez suffered?

Terry Buss and F. Stevens Redburn's study, *Shutdown at Youngstown* (1983), provides the best evidence to date. This is a detailed examination of the effects from the closing of Youngstown Sheet and Tube, a huge steelmaking operation in the industrial heartland of Ohio. Of course, we should always be skeptical of the results of a single case study (did the workers in Fluvanna County, Virginia, have the same experience?), but, unfortunately, social scientists have not completed many rigorous studies.

To critically judge their conclusions, we must first look at how Buss and Redburn conducted their study. In 1978 (one year after the closing began), they interviewed 284 randomly selected steelworkers, approximately one-half of whom remained employed at the plant while the other one-half were permanently laid off. Most of these workers and former workers were interviewed a second time one year later.

The respondents were given a battery of tests to measure twelve indicators of mental health, including anxiety, alcohol abuse, family relations, and depression. To measure anxiety, for example, respondents were asked to agree or disagree with the statement "I often feel all wound up" and nine similar statements. The researchers tallied the scores, producing a range from 0 (low anxiety) to 10 (high anxiety). Similarly, to measure family relations, the steelworkers in the sample responded to ten statements such as, "Our family is constantly in the midst of quarrels."

The results of this study do not show that these steelworkers generally had grave mental health problems. Few had high scores on any of the twelve mental health scales. But those who were still unemployed at the time of the survey did have moderately higher levels of aggressive feelings, anxiety, feelings of victimization, and alcohol abuse than did the other steelworkers who had kept their jobs, landed another, or retired. Any psychological costs, then, seem to reflect the effects of *continued* unemployment, not job loss itself. The reemployed or retired did not show signs of extra stress.

Why were these psychological effects relatively mild? These diagnostic tests may have been inadequate in assessing the workers' mental health. Obviously, they are blunt tools, although they are closely similar to standard tests used throughout psychological research. If major traumas were widespread, they likely would have registered greater indications of trauma than they did.

The distinctive circumstances in Youngstown also may have mitigated the distress. Because the city had other job opportunities, few workers had prolonged unemployment. Steelworkers also were eligible for a variety of unusually generous public and private programs, which substantially cushioned the financial blow of lost jobs. Added to this was the social cushion provided by a stable, well-integrated community life that included multigenerational family ties, ethnic organizations, the Catholic church, and a traditional political machine. All offered emotional comforts and eased reentry into the job world.

**Social Costs.**    When a plant closes, there are obvious ripple effects on the local economy. A management's decision to close a factory has inevitable economic consequences for others, not only for the laid-off workers. For example, the luncheonette across the street loses its clientele and local suppliers then lose a customer.

In a similar way, one can imagine that the displaced workers' economic and psychic stresses spill over into the community, robbing it of vitality and cohesion. In the aftermath of natural disasters, communities have often lost the power to regulate the antisocial activities of its members; crime, for example, may increase. At the national level, some types of crime also increase with higher levels of unemployment. Does a plant shutdown also cause such trauma for a community?

Russ and Redburn looked for evidence of community breakdown by examining trends in several social indicators. Comparing data for Akron before and after the strike, they found the following:

- no increases in traffic violations or arrests;
- a substantial decrease in the FBI's index for serious crimes, this at a time when the national rates for cities of similar size were increasing;
- no increase in liquor sales (adjusting for the effects of inflation);
- a small one-year drop in United Way contributions, although contributions subsequently rebounded to a record level; and
- no changes in domestic relations court cases, divorces, marriage license applications, and new court complaints.

Indeed, the Akron community seemed resilient in the aftermath of the shutdown. This is not surprising, however, because the most directly affected residents, the displaced workers themselves, could draw on programs to lessen the economic shock, and few had much personal trauma. Perhaps Akron is an unusually happy exception in community response to a large shutdown, but it at least suggests that gloomy predictions of community deaths—or substantial collective trauma—will not necessarily come true.

# A Declining Middle Class?

As we mentioned, industrial decline has been linked to an emerging two-tier society, one that is top- and bottom-heavy and with a diminishing middle. This is so because blue-collar production jobs, especially in unionized industries, pay relatively well and have long been the ticket to the middle levels of the overall income distribution. Certainly it is possible that economic change has had such effect, but the case remains in doubt.

To answer the question of whether the American middle class is declining, one might think we simply have to follow Detective Joe Friday's command, "The facts, ma'am, just the facts." But which facts are relevant to consider?

Consider, for example, the findings of Barry Bluestone and Bennett Harrison's 1986 study, *The Great American Job Machine: The Proliferation of Low-Wage Employment in the U.S. Economy,* which was prepared for the Congressional Joint Economic Committee. This study has been widely cited for its scholarly evidence of a shrinking middle class.

First, Bluestone and Harrison calculated the median wage and salary income of all wage and salary workers in 1973. They then created three earnings categories: *high earnings,* which were at least twice the median income; *middle earnings,* between half the median and twice the median; and *low earnings,* which were less than one-half the median.[3]

To determine how the earnings levels of jobs had changed, they then did the same for 1979 and 1984, adjusting the earnings cut-offs to account for inflation (rising prices) by using the consumer price index (CPI). Of course, a dollar today will not buy what it could a few years ago, and the CPI attempts to determine the actual purchasing power of a dollar for comparisons across years.

You can see their results in the left three columns of Table 11.1. From 1979 to 1984, the proportion of workers in the low-earnings category increased slightly, from 30.4 percent to 32.4 percent (see top panel). More notable are the types of new jobs that were created in this period. Bluestone and Harrison conclude that *"nearly three fifths of the net new employment generated between 1979 and 1984 was low wage, compared with less than a fifth during the preceding period"* (cited in Kosters and Ross, 1988, p. 12) (see bottom panel).

For all their statistical efforts, however, Bluestone and Harrison do not have the final word. We have related technical aspects of their study to show that fairly minor changes in methods and assumptions can lead to very different conclusions.

Marvin Kosters and Murray Ross (1988) reexamined the same data set. Their results are presented in the right three columns of Table 11.1. They conclude in a much more positive light: *"According to these data the share of employment in the low-earnings category has declined over time, that in the high-earnings category has increased, and it is difficult to see any trend up or down in the middle-earnings category"* (1988, pp. 14–15). (This follows from the numbers in the top panel.)

Even more discrepant is Kosters and Ross's finding that both middle-income and high-income jobs account for a larger proportion of new jobs than do low-income jobs—just the reverse of Bluestone and Harrison (see bottom panel).

---

[3]  Recall that the median is the middle value, the number for which one-half of the workers have a higher income and one-half a lower income.

**Table 11.1**    Employment Shares by Earnings Category

| | Bluestone and Harrison Study | | | Kosters and Ross Study | | |
|---|---|---|---|---|---|---|
| | Earnings (%) | | | | | |
| | 1973 | 1979 | 1984 | 1973 | 1979 | 1985 |
| Low | 31.8 | 30.4 | 32.4 | 30.1 | 29.2 | 28.9 |
| Middle | 51.6 | 53.1 | 52.7 | 50.5 | 51.9 | 51.6 |
| High | 16.6 | 16.5 | 14.9 | 19.4 | 18.9 | 19.5 |
| Total | 100.0 | 100.0 | 100.0 | 100.0 | 100.0 | 100.0 |

| | New Employment by Income Level (%) | | | |
|---|---|---|---|---|
| | 1973–1979 | 1979–1984 | 1973–1979 | 1979–1985 |
| Low | 19.9 | 58.0 | 23.7 | 24.1 |
| Middle | 64.2 | 47.5 | 60.8 | 47.3 |
| High | 15.9 | −5.5 | 15.5 | 28.6 |
| Total | 100.0 | 100.0 | 100.0 | 100.0 |

Source: Adapted from Tables II and V in Marvin Kosters and Murray Ross, "A Shrinking Middle Class?" *Public Interest* 90: 12, 25, Winter 1988. ©1988 by National Affairs, Inc. Reprinted by permission.

How could the same world look so different? The computers that Kosters and Ross used were given slightly different numbers: 1) revised data for 1979 to reflect additional information, 2) more recent data (1985 instead of 1984), 3) a slightly different version of the CPI to adjust for inflation in a way that did not unduly reflect changes in mortgage interest rates, and 4) some analyses (not reported here) defined high income as 150 percent of the median instead of 200 percent.

So which analysis is more believable? Faced with this question, some might be tempted to recall that famous saying, "There are lies, damn lies, and statistics." Everyone can say whatever she wants with numbers, so the reasoning goes. Thus, it is futile to even debate matters such as this.

As we argued in chapter 1, however, this view does little more than justify intellectual laziness. All good consumers of social science should reject it. Someone *can* say whatever he or she wants with numbers, but some people make better cases than others. We must evaluate whether an analyst has used reasonable methods and made sound inferences from the data.

In our judgment, the second analysis showing that there is no declining middle in the job structure is the more convincing. Social scientists may disagree about the particular methodological decisions that Kosters and Ross made, but each of their revisions seems sensible. Their data are more complete and recent, and their method of adjusting for inflation (developed by the U.S. Bureau of Labor Statistics) corrects for a widely recognized deficiency in accounting for the impact of mortgage rates. Also, no single difference in methods accounts for most of the difference in results.

The debate is not settled, but those who see a proliferation of bad jobs have yet to make a convincing case. It is a large exaggeration to say that a rising service economy has polarized the job world and created a two-tier system.

At the same time, we also should note that American society *is* becoming somewhat more unequal in the distribution of family incomes. In particular, the top quintile of all families has recently received a larger piece of the economic pie: 40.6 percent in 1969, but 43.7 percent in 1986. The slice going to the bottom quintile has gotten smaller in these years, dropping from 5.6 percent to 4.6 percent.

But this change cannot be attributed to increasing variation in wages or the increasing size of the service sector. Family incomes have become more unequal largely because of shifts in the demography of the work force, particularly the increases in dual-income families and families with women as sole breadwinners. Another contributing factor is the declining hours of work (hence, less income) among some segments of the labor force.

## Jobs and Power

Although the effects of recent economic changes are neither as pervasive nor as calamitous as some doomsayers have contended, the hardships for many American workers have been very real and painful. And yet these workers' troubles have sparked little political action. At the national level, the only proposal being actively considered is modest, requiring companies to provide workers with advance notice before shutting down. In 1988, however, this proposal was little more than a political afterthought, added to a larger trade bill in Congress. Finally, just before President Reagan left office, the sixty-day plant closure notice requirement was passed.

One critical point to recognize is that management has the right to shut down a business for whatever reason it deems adequate, no matter how much money it is making or losing, how many workers will be put on the street, or how the rest of the community may be affected. And no one has the right to a job. The intent of legislation requiring prior notice of a plant shutdown is to ease the hardships that follow the exercise of legitimate managerial discretion.

The displaced worker clarifies the reality of power relations in a capitalist society such as ours. Under capitalism, the means of production are privately owned, and production, prices, and income are largely determined by competition in marketplace. The abstract and seemingly neutral world of the economists' marketplace, however, rests on a social arrangement in which some groups systematically have more say than others.

Our laws and general beliefs encourage those with capital to invest their money however they see fit and wherever they want, all for their private profit. Americans further believe that the pursuit of profits in a free market promotes the public good. Because the market supposedly dictates what actions are profitable, consumers receive the goods and services they want at prices they are willing to pay. And as "greedy" capitalists seek profits, they generate jobs, thus increasing the general welfare.

In some overall calculation of benefits and costs, this virtually unrestricted use of capital may benefit society as a whole, as the capitalist ideology proclaims. That huge issue cannot be settled here, but private investment decisions clearly have inevitable social consequences, not all of them positive. The layoffs of 15,000 steelworkers in Chicago during 1979–1983 is estimated to have cost $444 million annually in lost tax revenues and $163 million in unemployment insurance and food stamps. This burden fell on taxpayers, not on the steel companies.

Such costs to governments can dramatically curtail vital public services. A large shutdown, for example, reduces a community's ability to pay for schooling; tax receipts decline and school budgets are cut, oft-repeated events throughout the industrial sections of Ohio during the last recession. Thus, a distant owner or executive can impose costs on others with impunity. No rationale is necessary for this decision; nor is any responsibility imposed.

The interests of capital for greater profits, then, can conflict with the interests of workers for secure income, often earned at jobs in which they "invested" themselves. The pursuit of maximum profits can also conflict with the interests of communities in having a stable economic base on which to build a communal life.

But American society has largely settled this conflict of interests: Capitalist interests are given precedence. As Robert Heilbronner (1985) recently wrote:

> Capitalism is the *regime of capital,* the form of rulership we find when *power* takes the remarkable aspect of the domination, by those who control access to the means of production, of the great majority who must gain "employment" [emphasis added] (p. 52).

That so many people believe that this regime is desirable or, at least, necessary goes a long way toward explaining our largely hands-off approach to the recent wave of plant closings.

Of course, the marketplace is not some pure world of private competition. Agricultural subsidies; import restrictions on steel, cars, and textiles; and tax incentives for home and office construction—all are governmental policies that benefit particular industries. All represent governmental interventions into the world of private enterprise. But Americans remain hesitant to interfere in the marketplace in ways that restrict the prerogatives of capital. Such interference is usually viewed as a recipe for economic disaster, and even as un-American.

The basic relations of power that underlie the capitalist regime are secure because they remain largely beyond challenge. Because business interests determine the economic health of our society, politicians and the public at large are inclined to think that what is good for business is good for society. After all, if business groups feel threatened, they may withhold investment, a move with disastrous consequences for the nation's economy and the reelection chances of political incumbents. Indeed, politicians generally see the need to favor business interests, not resist them.

At the same time, not all of the dislocated have quietly accepted their economic fates. Displaced steelworkers in Youngstown and the Monongahela Valley of Pennsylvania, for example, attempted to buy their former plants and run them as community-owned ventures. They energetically enlisted the support of local politicians, church groups, and a variety of grass-roots organizations. They also attempted to get federal governmental assistance for their proposals. But ultimately, they failed to secure the necessary financial backing, and the plants remained closed.

At the national level, labor groups have lobbied for advance notice legislation and increased funding for worker-retraining programs. Their efforts have met the active resistance of business groups such as the National Association of Manufacturers and the U.S. Chamber of Commerce. Fighting the general probusiness ideology as well as business's lobbying campaign, unions have lacked the power to bring about substantial change.

Looking ahead, we feel safe in predicting that basic managerial prerogatives will remain intact. A few states have enacted legislation that imposes notification requirements of business closings, and such laws may become more common. But Americans seem prepared to accept the social turbulence that has accompanied our capitalist economy—more so than the citizens in other capitalist societies. Most Americans value the dynamism of the system, especially its promise of growth and higher living standards, over the costs of lost stability in personal and communal lives.

# References

Bensman, David, and Roberta Lynch. *Rusted Dreams: Hard Times in a Steel Community.* 1987. New York: McGraw-Hill.

Bluestone, Barry, and Bennett Harrison. *The Great American Job Machine: The Proliferation of Low-Wage Employment in the U.S. Economy.* Report to the Congressional Joint Economic Committee. 1986. Washington, DC: U.S. Government Printing Office.

Buss, Terry, and F. Stevens Redburn. *Shutdown at Youngstown: Public Policy for Mass Unemployment.* 1983. Albany: State University of New York Press.

Heilbronner, Robert. *The Nature and Logic of Capitalism.* 1985. New York: Norton.

Kosters, Marvin, and Murray Ross. "A Shrinking Middle Class?" *Public Interest* 90: 3–27, Winter 1988.

Standohar, Paul D., and Holly E. Brown (Eds.). *Deindustrialization and Plant Closings.* 1987. Lexington, MA: Lexington Books.

# Suggested Readings

Bensman, David, and Roberta Lynch. *Rusted Dreams: Hard Times in a Steel Community.* This moving account of the shutdown of Wisconsin Steel in Chicago is largely based on qualitative interviews.

Buss, Terry, and F. Stevens Redburn. *Shutdown at Youngstown: Public Policy for Mass Unemployment.* This work explores the range of consequences and reactions following the large steel industry shutdown in Youngstown, using both qualitative and quantitative data.

Heilbronner, Robert. *The Nature and Logic of Capitalism.* A theoretical dissection of capitalism as a social system, this work is challenging and provocative.

Standohar, Paul D., and Holly E. Brown (Eds.). *Deindustrialization and Plant Closings.* This good collection of readings presents the main arguments about the validity of the deindustrialization thesis. Several readings address the pros and cons of related policy proposals.

# CHAPTER 12

# The Political Institution

## The Politics of Abortion

**F**or more than fifteen years now, the issue of abortion has received sustained and intense attention by politicians, the media, religious organizations, and various special-interest groups. The arguments for and against the legality and morality of abortions have produced picketing and bombings of abortion clinics, marches and demonstrations, lawsuits, legislation, and innumerable books and articles.

On the surface, the abortion controversy in the United States seems a simple question of whether women should be allowed to abort their pregnancies. A sociological analysis of this issue reveals, however, that other concerns are involved. Indeed, the narrow debate about the termination of pregnancies may not even be the most important issue in the debate.

In fact, this debate is symbolic of a larger and more divisive issue than whether abortions should be allowed. Politically, it is a dispute between those who see women as equal to men and those who do not. At the base of this issue is the question of relative power: to what extent should men and women share in the exercise of power and influence? On one side are those who see men and women as equals; on the other are those who view women and men as fundamentally different, with different rights and responsibilities. Each side wants its view to prevail.

AP/Wide World Photos

Sociological analysis of the Prolife–Prochoice debate suggests that it is less about abortion and more about the roles of women in society.

Sociologists argue that debates about abortion are fundamentally political. In this chapter, we discuss and analyze the politics of the abortion issue. Before doing so, however, let us consider how it is possible for this issue to be considered as a political one.

All politics involves power: how it is used and who is able to use it. Power may be defined in many ways, but in its role as the foundation of politics, it is best defined as "the *social capacity* to make *binding decisions* that have *far-reaching consequences* for a society (or community)" (Orum, 1983, p. 128). This definition makes clear that power is possessed by members of groups or by specific roles—that is, the "social capacity"— not by individual personalities. When groups of individuals such as physicians and judges have the power to make decisions that affect others, the identity of the doctor or judge making such a decision does not matter. What matters instead is that he or she occupies a particular role in our society, and any individual filling that role shares in its power. "Binding decisions" are those that are seen as legitimate, right, or proper by those who exercise power and those who are subject to it.[1] Finally, the "far-reaching consequences" of the exercise of power mean that indirect and long-term consequences are as important as the immediate and obvious consequences (Orum, 1983, pp. 127–128).

Having defined power, it is then possible to define politics or political action. "In the broadest sense, *political* acts are those which are oriented toward the acquisition and use of power and authority within a specified social system. . . . Making binding decisions or attempting to influence the content of such decisions are acts of political participation" (Wasburn, 1982, p. 145).

By these definitions, the abortion issue is indeed a political debate involving numerous organizations that directly attempt to influence legislation or judicial decisions; these groups include the National Right to Life Committee, the American Civil Liberties Union Reproductive Freedom Project, the Planned Parenthood Federation, and the National Abortion Rights Action League. Such lobbying groups are represented by spokespersons who attempt to convince those in power to sponsor or oppose particular laws.

As this news clip shows, many groups are involved in the effort to enact or prevent legislation or federal policy that governs access to and funding for abortions—the president of the United States, the U.S. Senate, special-interest groups, state governors, and Catholic bishops.

---

[1] Sociologists sometimes distinguish between power (the capacity to make decisions) and authority (the *legitimate* capacity to make decisions). That is, a group may be able to impose its will through coercion or other means but lacks the right to do so. Here the distinction is unnecessary because the political struggle over abortion focuses on the exercise of legitimate capacity, especially as represented in law.

# Abortion: Once More to the Fore

By Michael Satchell
with Michael Bosc
in Chicago

From clinic bombings around the country to massive protests in the nation's capital, from complex legal battles in the courts to rancorous debate on Capitol Hill, few issues over the past decade have engendered such passions and proven so divisive as abortion. At times, it has receded from the center of the political stage, but now, with an important court decision last week, a host of new regulations from the administration of Ronald Reagan and a growing number of restrictive local initiatives, the abortion issue seems poised to move front and center once again in a way not seen since the Supreme Court's landmark *Roe v. Wade* decision in 1973.

**Back to the High Court again?**

No one could have predicted the coincidence of the court ruling, which struck down a Minnesota requirement that minors 17 years and under must have parental or judicial permission to end their pregnancies. The ruling presages a possibly decisive abortion decision this fall in the U.S. Supreme Court, in which Reagan's controversial nominee, appeals-court Judge Robert Bork, could play a pivotal role. The court decision came in the same week that Illinois Governor James Thompson vetoed a bill designed to block the distribution of contraceptives to students in high-school clinics. Further fueling the debate is an administration plan to severely restrict federal funding for some 4,500 of the nation's birth-control clinics.

It is, by any standard, a dramatic gambit. The rules, expected to be published this week, would achieve by executive order what the President has been unable to accomplish in the Congress: Withholding money for clinics that even mention the word "abortion" when counseling women on birth-control or pregnancy options. The rules govern administration of something known as Title X of the Public Health Service Act, which this year will provide $142.5 million in federal support for family planning, mostly for the young and the poor. Title X is the only federal program directly underwriting domestic family-planning services. The clinics serve about 4.3 million women annually, and since 1970 Congress has prohibited program dollars from paying for abortion counseling or the actual surgical procedure; the clinics use private funds for these services. No federal money, in fact, can be used to pay for any abortion services, except when the mother's life is threatened.

The President's proposed regulations call for three changes in the way clinics must operate to qualify for funds. Counselors will be prohibited from even mentioning abortion as an option for pregnant women who do not wish to have their babies; nor can they refer clients to an abortion service if they are asked to do so. Critics say this is medically unethical, particularly in cases of high-risk pregnancies where the infants may be born severely handicapped, addicted to drugs or infected with AIDS.

Also, clinics that offer federally funded birth-control counseling and privately financed abortion services must have separate sites for each activity—a major expense if the clinic is located in a hospital. Third, federal money would be

continued

barred for "any program that encourages, promotes or advocates abortion," a catchall restriction that critics believe is unconstitutional because it violates the free-speech provisions of the First Amendment.

Abortion opponents, who have had few tangible gains to cheer during the Reagan administration—despite the President's fervid pro-life priorities—are encouraged but not enthralled by the latest maneuver. Douglas Johnson, legislative director of National Right To Life, insists that Title X was originally established by Congress as a contraception program and should be restored to that status. "A lot of the clientele for these clinics are adolescents, and when they find out they are pregnant, abortion is not only presented as an option, it's encouraged," Johnson says. "This is not what Congress intended."

The impact of the rules changes will be felt by pro-choice groups, particularly the Planned Parenthood Federation of America, the nation's largest birth-control-counseling agency. After a period of confusion and disruption, Planned Parenthood Executive Vice President David Andrews believes, the new rules will be overturned by the courts or rejected by Congress. "It's another attempt by the Reagan administration to destroy Title X," says Andrews, "which is one of the nation's best and most efficient programs serving the health needs of poor people."

For the anti-abortion forces, the battle in the courts has been tougher going. The setback in Minnesota, for instance, came when a federal appeals court struck down a state law colloquially referred to as the "squeal rule." It required women under 18 to inform their parents of a pending abortion, or get a judge's permission for the procedure. The decision will certainly be appealed to the Supreme Court, where a similar Illinois law is already scheduled to be heard during the fall term. Heartening pro-lifers—and heightening their anticipation of a major abortion decision in their favor—is the President's nomination of Bork to the Supreme Court. The

federal appeals-court judge, who faces fractious nomination hearings, has previously criticized several Supreme Court abortion decisions.

These latest developments in the battle over fetal life erupt at a time of mounting controversy over the introduction of birth-control services in health clinics at some of the nation's high schools. Spurring the move to put family planning services in school clinics are the rising numbers of unmarried teenage mothers and the increase in younger teens ending their pregnancies with abortion. On the encouraging side, the teen pregnancy rate leveled off in the first half of the 1980s. In 1984, the latest year for available statistics, there were some 469,700 births to women 19 and under and 401,100 abortions. In the 15-to-17-age bracket, the 200,500 abortions outweighed the 166,700 births.

Despite the relatively minuscule number of high-school clinics offering contraceptive advice, "right to life" advocates have long opposed them, though it's unclear if they will prevail. Pending in the U.S. Senate, for instance, is a bill that would expand the Title X program and add $10 million the first year for such school-based family-planning counseling. In Illinois, where Governor Thompson supports them as an important tool in preventing unwanted pregnancies and breaking the poverty cycle, three schools offer family-planning services and a fourth is due to start this fall. Opponents have attacked the program on questions of teenage morality, community rights, and legal and health issues. "The trend is going against these clinics," says a confident Phyllis Schlafly, head of the conservative Eagle Forum. "Out of 15,500 school districts in this country, the highest count I've seen is 115 clinics. We've killed them in most places." Says Cardinal Joseph Bernardin, the archbishop of Chicago: School-based contraceptive services encourage sexual behavior by "giving it a veneer of social acceptability."

**A President's legacy**

While abortion opponents press their offensive locally, they have long criticized Ronald Reagan for not doing more to further their cause. As the President's options dwindle with his time left in the White House, his best opportunity to leave his philosophical imprint may lie with the courts. That could be tested this fall if congress approves the nomination and the Court agrees to hear the Minnesota case and a related case involving an Illinois statute that is scheduled for the Court's fall term. Ironically, in the Minnesota case, the appeals court struck down the law, citing the very "family issues" Reagan has championed. The law, the court said, "may do more to fractionalize the family integrity than preserve it."

Still, regardless of what happens in the courtrooms, Ronald Reagan has a few more opportunities to influence the abortion debate. The best bet on the horizon: A program funded by the National Institutes of Health—and regarded as vulnerable by pro-lifers—to develop a so-called abortion pill to be taken after a woman learns she is pregnant. There are other executive-action orders—like the Title X rule changes—available to the President, but he apparently will keep them as reserve ammunition for the coming battles in what promises to be a major new offensive in the continuing war over who controls fetal life.

Abortion rights issues also figure into the platforms of candidates and political parties during election campaigns. As the following news-clip shows, candidates and political organizations (in this case, the Democratic party) are concerned that their positions on abortion are acceptable to their constituents.

Indeed, as the accompanying clip indicates, concerns about a candidate's position on abortion do matter to people in their decisions about whether to vote and for whom.

Why has abortion emerged in the late twentieth century as a political issue? How has a "private" issue become a "public" concern? What is at stake in this debate? What are the issues? What is the likely outcome of the debate? We will answer questions in our sociological analysis of the abortion controversy.

# The Issues of the Abortion Debate

Almost everyone seems to have strong feelings about abortion. Whenever the issue is raised, most people have fairly clear ideas of how they stand. But what is the issue? For some, it seems to be a question of when life begins—at birth? at conception? or somewhere in between? For others, it is a question of individual rights: Do people have the right to decide whether to abort the children they conceive? Some see the primary issue as one of privacy: Should government be permitted to in-

# Abortion: The Democrats Shift to the Right

Whatever his personal problems with women, Democratic presidential candidate Gary Hart was the favorite of many feminists because of his unequivocal support for legalized abortion, including federal funding for the procedure. But with Hart's abrupt departure from the race, the pro-choice lobby is left with some unsatisfactory choices. While recent party platforms have supported a woman's right to abortion, the Democratic field is divided over whether the government should pay for abortions for poor women.

Of the seven likely candidates, four—Sen. Joseph Biden of Delaware, Missouri Rep. Richard Gephardt, former Arizona governor Bruce Babbitt and Tennessee Sen. Albert Gore—say Medicaid shouldn't be used to underwrite abortions. The three others—Illinois Sen. Paul Simon, Massachusetts Gov. Michael Dukakis and the Rev. Jesse Jackson— would not ban Medicaid payments, but each has voiced personal objections to abortion.

The increased conservatism on abortion in part reflects a recognition of political realities. Democrats can't forget that former vice presidential candidate Geraldine Ferraro was attacked by her own Roman Catholic archbishop for her pro-choice stance in 1984. It also reflects the Democrats' new emphasis on "family issues"—an emphasis aimed at, among others, ethnic urban voters, many of them Catholic, and white Southern men. "For people who say they are personally uncomfortable with abortion, [opposing federal funding] is a way to walk the middle line," says Marla Bolotsky, executive director of Voters for Choice, a political-action committee in Washington.

But abortion lobbyists insist they won't let the Democrats evade the abortion issue. Says Richard Mintz, a spokesman for the National Abortion Rights Action League: "Our objective is that none of these candidates call themselves pro-choice unless they're for full choice." The results of such a litmus test may not please the pro-choice lobby, however, since the Democrats seem to think a less liberal position on abortion is where the party should be. "The politicians," says Democratic consultant Bob Squier, "are finally catching up with the people."

trude into the private affairs of individuals by regulating the permissible outcomes of their pregnancies? In fact, there is no single issue in the abortion debate. And when the history of this controversy is examined, it becomes clear that today's concerns are actually quite new when compared to the concerns about abortion one or two centuries ago.

To understand the political aspects of the contemporary debate, we must trace the long history of public concern, political struggle, and policies relating to abortion. Sociologist Kristin Luker has conducted the best analysis of this issue, and much of the following is taken from her work, *Abortion and the Politics of Motherhood* (1984).

# Politics and Abortion

## 'Family Issues' Play in the Race for the White House

Kenneth L. Woodward

Of all the issues that have emerged in the 1984 campaign, abortion has proved to be one of the most prickly—especially for the Democrats. Last week Democratic presidential candidate Walter Mondale defended his pro-choice stance as "an issue I've prayed over." But for other leading Democrats, notably vice presidential candidate Geraldine Ferraro and New York Gov. Mario Cuomo—both Roman Catholics—the issue could not be prayed away. A running argument on abortion between the governor and New York's Archbishop John J. O'Connor ballooned into a national debate last week when the president of the U.S. Roman Catholic hierarchy issued a statement criticizing Catholic politicians (like Ferraro and Cuomo) who say they personally oppose abortion but support freedom of choice.

The bishops' pronouncement underscored the extraordinary mix of religion and politics in this year's race for the White House. The religious factor began to emerge when Ferraro questioned whether President Reagan is really a "good Christian." Since then, hardly a week has gone by in which one candidate or another has failed to profess religious faith—or be photographed leaving a church. Black congregations and white fundamentalist churches have been busily registering voters, and both parties are presenting themselves as the custodians of traditional virtues and family values. But no issue cuts through the pious images and rhetoric quite like the vexing question of abortion.

In his brief statement, Bishop James W. Malone, president of the National Conference of Catholic Bishops, rejected as "simply not logically tenable" the argument of candidates who say "their personal views should not influence their policy decisions." That position, he wrote, would be as "unacceptable" as that of any office seeker who puts forth his personal views but no practical proposals to implement them. The statement affirmed the church's right to discuss the moral dimensions of public policies but stressed that bishops should not take positions on candidates. While acknowledging that Catholics may disagree over how moral principles should be applied to public policies, Malone seemed to rule out disagreement among Catholics with the church's opposition to the direct taking of innocent human life—"by abortion or by direct attacks on non-combatants in war."

Malone's statement had been prepared weeks ago but was released last week in part because of the escalating debate in the New York press between O'Connor and Governor Cuomo. During a televised press conference last June, O'Connor had said that although he would not tell Catholics how to vote, he personally could not "see how a Catholic in good conscience can vote for" a candidate who supports abortion. In Cuomo's view, the archbishop was saying that no Catholic could vote for politicians like Sen. Daniel Patrick Moynihan or himself because—though personally opposed to abortion—they support freedom of choice. When the

continued

archbishop responded that the governor had "misinterpreted" his comment as a directive to his flock, Cuomo accepted the "clarification" but vowed to continue the argument over religion in politics.

**'Straw Man':** Last week in his Albany office, Cuomo reviewed Malone's statement and concluded that "there isn't a line I can disagree with. The bishops are saying they won't take positions on candidates and that officeholders should make decisions based on conscience." As Cuomo saw it, the bishops "outlined a straw man" in describing candidates who take personal positions but do not act on them. "It certainly doesn't apply to me," he insisted. "I don't think it's good that society aborts its young," he declared, "but for a public official, the question is where you draw the line between the beliefs you hold personally and those you pursue in public policy."

In the 10 years since abortion was declared legal in the United States, leading liberal Catholics in the Democratic Party—notably Sen. Edward Kennedy, Speaker of the House Thomas P. (Tip) O'Neill and Congresswoman Geraldine Ferraro—have drawn the line in a way that allows them to stand on both sides of the abortion issue. Ferraro summed up that position five years ago on the floor of the House: "As a Catholic, I accept the premise that a fertilized ovum is a baby . . . [but] I have no right to impose my beliefs on [others]." It is precisely this position which the Catholic bishops now find illogical and untenable. It is also the line that President Reagan has repeatedly attacked. During a recent spaghetti dinner at a Roman Catholic church in New Jersey, for instance, the president hit back at Cuomo's charge in his keynote address to the Democratic convention that the Republicans lack compassion. "Why do those who claim to represent the party of compassion feel no compassion whatsoever for the most helpless among us—the unborn?" Reagan asked rhetorically.

**Church and State:** But the Catholic bishops themselves are in a bind. Thus far, the Republicans have shown no mind to heed the hierarchy's equally pointed criticism of the Reagan administration's cuts in welfare programs, its policies in Central America or its posture on nuclear weapons. Moreover, by insisting that Catholic politicians of both parties form their consciences according to Catholic principles, the bishops risk criticism that they seek to dictate to Catholics in public life—a charge that the election of John F. Kennedy had seemingly laid to rest. Last week, for example, Ferraro defended her support of "reproductive freedom" as congruent with the independent position staked out by President Kennedy 24 years ago. "He believed in the separation of church and state," Ferraro said. "I do, too." Moynihan allowed that "we live in mild times" compared with past eras when bishops spoke out more often on politics. And O'Neill offered his own rationale for ignoring the hierarchy: "Historically, most archbishops have voted for the Republican Party while the nuns and priests who work in the vineyard have voted for the Democrats."

Perhaps the calmest voice in the evolving debate belonged to former Sen. Eugene McCarthy, a Catholic who twice ran for the Democratic presidential nomination. McCarthy recalled that church leaders influenced political debates on civil rights, capital punishment and the war in Vietnam. Of the debate between Cuomo and O'Connor, McCarthy observed, "Governor Cuomo was wrong to say that the church shouldn't exert its influence on political issues, and Archbishop O'Connor is guilty of great oversimplification because abortion is not the only issue on which voters have to judge candidates." Nonetheless, McCarthy argues, "abortion is a legitimate political issue and far from sectarian, since more than just Catholics oppose it."

**Voice:** In a campaign year that has already heard from newly politicized fundamentalists and freshly active blacks, the Catholic bishops' voice is only one among a chorus of concerned religious constituencies. But it is a voice that claims to speak for some 52 million Americans on an issue—abortion—that continues to be the nation's most agonizing moral dilemma. Whether that dilemma permits a purely political solution is highly doubtful. But at this moment in campaign '84, it is the issue that most severely tests both parties' capacity for civility—and political dexterity.

# The History of the Abortion Issue

The abortion controversy is not new. Although no legislation governed the procedure in 1800, one century later every state forbade abortion at any stage of pregnancy. What happened during the nineteenth century to produce such laws?

Physicians became the single most important group to call for legal restrictions on abortions, according to Luker. During the nineteenth century, medicine was far different than it is today. To now call oneself a physician and practice medicine, one must graduate from an accredited medical school, pass rigorous examinations, and be licensed. Throughout the 1800s, there were no licensing requirements for doctors; anyone who wished to could "practice" medicine. Although there were highly trained doctors, many quacks also competed for patients. Doctors thus had relatively low status. Trained physicians sought some way to regulate those who could practice medicine.

The American Medical Association (AMA) was founded in 1847 to improve the standing of doctors. In 1859, a resolution was passed by the association that condemned abortion. At this time, Luker estimates, one-third of all pregnancies were so terminated (p. 191).

The AMA condemned the practice for two reasons. First, it argued that women aborted because they believed that a fetus was not alive before "quickening"—that is, before movement by the unborn was perceptible (this occurs at about four months into a pregnancy). Women lacked the knowledge that a fetus was "alive" from conception, according to the AMA. Second, the association claimed that new medical discoveries showed that an embryo is a child from the very moment of conception.

These claims were astonishing, especially because neither was true. First, the general public knew that pregnancy was a continuous process that began at conception—the idea was firmly established in the early part of the century. Second, no new medical discoveries demonstrated whether an embryo was a child. Why did the AMA make such claims to support its opposition to abortion?

By making these assertions, physicians were arguing that women were ignorant of the facts. The question of abortion became one of facts, not values, and thus of who had the facts. Physicians could now claim to have superior knowledge. And more important, the need for licensing was easily shown. Charlatans did not have access to the facts and therefore should not be permitted to perform abortions.

In the mid-nineteenth century, legitimate physicians actually had little more to offer their patients than did quacks. Abortion, however, offered an area in which true physicians could distinguish themselves from other "doctors" through the sole possession of expert knowledge. As Luker notes, physicians did not seek to ban all abortions. Instead, the AMA argued that doctors be allowed to decide *when* an abortion was permissible by evaluating the mother's health.

> The physicians' choice of abortion as the focus of their moral crusade was carefully calculated. Abortion, and only abortion, could enable them to make symbolic claims about their status. Unlike the other medico-moral issues of the time—alcoholism, slavery, venereal disease, and prostitution—only abortion gave physicians the opportunity to claim to be saving human lives. . . . What was at the core of their argument, therefore, was a *reallocation* of social responsibility for assessing the conditional rights of the embryo against the woman's right to life, both narrowly and broadly defined. From the late nineteenth century until the late 1960s it was doctors, not women, who held the right to make that decision (1984, pp. 31–35).

In short, the regulation of abortion as prompted by physicians' claims of expert knowledge was actually a struggle over power and privilege. In particular, physicians struggled to enhance their standing relative to others in society and to acquire the right, or power, to make binding decisions with long-range consequences for large numbers of people.

In fact, physicians did acquire this power. By the end of the nineteenth century, abortion had become only a medical issue. Abortions were performed only to "preserve the mother's life." But mothers were not the ones who decided what that meant. This situation continued, more or less unchallenged, for some three-quarters of a century. Only in the 1960s did people begin to question the authority of physicians over abortion. One question that Luker sought to answer in her study was, "Why so little public discussion about abortion from the beginning of the twentieth century until recently?"

# The Twentieth Century

According to Luker, one reason that the abortion issue received little public discussion was its casting as an issue that concerned facts, not morals. And because doctors were the ones who had these facts, ordinary citizens lacked the information necessary to enter the discussion. Abortion also was seen as pitting the interests of a woman against those of her fetus, and so a woman's desires were not seen as objective.

With real advances in modern medicine in the twentieth century, medical threats (other than a woman's mental health) that could have been used to justify an abortion became less serious. Tuberculosis, cardiovascular diseases, and renal diseases became treatable conditions that were manageable without threatening the mother's life or that of the fetus, when given adequate care.

Finally, and most important, there were no real obstacles to obtaining abortions. Many physicians were quite liberal in their interpretation of the necessity to perform abortions—saving the mother's life. Many doctors interpreted this to mean that an abortion could save the mother's mental health. So prevalent was abortion that in 1948 20 percent to 25 percent of all women who had ever been married reported having had had an abortion (Luker, 1984, p. 49).

The reasons for abortions in the early twentieth century shifted to the psychiatric and social. Decreasing numbers of abortions were performed expressly to preserve physical life. As a result, the medical profession's authority over who could obtain an abortion and for what reasons became less justifiable. Indeed, many doctors themselves began to question the entire issue. Some began to feel, as did others of the public, that abortions were justified only to save physical life; others, however, felt it justified in cases of severe fetal deformity or where pregnancy and childbirth threatened a woman's mental health (for example, when pregnancy resulted from rape or incest). Abortion "liberals" felt that abortion was justified for a wide range of psychiatric or social reasons, while abortion "conservatives" felt it justified only to save a woman's life. As Luker notes, "Both extremes on the continuum had assumed that their views were representative of public opinion" (1984, p. 65).

But despite the wide differences of opinion about justifications, there was no public discussion in the first half of the century. So what brought the debate out into the open?

## Abortion as a Public Issue

Beginning in the 1950s, hospitals established therapeutic abortion boards of internists, psychiatrists, obstetricians, and other physicians to rule on abortion requests. In other words, each woman seeking an abortion applied to the board for its approval.

Luker reports that the criteria used by these boards lacked uniformity—that is, some hospitals might approve a request while others would not. Such uncertainty about which conditions were justifiable inevitably led to public awareness of the situation's ambiguities. One particularly well-publicized case in 1962 involved a mother's request to abort a seriously deformed fetus; public attention focused on the fact that some doctors granted abortions for largely social and psychiatric reasons while others granted them only in cases of clear threat to the mother's life. With this case and its publicity, "what had been a trickle of public interest in the issue of abortion became a torrent" (1984, p. 65). Clearly, some reform was needed.

As had been true in the nineteenth century, physicians were the ones who first pushed for abortion reform. In particular, they sought an acceptable legal definition of a permissible abortion. After several years of open debate among professionals, California enacted a law in 1967 that allowed an abortion by a qualified physician (M.D.) in a hospital certified by the American Hospital Association if it was done to prevent mental or physical damage to the woman. Once this law was in place, abortions were generally available. By 1970, more than 99 percent of women who applied for abortions had them granted (Luker, 1984, pp. 88, 94). One would imagine that the issue was settled.

## The Abortion "Rights" Movement

Physicians, however, were not the only interest group involved in this debate. In the mid-1960s, growing numbers of women began to argue for equal rights. In many states, organizations of women called for the abolition, not modification, of abortion laws—abortion, they argued, should be a woman's right. "In the 1960s women began to claim that no man (including most physicians of the time) could make an 'objective' decision on abortion, and, further, only the woman herself could legitimately decide whether or not an abortion was 'necessary.' A new era had begun." (Luker, 1984, p. 99). After so many years, why did women begin to organize and demand abortion as a right?

Before the 1960s, the idea that a woman might pursue a career rather than define herself solely as wife and mother was not widely accepted. In general, a job or career was expected to assume secondary importance in a woman's life. Her first and primary responsibility was to be a good mother. This "traditional" idea was accepted by most men and women, but during the 1960s, women in particular began to challenge this tradition.

Women began to enter the paid labor force for many reasons. Many completed high school and college and therefore expected to pursue careers. Divorce rates increased, thereby forcing more women to work just to support themselves. People also married later, which meant that women needed to work in order to support themselves. Birth rates dropped during the 1960s, which further freed women to leave home to enter the work force. And perhaps most important, because of macro-economic forces, the average American family needed more money to sustain an average middle-class life-style. More than anything else, women entered the labor force out of necessity. (See Suzanne Bianchi and Daphne Spain's *American Women in Transition* [1986] for a discussion of these trends.)

When women began to see jobs or careers as options and to think about combining them with family life, many realized that they were treated unfairly in the workplace because they were mothers or potential mothers. For women who sought equality with men in their jobs or careers, childbearing obviously was a highly important issue. Because control of childbearing was so essential to working women, who could make that decision became a matter of political power. Antiabortion laws came to be viewed as a restriction on women's abilities to control their lives, especially their work lives.

Remember, however, that abortions were available. As already shown, 99 percent of women requesting abortions in California were granted them. So if women had no trouble obtaining abortions, why were there organized efforts to abolish abortion laws? What purpose would be served by achieving such a goal?

# The Symbolic Meaning of Abortion

The answer is that women were fighting a *symbolic* battle for equal rights as much as anything else, at least with respect to abortion laws. Their goal was to redefine the authority governing abortions. They sought to change the power relations in society, to shift the ability to control abortions from one group—physicians—to another—themselves.

Why women's groups fought so hard for the abolition of state abortion laws is easy to understand. Although laws are often enacted to cause or enforce a certain type of behavior, this is not their only, or even principal, purpose. Speed limits were lowered in the United States from 65 to 55 miles per hour in the late 1970s to conserve energy. But motorists did not slow down, continuing to drive 65 mph or faster on interstate highways. Thus, in 1987, speed limits were raised back to 65 mph because the law had been inconsistent with Americans' behaviors. This is often the case. Laws rarely will make people behave in fundamentally different ways. They will obey laws that they consider sensible and just, otherwise they will not. And no law can be enforced in the face of widespread public opposition. Thus, laws symbolically reflect the way "we" do things.

When the law allowed physicians to decide whether a woman could obtain an abortion, almost every woman who requested one had it granted. But women were denied the power to make these decisions alone. The law allocated that power to physicians, and in doing so announced that "This is the way we do things." The law embodied the collective decision that power be allocated to one group rather than another. "We" gave physicians this power—our society, our state, our community, we as voters, we as citizens. By seeking to abolish these laws, women's groups thus made a different symbolic statement about how "we" should do things. Their goal was to embody the collective sentiment that women had the sole power to decide about abortions.

The movement to abolish state abortion laws gained momentum through the 1960s as the women's movement gained in numbers and influence. Although abortion laws were only one issue on which the movement focused, abortion rights were extremely important to feminists. It was not surprising, therefore, when the U.S. Supreme Court agreed to hear such a case.

In *Roe* v. *Wade,* the constitutional issue presented to the court was whether legislation that denied abortions infringed on a woman's right to privacy. Such a right is not specified in the U.S. Constitution, but the Court had established such a right in its interpretation of the Bill of Rights in the case of *Griswold* v. *Connecticut* (1965). That case had involved a challenge to a Connecticut law that prohibited the distribution or sale of contraceptives. In its decision, the Court overturned a lower court, ruling that the law had unconstitutionally restricted a couple's right to privacy. For the first time, this decision established a constitutional right to privacy for married couples. A subsequent U.S. Supreme Court decision, *Eisenstadt* v. *Baird* (1972), extended that right to unmarried persons. The constitutional right to privacy is a fundamental right, which means that states may restrict it only for "compelling reasons."

The January 1973 decision in *Roe* v. *Wade* was not a clear-cut victory for those seeking to abolish abortion laws or for those seeking to establish or maintain them. The Court ruled that the decision to obtain an abortion must be left solely to a woman and her physician during the first trimester (three months) of pregnancy. States have no compelling reason to restrict access to abortion, and thereby restrict a woman's privacy, during this stage of pregnancy. During the second trimester, the Court said, states have an interest, a compelling reason, in protecting the life of the mother and may regulate where and how abortions are performed; and during the third trimester, the fetus has the potential of life and a state has a compelling interest in protecting this potential life and may prohibit abortions at this late stage of pregnancy. For all intents and purposes, *Roe* v. *Wade* eliminated most state laws that prevented a woman from obtaining an abortion, except in the late stages of pregnancy. The decision was hailed as a victory for both abortion rights and feminist groups, and as a disaster for those opposed to abortion.

By making abortion legal, the Court restructured the power relations that had prevailed to that time. Professionals (physicians) were no longer the gatekeepers entrusted with the authority to approve or deny this procedure. The political efforts of the prochoice groups brought the issue before the Court, where their arguments prevailed.

*Roe* v. *Wade* also had tremendous symbolic importance. In particular, the decision was a major victory for women who viewed motherhood as an option in their lives and childbearing as something that will fit into the other roles they occupy. By legalizing abortion, the Court granted women the right to redefine motherhood as something controllable and manageable along with other responsibilities. At the same time, for women (and men) who viewed motherhood as the natural, central, and defining role of women, the decision was a symbolic rejection of their view of the world.

Since the 1972 decision, the political struggle has continued. Those who wish to see abortion restricted or prohibited (prolife) and those who wish to see abortion rights unchanged (prochoice) have each organized to seek to preserve or alter the distribution of power on this issue. Prolife activists wish to see the state empowered to decide who can obtain an abortion, while prochoice activists seek to maintain women's power. Luker studied both prochoice and prolife activists and found that they disagree with one another in fundamental ways.

Prolife people view a fetus as a human being from the moment of conception. Prochoice people, however, see the fetus as a potential human being until it is actually delivered. The Court did not consider this issue—there is no demonstrable way to show when during development the human organism becomes a person. But since *Roe* v. *Wade,* the question of when life begins has figured prominently in the argument to outlaw abortion. By the logic of prolife groups, abortion amounts to murder.

More dramatically, prolife activists believe men and women to be intrinsically different in their social roles. Women, such individuals believe, are destined to be mothers first and foremost. Because motherhood is women's natural role, anything that makes it less central or less important makes women less important.

On the other hand, prochoice activists believe that men and women are basically equal. The roles that each occupy in the family are negotiable and not a reflection of innate differences. As with other adult female roles, motherhood is something over which a woman should have control. Anything restricting that control makes women unequal to men, handicapping them in a way that men are not.

This symbolic meaning of abortion is what accounts for the extreme emotion seen in the debate. As Luker notes:

> In a world where men and women have traditionally had different roles to play and where male roles have traditionally been the more socially prestigious and financially rewarded, abortion has become a symbolic marker between those who wish to maintain this division of labor

and those who wish to challenge it. . . . In order for pro-choice women to achieve their goals, they *must* argue that motherhood is not a primary, inevitable, or "natural" role for all women; for pro-life women to achieve their goals they *must* argue that it is. In short the debate rests on the question of whether women's fertility is to be socially recognized as a resource or a handicap (1984, p. 202).

To investigate the argument that motherhood is symbolic of views of male–female equality, Steven Nock (1987) examined the relationship between women's opinions on the issue of equality and the number of children they had or hoped to have. The question he asked was whether opinions about sexual equality affect whether a woman has or desires children, and if so, how many. In a national sample, very traditional women—those who saw male and female roles as quite different—had more children and reported larger numbers of children as ideal. For example, 38 percent of very traditional women had three or more children, but only 14 percent of nontraditional women—those who believe males and females are substantially equal—had as many children. Similar differences were found between the two types of women in the number of children that they consider to be ideal. In other words, motherhood is strongly related to views about sexual equality: Those who subscribe to traditional views of male and female roles in society have more children than those who see males and females as being equals (see Table 12.1).

The abortion debate pits traditional women and men against nontraditional men and women. In a very real sense, the argument is over how we as Americans view women: Are they equal to men? When a man and a woman conceive a child, the man is required by neither law nor custom to significantly alter his life. If we forbid abortions, then, only a woman would be required to make such significant changes, even if she does not wish them.

By allowing women to decide whether they will have children they have conceived, we seem to say that motherhood should not necessarily be more important than other things to a woman. This is the very opposite of what traditional, prolife individuals believe. To them, motherhood is the most important function a woman has and is, indeed, her obligation.

Public opinion, however, is not as divided as the prochoice and prolife groups have suggested. Only 38 percent of Americans believe that a woman should be allowed an abortion "for any reason," but 85 percent believe an abortion should be allowed if a woman's health is endangered by her pregnancy. When there is a strong chance of a serious defect in the baby, 77 percent of Americans believe a woman should be allowed an abortion. Only 40 percent believe an abortion should be allowed simply because a woman does not want more children (National Opinion Research Center, 1987). In short, abortion rights have both considerable

**Table 12.1** Traditionalism and Numbers of Children, Actual and Desired, for Women Ages 45 and Younger

| | Numbers of Children | | | | | | | |
|---|---|---|---|---|---|---|---|---|
| | Actual (%) | | | | Ideal* (%) | | | |
| Level of Traditionalism | None | 1–2 | 3 + | Total | None | 1–2 | 3 + | Total |
| Very traditional (N = 91) | 22 | 40 | 38 | 100 | 1 | 57 | 42 | 100 |
| Moderately traditional (N = 186) | 27 | 51 | 22 | 100 | 0 | 64 | 36 | 100 |
| Very nontraditional (N = 153) | 42 | 44 | 14 | 100 | 3 | 70 | 27 | 100 |

*The question was worded, "What do you think is the ideal number of children for a family to have?"
Source: Nock, Steven L. "The Symbolic Meaning of Childbearing." *Journal of Family Issues* 8: 373–393, December 1987.

support and considerable qualification. Only certain justifications are allowed for an abortion, and yet few Americans favor outlawing all abortions. Clearly, the prolife and prochoice activists are on the extreme ends of the spectrum.

According to our sociological analysis, the abortion debate will continue so long as there are strong views about whether women should be treated as the equals of men. Because the claim to sexual equality is actually quite new, having begun on a widespread scale only during the 1960s, a resolution is unlikely in the near future.

# Summary and Conclusion

We began this chapter by asking several questions:

First, why is this "private" issue a "public concern?" We have seen that abortion is *symbolic* of a larger, more controversial issue than whether women can obtain legal abortions: Who has and exercises power? In particular, it involves questions about the relative power of women and men.

Second, "What is at stake in this debate?" Nothing suggests that abortion laws have much to do with the number of abortions that are performed. Even before the legalization of abortion in *Roe* v. *Wade*

(1972), abortions were widely available to those women who were willing to take the steps required to obtain one. In other words, the actual number of abortions performed is not likely to be affected by the outcome of this debate. Instead, our society's definition of motherhood and its role in women's lives is at stake. Are women in the United States viewed primarily—perhaps solely—as mothers? Or is motherhood only one of many adult roles that women may occupy?

Third, "What are the issues?" On its face, the abortion debate appears to be about when life begins—at conception or later? But, as we have seen, it also involves questions about privacy. Is a woman's decision about whether to bear a child a private one? And, most important, the debate concerns power. Who is to have the authority to make such decisions—doctors? courts? women? or who?

Fourth, "What is the likely outcome of the abortion debate?" This amounts to asking whose views will prevail. The activists involved (prolife and prochoice groups) are at the opposite and extreme ends of the issue and offer little hope of compromise. But activist groups do not represent popular public sentiment about abortion. Most Americans are neither prochoice nor prolife. Few favor either the complete abolition of abortion or its unrestricted use.

More directly, the outcome of the abortion debate depends on Americans' views about motherhood and male–female equality. As long as significant numbers believe women and men to be fundamentally different and with differing "natural" roles in life, women's rights to decide about their own reproduction will be contested. Although there is evidence that growing numbers of Americans accept the ideal of male–female equality, it is a relatively new idea and large numbers of people still disagree. The future will see increasing numbers of individuals committed to substantial male–female equality, but when this idea will be commonly accepted is only a guess.

# References

Bianchi, Suzanne, and Daphne Spain. *American Women in Transition.* 1986. New York: Russell Sage.

Luker, Kristin. *Abortion and the Politics of Motherhood.* 1984. Berkeley: University of California Press.

National Opinion Research Center. *General Social Survey.* 1987. Chicago: University of Chicago Press.

Nock, Steven L. "The Symbolic Meaning of Childbearing." *Journal of Family Issues* 8: 373–393, December, 1987.

Orum, Anthony M. *Introduction to Political Sociology.* 1983. Englewood Cliffs, NJ: Prentice-Hall.

Wasburn, Philo C. *Political Sociology.* 1982. Englewood Cliffs, NJ: Prentice-Hall.

## Suggested Readings

Luker, Kristin. *Abortion and the Politics of Motherhood.* A sociologist argues that the abortion debate reflects fundamental values about the appropriate roles of women in society. The argument developed by Luker is the basis for the argument used in this chapter.

# CHAPTER 13

# Social Movements

## MADD's Anti-Drunk Driving Crusade

**E**ach year, some 25,000 Americans are killed in automobile accidents that involve a drunk driver—one-half of all automobile fatalities. Is it any wonder, then, that federal, state, and local governments are getting tough with drunk drivers? Or that citizens have organized massive campaigns designed to publicize and dramatize the problem? Or that organizations pay professionals to lobby state and federal officials to pass stiffer laws to punish drunk drivers? Or that throughout the nation—on television, on automobile bumper stickers, and in schools—the message is "Don't drink and drive"? Is it any wonder that within the past six years every state in the union has raised its minimum drinking age to 21?

The answer to all of these questions is, "Yes, it is a wonder that such things have happened." Indeed, it is astonishing how quickly the issue of drunk driving emerged as a national problem and how effective organized groups have been in having legislation enacted to combat it. Before 1980, there was virtually no citizen involvement in curbing drunk driving. Since that time, citizen groups have dominated the debate over how to combat this menace. Once these groups became involved, laws were passed, judicial practice was amended, enforcement strategies of police were changed, and, most important, attitudes about drinking and driving were altered.

Tom Cheek/Stock, Boston

The crusade against drunk driving led by MADD continues to gain more and more attention. One theme of the movement is that drunk driving "accidents" are, in fact, crimes.

If one examines the nature of the drunk driving issue over time, one finds that it has been a recognized problem since the widespread adoption of the automobile. In 1911, California first passed a law prohibiting driving under the influence of alcohol (DUI). In the 1930s, the first scientific research on the relationship between driving ability and alcohol consumption confirmed the common sense observation that drinking impairs driving. During the 1960s, substantial evidence also affirmed this link, provided by scientists studying the issue. So great was national concern over drunk driving in the 1960s that the federal government instituted massive programs to provide the states with money to combat the problem. And throughout the 1970s, federally funded alcohol safety action projects (ASAP) sought to enhance local police enforcement efforts. Despite all this, drunk driving did not become a significant public issue until the 1980s. Almost all previous efforts were made by government officials, and the public simply did not define the issue as a problem. This all changed around 1980.

Statistically, there was nothing particularly noteworthy about 1980. Alcohol-related traffic fatalities did not increase significantly that year. There was no major discovery linking alcohol and traffic safety. No major legislation relating to drunk driving was passed. So why did drunk driving become such an important topic then?

This chapter explains the emergence of a *social movement,* this one directed to the problem of drunk driving. Of all the serious problems facing us, why did drunk driving emerge as one worthy of national attention? After so many years of drunk driving fatalities, why did something happen in 1980? And why has the citizens' movement been so successful in its goals of legislative and judicial reform?

Sociologists apply resource mobilization theory to explain the emergence and success or failure of social movements. Briefly, this theory stresses the importance of money, time, and people for a social movement. Successful movements are able to mobilize, or gain access to, such resources through a variety of methods. The psychological motives for crusading for or against an issue are less important than they might first appear. We will show that the emergence of the anti–drunk driving movement in 1980 depended more on the ability of activists to secure resources than it did on any objective change in public perception of the problem.

# History of the Movement: Who "Owns" the Problem?

To understand what happened in the 1980s, we must consider historical attempts to curb drunk driving and traffic accidents. According to sociologist Joseph Gusfield (1988), three trends converged in the 1980s to make drunk driving a major focus of attention in the United States. These trends represent three different perspectives on drunk driving, each contributing to different evaluations of the seriousness of the problem and the types of solutions needed.

## The Automobile Safety Perspective

The first trend was the movement to enhance automobile safety. Beginning in the early 1900s, states assumed responsibility for traffic safety by passing speed limits and laws governing highway use. The construction of safe roadways and the passage and enforcement of traffic laws dominated the early automobile safety movement in the United States.

Beginning in the 1960s, attention shifted to the safety of the automobile itself. The creation of the federal Department of Transportation in 1960 and the National Highway Traffic Safety Administration (NHTSA) in 1966 marked the beginning of governmental concern with vehicle safety as it directed its efforts at the automobile-manufacturing industry rather than the driver. From this perspective, drunk driving laws were seen as one of many possible ways to enhance traffic safety. In fact, these laws have been seen as secondary to efforts that required safer automobiles. As activist Ralph Nader said, an automobile designed to be safe "under the assumption that fools and drunks would drive it" would be more effective in saving lives (Gusfield, 1988, p. 115).

The automobile safety perspective has promoted numerous laws that have been designed to protect both drivers and pedestrians—laws pertaining to speed limits, stop lights, posted signs, highway markings, driving under the influence, and seat-belt use. But from this perspective, the drunk driver is no more reprehensible than the driver who does not maintain a safe vehicle, is sleepy, or fails to use seat belts. In short, drunk driving is part of the problem when viewed from this perspective, not the overriding issue.

## Health and Alcohol Use Perspective

Concern over drinking, alcoholism, and intoxication is part of a larger public health emphasis in the United States. Public attention to the problems associated with alcohol use is widespread. Every state regulates the sale of alcoholic substances, forbidding certain individuals (minors and convicted felons) from purchasing them, declaring times and days when alcohol may be purchased, and regulating the conditions under which alcohol can be sold.

The history of public concern about alcohol reveals a curious fact: Most of the attempts to control alcohol have been directed at reducing its use and availability even though a majority of Americans condone drinking, celebrate important events with alcohol, and admit to drinking on a regular basis. From 1917 to 1933, the sale or possession of alcohol was illegal throughout the United States. But federal efforts at Prohibition were generally viewed as complete failures, much as are contemporary attempts to prohibit the sale or use of marijuana. Most Americans accept the consumption of alcohol as a legitimate form of behavior and without concern. It is *excessive* drinking and alcoholism that are so worrisome.

In the 1960s, the federal government became involved in public health efforts to combat alcoholism, and in 1970, the National Institute for Alcohol Abuse and Alcoholism was established. Since the middle of the century, health professionals have sought to define alcoholism as a disease rather than as an individual's moral failure. Alcoholism treatment programs are found in every state, often funded through federal and state taxes. Throughout the country, alcoholism is now recognized as a serious health issue.

Viewed from the public health perspective, drunk driving is one of many problems caused by alcohol. From this perspective, two solutions are needed: a method of "curing" the disease of alcoholism, and better ways to control access to alcohol. During the 1970s, programs that attempted to prevent alcohol problems were popular: Legislation restricted the sale of alcohol (for example, so-called happy hours, during which time discount drinks are purchased, were widely eliminated); increased liquor taxes, thereby making it more expensive to drink; and treatment programs established for chronic alcohol abusers or alcoholics.

Both those who were concerned about alcohol and health and traffic safety were aware of the problems associated with drunk driving. But each group saw the problem differently, one as a highway safety issue, the other as a health concern. Both groups desired to see drunk driving eliminated, and offered programs to accomplish that goal. But neither group focused sole attention on the drunk driver as a drunk driver. That is, neither orientation saw the drunk driver as the specific problem. Instead, each saw alcohol and its abuse as part of a larger concern. In contrast, the third orientation saw drunk driving as the sole focus of concern. Moreover, the third orientation focused on the individual drinker, not on the substance.

## Morality and Justice Orientation

Consider three different statements that people might make about a certain driver: He drives faster than the speed limit, he does not properly maintain the brakes on his vehicle, and he drives while under the influence of alcohol. Although each action endangers others, drunk driving is condemned far more than the other two. In fact, it is viewed as a *moral* offense against innocent citizens. The drunk driver, but not the speeder or the driver of an automobile in bad repair, is guilty of a moral transgression.

From the morality and justice perspective, the drunk driver knowingly endangers the rest of us and should be severely punished for reckless disregard for our lives and those of our children. And if the drunk driver causes injury, he should receive a penalty that reflects his commission of a serious violent crime and not an accident.

Central to this view is the concept of "malevolent assumption" (Collins, 1982). This assumes that if an injury results and alcohol is involved, then alcohol was the cause of the injury—in short, the injury would not have resulted if there had been no alcohol. Once this assumption is accepted, every accident in which a drunk driver is involved is blamed on the driver's consumption of alcohol, whether the alcohol caused it or not. Seen this way, such accidents are preventable because individuals can choose whether to drive or to drink. There is no such thing as a drunk driving "accident" because there is nothing accidental about someone's decision to drive after drinking. Instead, any personal injury caused by a drinking driver is viewed as a violent crime and the perpetrator as a criminal. Once one accepts the assumption of malevolence, one accepts the idea that something can be done about alcohol-related injuries and deaths. There is now a clearly defined course of action to be taken: The drunk driver must be controlled. Little else is required.

Unlike the objective views of drunk driving held by the traffic safety or the health orientations, the morality and justice orientation is anything but detached. It is emotional, personal, and angry. Proponents of this orientation demand justice for innocent victims who are injured or killed by wanton criminals using automobiles as their weapons. Where the health orientation focuses on the health of the drinker, and the traffic safety approach focuses on the safety of an automobile's occupants, the morality approach has no concern for the drunken driver, except that he be punished according to the severity of the actual crime committed. Only when drunk driving is penalized for what it is—a violent crime such as rape or murder—will drunk driving stop.

All three approaches propose strong measures to curb drunk driving, but for different reasons. Each represents a different group of interests: the first on safety, the second on health and alcoholism, and the third on justice and retribution. Until recently, each orientation pursued its goals more or less independently. No one really "owned" the problem of drunk driving—it did not belong to one particular concern but was part of all three. This changed in the 1980s, however, when the morality and justice orientation claimed undisputed ownership of the drunk driving problem.

# Mothers Against Drunk Driving

> It was a typical spring day. The date was May 3, 1980. Cari and her friend Carla were walking to a nearby school carnival. Suddenly, Carla heard a thump. She turned to ask Cari what happened—but Cari was no longer there, only her shoes remained. Cari was thrown 125 feet and left in the road to die. Cari's killer was a multiple repeat offender, a hit-and-run drunk driver. Cari's obituary read, "Cari Lightner, age 13, died the victim of a traffic accident." But Cari was not the victim of an accident; she was the victim of a violent crime—a crime that kills 25,000 people each year in the United States (Lightner, 1985, p. 1).

The words above were written by Candy Lightner, mother of the child killed by the drunk driver and founder of Mothers Against Drunk Driving (MADD). Lightner discovered that the driver was on probation for previous drunk driving convictions and had been out on bail for another hit-and-run drunk driving offense several days earlier. As she followed the case against the driver, Lightner became outraged by the leniency shown the killer of her daughter—indeed, by the extremely lenient penalties that were routinely given for drunk driving offenses generally. She directed her grief and anger toward securing tougher treatment of DUI offenders through harsher laws and stiffer penalties, and toward changing both law and judicial practice. Three months after Cari Lightner's death, MADD incorporated as a nonprofit organization in California.

Candy Lightner began to call press conferences in order to bring the situation to the public's attention. Her grief and anger were compelling. The stories she recounted of innocent children killed by drunk drivers who were released with little more than a "slap on the hand" aroused sympathy and concern. So moving was her story that, within a year, she had appeared on nationally televised talk shows on all the major networks, had been the subject of front-page stories in national newspapers, and was featured in stories about MADD in *Newsweek*, *Time*, and *The Nation*, among other publications. Hers was the "voice" of the victim. She asked that punishment fit the crime of drunk driving, calling the drunk driver a criminal and his actions a violent crime.

She contacted legislators in the state house, spoke with the governor of California, and began to lobby for tougher laws against drunk driving. According to her own accounts, these initial contacts with state legislators were frustrating and often unproductive; she was neither politically knowledgeable nor skilled in the art of lobbying. But a few sympathetic legislators took her under their wing and gave her the basic strategies for effective political persuasion. The principal obstacle to her efforts was the belief among lawmakers that drunk driving was something about which little could be done. Almost anyone who drinks has at some time driven while intoxicated—including legislators, judges, and juries. How could citizens be motivated to support measures that were designed to punish people for things these citizens themselves had sometimes done? Undaunted by this initial opposition, Candy Lightner continued her media campaign. Sympathetic victims of similar drunk driving accidents joined forces with her and worked to enlarge the organization. A board of directors was created and applications for funding were prepared. Lightner invested the insurance settlement from her daughter's death in the fledgling organization, and NHTSA provided a $65,000 grant to organize local MADD chapters. Private foundations also began to fund MADD's activities. A direct-mail fund-raising firm was hired to solicit money, and within a year of MADD's incorporation, the money poured in. In its first year, MADD had raised more than $500,000 and started chapters in eleven states; within five years of its founding, MADD had more than 600,000 members, 360 chapters in all 50 states, and a budget of $10 million administered by 20 full-time professionals (Reinarman, 1988, pp. 98–99). Each local chapter is affiliated with the national office but pursues MADD's mission within its own locale. Candy Lightner had recruited fund raisers, organizers, media specialists, and lobbyists for MADD's professional staff, many drawn from other charities or social movement organizations.

Now there was a visible victim—Candy Lightner. Despite years of growing concern about drunk driving, there had never been a convincing voice, face, or family with which the public might associate the problem. How could anyone argue with this convincing woman? Her tragedy was real, her suffering severe, her anger justified. The hundreds of articles written about Lightner and MADD in the first years of the crusade supported her cause. Indeed, how could anyone oppose her message?

Shrewdly, MADD focused its efforts on the drunk driver rather than the alcohol industry, purveyors of liquor, automobile manufacturers, or other seemingly related groups. There was no traffic safety or public health message. The drunk driver was not portrayed as a victim of alcoholism but as a deviant. MADD did not call for treatment for the drunk but for punishment. The message was short and simple: Drunk drivers are villains and must be dealt with accordingly.

Within five years, MADD had moved an issue fully into the public spotlight. And with the widespread public support, MADD began to reap major victories with executives and legislators throughout the country. The organization's supporters were a constituency that politicians recognized.

A commission on drunk driving was appointed in early 1984 by President Reagan. By late 1984, this commission had recommended that every state be required to raise its minimum drinking age to 21. In 1985, a bill with this provision was introduced in Congress, requiring a state to so raise its drinking age or to lose a portion of its federal highway funds.

With MADD's vigorous lobbying on its behalf, the bill was signed that same year by the president. By 1988, every state had complied with the law, and more than 230 new anti-drunk driving laws had been passed at local levels, almost all at the insistence of MADD (Reinarman, 1988, p. 100).

Both police and judicial practices began to change—not dramatically, but noticeably nonetheless. Enforcement of drunk driving laws increased, judges became less willing to permit plea-bargaining of DUI offenses, mandatory jail sentences were given for offenses, licenses were suspended, and entirely new definitions of such offenses were established. In particular, MADD championed the use of "per se" laws, which define driving with a blood alcohol level of a certain amount—usually 0.10 percent, or an alcohol content of 1 part per 1000 parts of blood—as a crime. In contrast to older laws, per se laws do not require proof of impairment; the simple fact of a certain alcohol content in the blood proves the driver guilty, period.

MADD has stated, "Tougher alcohol countermeasure laws are intended to play a vital role in achieving MADD's goals of reducing drunk driving tragedies" (MADD, 1988). Indeed, to the extent that MADD has been a success, it is because of its accomplishment of legislative and judicial changes. Whether drunk driving injuries and fatalities have been reduced is another matter altogether, one that we address at the conclusion of this chapter. A summary of MADD's proposed measures includes the following.

- *Victim compensation:* This provides state-funded compensation for the financial losses suffered by DUI victims and their families.

- *Victim's bill of rights:* This guarantees the victims of drunk driving accidents their rights within the legal system.

- *Administrative revocation:* This requires the immediate suspension of the driver's license when a driver is caught with a blood alcohol level above the legal limit.

- *License plate confiscation:* License plates are removed from the automobiles of habitual drunk drivers or those who drive on suspended licenses.

- *Mandatory incarceration of repeat offenders:* For those convicted more than one time for drunk driving, this guarantees confinement that cannot be suspended or reduced to probation.

- *Open container laws:* These prohibit the possession of open containers of alcohol by any occupant of an automobile.

- *Color-coded plastic licenses:* These unalterable licenses clearly indicate whether a driver is of legal drinking age.

■ *Dram shop laws:* These allow the victims of drunk drivers to file lawsuits against individuals who served alcoholic beverages to the drivers.

Will MADD be successful in having such laws passed? Probably. MADD and its goals seem to have little opposition. Indeed, achieving a nationwide change in state drinking ages testifies to this organization's immense power.

## MADD and Resource Mobilization Theory

How are we to account for MADD's dramatic success in achieving its legislative goals? More generally, how are we to explain the sudden emergence of this social movement organization? Was it caused by Candy Lightner? Was this entire movement and the organization the result of one person?

Indeed, Lightner was the immediate cause—the catalyst for the movement and its organization. But far more was required to make MADD a national social movement organization. After all, many other antidrinking campaigns had been launched only to fail, and other problems of greater significance have spawned no social movement at all. As mentioned earlier, sociologists explain the success or failure of social movements by resource mobilization theory (see especially McCarthy and Zald, 1977). In this section, we present this theory's basic principles and show how MADD illustrates them.

First, we must define a few terms. A *social movement* refers to a large number of people who have joined together to bring about or resist some social change. A *social movement organization* (SMO) is a formal organization that attempts to implement the social movement's goals. Typically, there are several SMOs within any social movement.

Resource mobilization theory differs from conventional explanations of social movements that focus on the psychological grievances of the participants in the movement. Common sense might suggest that an SMO arises when a problem becomes intolerable and the potential beneficiaries of a movement are motivated to take action on their own behalf. In contrast, resource mobilization theory stresses that grievances are a constant—usually, enough unhappiness exists to justify a movement to correct the problem. As we have seen with MADD, drunk driving was not a new problem in 1980. There was no great increase in its incidence, no significant change in the state of affairs to stimulate a social movement. And, for that matter, the participants in MADD did not stand to gain directly from the actions of the organization. The passage of stiff drunk driving legislation does not directly touch the lives of MADD's members.

Other important social movements have emerged when events or situations have appeared to be improving or, at least, remaining the same. The civil rights movement of the 1960s was not spawned by a significant deterioration in race relations in the United States; the Civil Rights Act of 1964 was not the end of the movement, but part of its early stages, marking the beginning of possibilities for better race relations. Furthermore, many of the civil rights activists (Northern white liberals) stood to gain nothing directly by the accomplishment of racial equality. Much the same is true of the women's rights movement, which began in the late 1960s. At that time, women were seeing improvements in their status through higher education, employment, and the beginnings of political participation. In 1963, for example, Congress had passed the Equal Pay Act, which required that men and women doing the same jobs must be paid the same wages.

Rather than arising out of a sudden increase in grievances, resource mobilization theory holds that SMOs arise because of changes in group resources, organization, and opportunities for collective action (Jenkins, 1983). The most important factors that account for the rise of an SMO are the availability of individuals to work in the organization, the ability to organize these individuals, and the money to pursue a goal.

With these considerations, the real question becomes, How does a social movement organization "mobilize" the resources it needs? The following principles, taken directly from John McCarthy and Mayer Zald's theory of resource mobilization (1977), may provide some answers.

## Resource Mobilization Principles

**The Social Environment.**    Aside from the specific issues addressed by any SMO, the social environment must be conducive. Social movements hold low priority to most individuals no matter how important their cause may seem to specific individuals. Not until people satisfy their basic wants and needs will they contribute time or money to a cause. Thus, social movements are more common in times of abundance—that is, when people can afford the "luxury" of working for a cause. This explains why SMOs are relatively uncommon in undeveloped nations and during harsh economic times. In general, there must be a public with sufficient discretionary income and time to support an SMO.

The social environment also contributes directly to the ability of a social movement to succeed. In particular, the development of media permits the spread of a message. The widespread use of such communications technologies as the telephone and direct mail further supports the goals and methods of resource mobilization. SMOs that are able to use advanced methods of communication fare much better than those that cannot. As we saw, MADD availed itself of such tactics in 1980, its first year, when direct mail and telemarketing were still in their infancy. In other words, changes in the social environment assisted the mobilization efforts of MADD independently of the SMO's specific goals.

**The Role of Indirect Beneficiaries, or "Outsiders."** One clear objective of every SMO is to turn its sympathizers into contributors. When we think of a social movement, we tend to focus on the individuals who stand to benefit from the achievement of the movement's goals. But resource mobilization theory holds that individuals who do not stand to directly benefit are the ones who matter most to the SMO, the so-called conscience constituents. They are crucial because they typically have the most resources. Individuals who need a social movement, the potential direct beneficiaries, tend to be needy in many ways, often lacking organizational skills, high incomes, or high levels of education. An SMO that depends only on its beneficiaries is less likely to mobilize all its resources for success.

This reliance on "outsiders" or conscience constituents raises a troubling issue. If people stand to gain nothing from contributing time or money to a cause, why would they? More generally, when an organization is committed to accomplishing a collective goal, one that benefits many people, what reason does anyone have for giving time or money? Clearly, the goal will be pursued whether or not a person contributes time or money, and regardless of his or her efforts, the person will still benefit from the goal's achievement. Furthermore, the person's contribution is so marginal to the entire mission that it cannot make a significant difference whether it is made or not. This is the "free rider" problem first discussed by economist Mancur Olson (1965).

According to Olson, most rational individuals will not give time or money to accomplish a collective goal (defined as one that benefits everyone and cannot be experienced by only some—that is, a goal that is not divisible) because it is more rational to "ride free." Rational self-interest would rule out contributing to a cause that cannot return greater benefits to those who contribute than to those who do not. Why not simply let others do the work? The benefits will be the same anyway. Indeed, studies have shown that the overwhelming majority of people do ride free in social movements. So how can an SMO motivate conscience constituents?

The answer is that successful SMOs offer benefits to contributors that go beyond the specific goals of the organization—personal benefits beyond the collective goals. The most important is the sense of purpose and belonging that people experience when they participate. Their efforts on behalf of a moral goal and their relationships with other group members are felt to be gratifying (Jenkins, 1983).

Within MADD, most activists are victims, relatives of victims, or acquaintances of victims of drunk driving accidents. While pursuing the collective goals of stiffer laws and the deterrence of drunk drivers, members also find comfort and solace in their ability to take action after a loss or injury, to *do something*. MADD activists have the opportunity to share their experiences with others who have suffered similar losses. Even those MADD members who are not victims experience solidarity with others who are committed to solving the same moral objective.

Another group of outsiders are those institutions or organizations that must be tapped for resources—government and private agencies, philanthropies, and religious organizations, all of whom may provide financial backing. Media organizations that provide free publicity and forums, such as schools in which the message can be disseminated, also are important. In short, resource mobilization theory states that not only must a successful SMO have large numbers of conscience constituents, but also it must convince outside organizations and institutions to lend support.

As we have seen, MADD was extremely effective in its efforts to involve such outside organizations and institutions. In its first year, MADD received funding from federal and private agencies; the press media were more than willing to tell Candy Lightner's story, which is a message with immense appeal. By describing the mission as one organized by mothers, the appeal also was successful in recruiting many nonvictims and others who had never before been active in social movements. Direct-mail solicitations to supporters of Christian missions were successful in painting MADD as a moral crusade, enlisting the support of many conscience constituents. Public schools also became involved with their own programs, such as Students Against Drunk Driving (SADD).

Virtually every social movement faces opposition from some sector. Resource mobilization theory holds that successful SMOs are able to neutralize such opposition. A crusade against drunk driving might be thought to challenge the liquor industry, for example. But MADD's strategy neutralized such opposition by focusing its message on the deviant individual rather than on the industry responsible for promoting the consumption of alcohol. MADD made a strategic choice in not attacking drinking per se as the public health orientation had done. Unlike other anti–drunk driving organizations such as Stop Marketing Alcoholic Beverages on Radio and Television (SMART) and the program of the Center for Science in the Public Interest, MADD did not attempt to limit the sales or advertising of alcoholic beverages. By placing the problem on the individual, MADD was able to avoid the appearance of attacking a major commercial industry. Indeed, Anheuser–Busch and Miller brewing companies both contributed money to MADD. The liquor industry participated willingly in the campaign because it deflected attention away from the problems related to consumption of their products in general (Reinarman, 1988, p. 102). Thus, MADD's strategy not only neutralized opposition, but also increased its support from outside organizations.

**Structure of the Social Movement Organization.** The important organizational distinction for successful SMOs is whether they are "federated." A federated SMO has chapters located near its members (a nonfederated SMO typically has one main office and communicates with its members from afar). Resource mobilization theory holds that federated SMOs are more successful in sustaining membership and mobilizing resources generally.

A federated structure is particularly important for conscience constituents whose primary incentive for participating is the sense of solidarity they derive from interacting with other members in face-to-face settings. When SMOs are not federated, members rarely have such opportunities and thus derive fewer benefits from their membership.

This has important consequences for the SMO's ability to mobilize effort and money from its constituents. Because most social movements contain several SMOs, constituents of one are more easily swayed by the advertising strategies of competing SMOs. In the absence of personal contact, members may be convinced that their SMO is not successful or not *as* successful as its competitors. Members have no way to evaluate what they get for their money because no "solidarity" benefits are derived from their participation in the SMO. Conscience constituents may be convinced to switch their support to another SMO that is pursuing similar goals or even to one that is pursuing entirely different goals.

As a result of these considerations, nonfederated SMOs must spend a greater portion of their resources on both advertising and keeping their members informed of accomplishments. These SMOs also must contend with a less stable base of support as their constituents shift their allegiances or balance their contributions to the SMO against other claims on their time and money. In short, nonfederated SMOs are unable to convert as many resources directly into their goals and so become less successful. Undoubtedly, much of MADD's success can be attributed to the aggressive federation of chapters that were begun in its first year and that have continued ever since. Local chapters provide face-to-face contact among constituents and offer evidence of success in achieving goals. Indeed, most MADD goals (or objectives) are local, requiring the passage of state or local ordinances. Success in such endeavors is immediately obvious to local chapter members.

**The Life Course of Social Movements.** All major social movements pass through specific stages of initial growth, establishment, and decline. The early days are difficult because the message is new and people must be taught to see the problem as legitimate and solvable. Eventually, the message may be accepted, and the movement then is seen as legitimate and thus established. Ultimately, however, all movements decline. Those that accomplish their objectives pass from view as they are no longer needed; those that do not meet their goals come to be seen as ineffective. No social problem will capture the attention of the American public forever. Sooner or later, the problem is either solved or abandoned as unsolvable. This rise and fall is referred to as the "life course" of a social movement.

In the earliest days of any movement, there may be only one or two organizations. But as a movement gains legitimacy, increasing numbers of people are attracted, and more organizations are formed to participate in the cause. Eventually, an entire social movement industry comprises all of the SMOs within the movement. In a very real sense, each SMO must compete with the others for the same resources, and not all survive.

Resource mobilization theory specifies that the older, more established SMOs are most likely to survive the rise and fall of the social movement industry. New organizations have difficulty in distinguishing themselves from the older, better-known SMOs. The older organizations also are better able to modify their mobilization strategies to deal with changes in the political and social climate.

MADD, the oldest anti–drunk driving crusade, illustrates this point. Because MADD is so well known, newer SMOs have been forced to establish far narrower goals in order to distinguish themselves. Crusades against the advertising of liquor, for example, or for alcohol-free high school proms share the movement's overall mission. But their goals are narrower than MADD's, and their ability to mobilize resources is considerably less. Many such movements simply fail.

Now a decade old, the anti–drunk driving movement is showing signs of decline. Most notably, media attention has fallen sharply. The movement may be in its last years. Even within MADD, internal dissension is obvious: Candy Lightner was recently removed as president in a battle over strategies and personalities. But MADD continues to survive even as other anti–drunk driving organizations fail. In all likelihood, MADD will be the last to die.

This brings us to our last question: If the anti–drunk driving movement is beginning its decline, is this because it has accomplished its objectives or because the public has become convinced that the drunk driving problem is not solvable? The answer is, yes, both statements are true in part.

# The Success of the Anti–Drunk Driving Social Movement

After existing for a decade, it is now possible to evaluate the movement's effects and success. Measured by changes in laws, police enforcement, and judicial practices, there is little doubt that the movement has been tremendously successful: Numerous laws against penalties for drunk driving now exist where none had ten years ago. Most of these resulted from the movement, MADD in particular.

But if success is measured in terms of reduced injuries and fatalities from drunk driving, the conclusion is more equivocal. MADD and other SMOs point with justifiable pride to the yearly reductions in fatalities and injuries. But the trend to fewer such cases had begun long before MADD came into existence. Through the 1970s, alcohol-related injuries and fatalities declined annually. The movement cannot take credit for this.

The primary goal of MADD is *deterrence*. When drivers know that it is legally risky to drive drunk, the logic goes, they will be unwilling to take to the road after drinking. Indeed, there is good evidence that when drivers believe in a high probability of being caught, they are less likely to drive drunk. Thus, the American public has been educated about drunk driving, and most Americans now accept the malevolence assumption and are more willing to view drunk driving as a serious crime.

The probability of being apprehended while driving drunk is about 1 in 1,000 (Ross, 1985). Vigorous enforcement programs that seek to increase such odds may indeed double, triple, or even quadruple them. Some evidence suggests that in the early period of a crackdown on drunk driving, drivers believe that the likelihood of being caught is greater. As a result, they refrain from driving under the influence. But within a few months, the secret is out, and drivers realize that the odds of being caught are still low. As a result, the deterrent effects from such crackdowns are minimal in the long run. The policy implications of this finding are clear: To deter drunk driving, states must sustain the perception that such offenses will result in arrests. Pragmatically, this does not seem possible.

Other deterrent strategies fare even worse in research. Studies of communities that have instituted road block checkpoints (where drivers are randomly tested for drunkenness) show no effects. The consequences of tougher penalties are equally disappointing. Initially, these laws appear to have the desired effect, but in short order the deterrence element disappears as motorists realize the extremely low chances of being apprehended. Deterrence works only to the extent that people are rational and risk-aversive. But those who are likely to drive while impaired probably are neither.

The assessment of the anti–drunk driving movement and MADD in particular is a matter of perspective. MADD has given a voice to the victims of the crimes committed by drunk drivers. It has offered comfort to thousands, brought a problem to national attention, and motivated countless individuals to combat the problem. It has had tremendous effects on state and national laws. In the end, the real goals of the movement are "changing attitudes and social norms," "making drunk driving socially unacceptable," and "creating a society in which impaired driving is not only unacceptable but also unnecessary" (Donelson, 1988, p. 36). In short, people must be changed more than laws and regulations.

# References

Collins, James. "Alcohol Careers and Criminal Careers." In *Drinking and Crime*. J. Collins (Ed.). 1982. London: Tavistock.

Donelson, Alan C. "The Alcohol–Crash Problem" In *Social Control of the Drinking Driver*. M. D. Laurence, J. R. Snortum, and F. E. Zimring (Eds.). 1988. Chicago: University of Chicago Press.

Gusfield, Joseph. "The Control of Drinking Driving in the United States: A Period of Transition." In *Social Control of the Drinking Driver*. M. D. Laurence, J. R. Snortum, and F. E. Zimring (Eds.). 1988. Chicago: University of Chicago Press.

Jenkins, J. Craig. "Resource Mobilization Theory and the Study of Social Movements." In *Annual Review of Sociology*. 1983. Palo Alto, CA: Annual Reviews, Inc.

Laurence, Michael D., John R. Snortum, and Franklin E. Zimring (Eds.). *Social Control of the Drinking Driver*. 1988. Chicago: University of Chicago Press.

Lightner, Candy. "When a Crash Becomes a Crime." *MADD National Newsletter* 5(2): 1, Fall 1985.

MADD. "Summary: MADD Legislative Goals." 1988. Mimeograph.

McCarthy, John, and Mayer Zald. "Resource Mobilization and Social Movements: A Partial Theory." *American Journal of Sociology* 82(6): 1212–1241, May 1977.

Olson, Mancur. *The Logic of Collective Action*. 1965. Cambridge, MA: Harvard University Press.

Reinarman, Craig. "The Social Construction of an Alcohol Problem: The Case of Mothers Against Drunk Driving and Social Control in the 1980s." *Theory and Society* 17(1): 91–120, May 1988.

Ross, H. Laurence. "Deterring Drunken Driving: An Analysis of Current Efforts." *Journal of Studies on Alcohol* supplement 10: 122–209, July 1985.

_____. *Deterring the Drinking Driver*. 1982. Lexington, MA: Lexington Books.

# Suggested Readings

Laurence, Michael D., John R. Snortum, and Franklin E. Zimring (Eds.). *Social Control of the Drinking Driver.* This collection of articles addresses and assesses the nature of the drunk driving problem, the situation in other countries, and the methods of combatting it.

Ross, H. Laurence. *Deterring the Drinking Driver.* A sociologist considers the law as a form of deterrence for drunk driving. He concludes that such laws offer extremely limited deterrence.

CHAPTER 14

# Population

Crime and Divorce: Blaming
the Baby Boom

# Divorce Rate Going Down?
# Dallas Doesn't Believe It

By Lori Montgomery
OF THE TIMES HERALD STAFF

Newlyweds, take heart. The widely held
notion that half of all American marriages end in divorce is way off, according to a Harris poll released Sunday.

The idea that half of all marrying
couples are doomed even as they approach the altar is "one of the most spe-
cious pieces of statistical nonsense ever
perpetrated in modern times," pollster
Louis Harris told the Associated Press.

Harris said government statistics
and his new survey show that only one of
every eight marriages will fail. And in
any given year, Harris said, only about 2
percent of married couples will wind up
in divorce court.

In Dallas, the world's divorce capital according to a 1986 study, Harris
drew skepticism from marriage counselors who said his findings fly in the face
of 20 years of research.

"One in eight does not sound right;
one in eight does not even sound close,"
said marriage counselor Jim Spruiell.

And marriage therapist Anna Beth
Benningfield asked, "By astronomical
odds, did he hit all the people in this
country who have never been divorced?
And if his survey is well-designed, I want
to know where all the others have been
coming from all these years."

continued

Danny Lyon/Magnum Photos

Most criminals are young males. As the baby boom came of "crime-producing" age, the crime rate predictably increased. Since then, as the population has aged, the crime rate has decreased.

The commonly quoted statistic that 50 percent of marriages fail first appeared in 1981, Harris said, when the U.S. National Center for Health Statistics reported that 2.4 million couples wed that year, but 1.2 million couples untied the knot.

"One critical element left out of the equation," Harris said, is that "a much, much bigger 54 million other marriages just keep flowing along like Old Man River."

A statistician with the U.S. Census Bureau, Arlene Saluter, agreed with Harris that the 50-percent figure is misleading because it can be applied only to recent years and cannot be projected into the future.

"If you take in marriages that occurred 30 and 40 years ago and combine them with recent marriages, it certainly wouldn't turn out to be 50 percent, because it's just in recent years that (divorce) has really soared," said Saluter, of the bureau's Marriage and Family branch.

Census statistics recorded so far in the 1980s show that the number of marriages has actually increased each year while the number of divorces peaked in 1981 and has been declining ever since.

From *The Dallas Times Herald*, June 29, 1987. Reprinted by permission.

**A**s indicators of the general health of our society, the prevalence of divorce and crime are viewed by many as "diseases" that afflict our culture. When divorce and crime rates increase, most people begin to look for explanations because these trends seem to indicate decadence or disintegration. Both divorce and crime are almost always viewed as pathologies needing correction.

Although both phenomena share pathological connotations, that is where their apparent similarity ends. Family breakdowns and crimes committed by adults do not seem closely related. There also is no evidence that criminals have greater divorce rates than law-abiding citizens. Divorce and crime rates thus would seem to reflect different processes, one breaking families apart and one leading people to break the law.

Indeed, there may be completely different processes involved in the generation of crime and the generation of divorce, but there is also an important and common causal element—a demographic cause—for both types of problems. In particular, crime and divorce are most common among people of a particular and narrow age group. When the numbers of people in that age group increase to form a large segment of the total population, there will be increases in both types of problems. Additionally, people born during the 1950s and early 1960s share certain experiences that may partially explain their divorce and crime rates.

In this chapter, we consider three demographic explanations and then apply them to the national divorce and crime rates since 1960. Finally, we make projections for the future based on what we know about people who are now in their late teens and early twenties.

# Robbery Figures Skyrocket as State Crime Rate Rises 14.9%

By Evan Moore
HOUSTON CHRONICLE

On March 6, Opal Zacharias became one of the 50 percent.

On that day, Mrs. Zacharias, 64, a woman who donated to her church and the PTA, was shot and then run over with her own station wagon when she surprised burglars at her home. The men who robbed and killed her remain at large.

Her husband, Herbert Zacharias, plans to offer a $5,000 reward for information leading to the indictment of her killer. Police have issued composite drawings of one of the men, based on witnesses' descriptions, and have recovered her abandoned car and emptied purse.

But Mrs. Zacharias remains the same—one of the 5,000-6,000 individuals Houston police project will become targets of robberies in the city this year, making up 50 percent of the 11,200-12,000 robberies police expect to be inflicted on individuals and businesses in the city in 1987. Unlike most of them, she was murdered.

Those crimes appear to be a large part of increasing crime in the state. A report released Monday by the Texas Department of Public Safety shows a 14.9 percent increase in the state crime rate last year, and the largest increase in the major categories of crime was in robbery, which rose 26.3 percent.

Increases were smaller in Houston, where overall crime increased 7.8 percent between 1985 and 1986, but correspond in showing increases in most categories.

From the *Houston Chronicle*, March 24, 1987. Reprinted by permission.

## Demographic Explanations

When demographers explain trends in divorce or crime rates, they distinguish among three general classes of effects that may produce them: age, period, and cohort.

### Age Effects

The age composition of our population often explains why birth, marriage, divorce, or crime rates increase or decrease. Whenever divorce or crime is more common for a particular age group, changes in the proportion of the population that age may explain changing demographic rates. This is known as an *age effect*.

## Period Effects

Rates sometimes change in ways that are unrelated to the population's age structure. The social conditions of a particular time in a society may affect the rate at which some phenomenon occurs. For example, divorce rates are known to decrease and some types of crime rates increase during harsh economic conditions such as recessions and depressions. When this occurs, the changes are caused by a condition that is associated with a particular *period* of time and are known as *period effects*.

## Cohort Effects

Individuals who are born in roughly the same time period belong to the same age cohort. For example, all people born between 1970 and 1979 in the United States are members of a demographic cohort as are people born between 1960 and 1969. Sometimes, individuals of a particular cohort experience common historical events that shape their lives in similar ways. For example, many teenagers who grew up during the Vietnam War came to view their society differently from other people. Something about their experiences may have made them more tolerant of divorce and more willing to seek divorce. To the extent that such different attitudes or behaviors persist over their lifetimes, their cohort will stand out as being distinctive even while its members grow older. Demographers call this a *cohort effect*.

# The Trends

The trends in divorce and crime are easily summarized by Figures 14.1 and 14.2. Figure 14.1 shows divorce ratios. The divorce ratio is defined as the number of divorced persons per 1,000 people who are married and living with their spouses. This is an example of what demographers call a "refined rate"—only individuals who are "at risk" of divorcing are included in the denominator. For example, in 1986 there were 13,555,000 divorced persons and 103,408,000 persons married and living with their spouses, yielding a ratio of 131 per 1,000.

Figure 14.2 presents the FBI's crime index rate, which is calculated by totalling the number of reported murders and manslaughters, rapes, robberies, assaults, burglaries, larcenies, and vehicle thefts, and then dividing by the total population and multiplying by 100,000. For example, in 1985 there were 12,430,000 reported cases of index crimes and 238,740,000 Americans. Multiplying the rate (0.052065) by 100,000 gives the figure 5,206.5, which indicates the number of crimes per 100,000 Americans. This is a "crude rate," because the denominator includes the entire population, including those persons who are not at

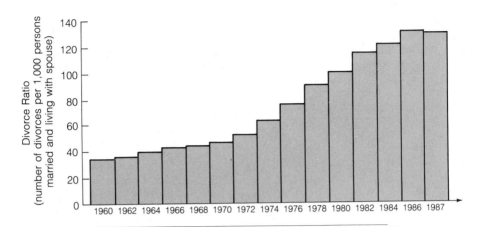

**Figure 14.1** Divorce ratios in the United States,
1960–1987 *Source: Historical Statistics of the United States,
Vol. I, 19. Tables B216–B220. Washington, DC: U.S. Bureau of
the Census. Statistical Abstract of the United States, 1972, 1973,
1974, 1975, 1976, 1977, 1978, 1979, 1980, 1981, 1982, 1983,
1984, 1985, 1986, and 1987.*

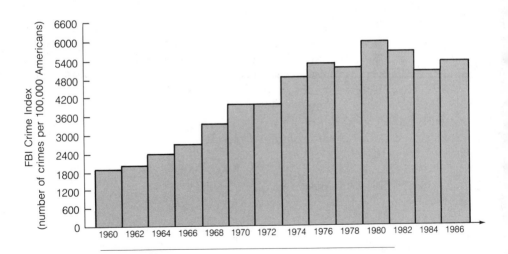

**Figure 14.2** Index of crime in the United States,
1960–1986 *Source: Federal Bureau of Investigation. Crime in
the United States—Uniform Crime Reports. 1988. Washington, DC:
U.S. Government Printing Office.*

risk of being victims of certain crimes (for example, males cannot be legally raped and people who do not own cars cannot be the victims of auto theft).

The divorce ratio has climbed steadily since 1960, with the most marked increases occurring between 1970 and 1980. Since 1980, the increase has been slower, and since 1986, there has actually been a very small decrease in the divorce ratio.

The crime index rate also has climbed steadily since 1960, with the most marked increase occurring between 1968 and 1980. Likewise since 1980, the crime index rate has declined noticeably.

Both the divorce ratio and the crime index rate have followed closely similar patterns for the approximately three-decade period shown in the figures: a long period of rapid and pronounced increase beginning around 1968–1970 and ending around 1980, with both trends showing the beginnings of decline in recent years.

How do we interpret these trends? In fact, there are several possible interpretations. First, the decade of the 1970s may have been particularly difficult. Some set of forces in that period may have fostered unusually bad marriages and large numbers of criminals. If so, we see an example of a period effect. Second, the divorces and crimes of the 1970s may have been the product of a particularly unusual cohort of individuals who were born in the 1950s—that is, the "flower children" and "hippies" of the late 1960s and early 1970s. If so, this would be an example of a cohort effect. Finally, divorces and crimes may be practiced more by people of a particular age or ages. There may have been many more people of these ages in the 1970s. If so, this would be an example of an age effect. Which, if any, of these explanations is the most plausible?

To answer this question, we must turn our attention to the age structure of U.S. society. Because so much of what people do depends on their age, it is of tremendous importance to know the relative numbers of people of differing ages in a society. Furthermore, if age cohorts differ in their behaviors, we must examine the history of each cohort to understand it: Does it constitute a particularly large or small cohort, and how old were its members at important times in our history?

# Age Structure of the United States

The age structure of a society refers to the relative size of different age groups over time. If we define ages 1 to 5 years as an age group of interest to us for some particular reason (for example, as an indicator of the demand for day-care facilities), we would examine the age structure of the United States over time in order to see what proportion of Americans fall into the 1–5 age group. The proportion might grow, shrink, or remain stable. Each possibility implies different consequences for the issue under consideration.

The age groups we work with in this chapter are those used by the U.S. Bureau of the Census. They correspond to conventional ages of certain important life-cycle transitions. Thus, for example, the first age group comprises all individuals under age 5. These children are rarely in school. The second age group includes ages 5 to 13. These individuals are in primary and intermediate grades of school, and most have not yet reached adolescence. The third group includes young people ages 14 to 17. Most of these teenagers are in high school and have a distinctive subculture of their own but are not yet emancipated from their parents' homes. The next group includes people ages 18 to 24. This category includes most young adults, who, during these years, begin to work full-time whether or not they attend college; most of them no longer live with their parents. Subsequent age categories are divided into ten-year age groups.

The age structure for the United States in a particular year is determined by taking the number of individuals in each age category and dividing by the total number of Americans that year. This has been done for even-numbered years since 1960. For example, in 1986 there were 14,792,000 teenagers aged 14 to 17. The total population of the United States that year was 239,374,000. Therefore, teenagers aged 14 to 17 were 0.062 (6.2 percent) of the total population. The following year (1987), people of that age made up only 6.0 percent of the total population.

The relative size of age categories changes over time for several reasons. First, natural or unnatural disasters (plagues and wars) will kill large numbers of people of particular ages. Second, immigration is often concentrated among young people who in our history have significantly affected the age structure of the population. But the most important reason is the number of children that women have in any particular year. Demographers refer to females' *fertility* to describe the number of children they bear.

For example, suppose that American men and women went on a "baby binge" for a few years, producing children in unprecedented numbers. Instead of the average woman bearing two children during her lifetime, let us suppose the average woman bore three or four children. Furthermore, suppose this trend continued for ten or fifteen years. The children born to these adults would swell their age group throughout their lifetimes. Thus, in the first five years of this baby binge, the proportion of Americans under age 5 would swell and other age groups would proportionally shrink. In another five years, the proportion of Americans under age 10 would swell, and five years later the proportion of those under age 15 would grow. Those individuals who were born during this baby binge would swell the ranks of each successive age group as time passed.

In fact, there was just such a baby binge beginning in 1947 and continuing until 1960. Unusually large numbers of children were born in this period, which now is called the Baby Boom. Not that people had large families (five or more children) during the Baby Boom—instead, it was that higher proportions of women had at least one child and many had three or four. Adults married at somewhat younger ages and had children earlier in their lives. The combined effect of these trends was very large numbers of children born between 1947 and 1963. For each of the seventeen years in this interval, the *total fertility rate* (the total number of children the average woman is predicted to bear in her life-time) was 3.0 or greater. Because the average number of children born per woman was lower both before and after the Baby Boom, the baby boom cohort is disproportionately large, regardless of the age of its members.

Look at Figure 14.3, the population structure of the United States since 1960.

Consider three of the fourteen bars: the first (1960), sixth (1970), and eleventh (1980) represented in the figure. In 1960, the children of the Baby Boom were younger than 13. In 1970, members of the Baby Boom cohort were ten years older, between ages 7 and 23; by 1980, between ages 17 and 33. By 1990, the Baby Boom generation will be between ages 27 and 43. The age structure shown in Figure 14.3 reveals that as the Baby Boom matured, the proportion of individuals in their age range increased.

For each age group, the figure has bars representing the proportion of Americans that age for every other year since 1960. To illustrate, consider three bars showing the proportion of Americans younger than age 5 (the first age group in the figure). The first bar over that group shows that 11.2 percent of Americans were that age in 1960. The tenth bar for that group shows that 7.1 percent of Americans were that age in 1978. The last bar represents 1986 and shows that 7.6 percent of Americans were younger than 5 years old that year.

Let us briefly trace the history of the Baby Boomers. In 1960, these individuals were ages 13 and younger. Children under 5 that year were a greater proportion of all Americans than that age group has been in any year since. This makes sense: 1960 was near the end of the Baby Boom—children under age 5 that year had been born between 1956 and 1960. As the Baby Boom drew to a close with the approach of 1963, fertility began to decline. As a result, the proportion of Americans under age 5 also began to decline, as is seen clearly in the figure (the height of bars over the "Under 5" category is progressively lower for succeeding years).

The aging of the Baby Boom cohort also is obvious in the next category, ages 5 to 13. People of this age group in 1960 were born

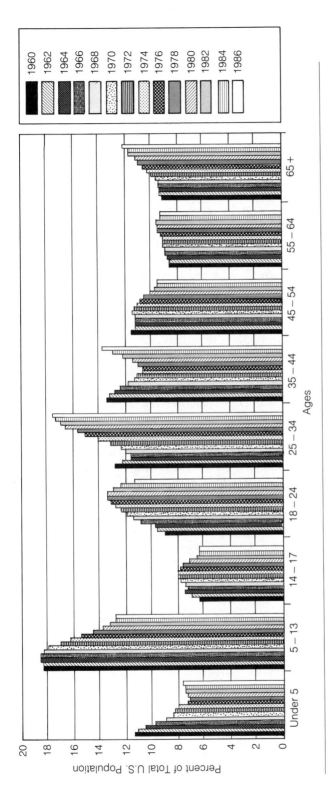

**Figure 14.3** Age Structure of the United States

*Sources: For 1960–1973, "Estimates of the Population of the United States by Age, Sex, and Race: April 1, 1960, to July 1, 1973." Current Population Reports, series P–25, no. 519 (1974). Washington, DC: U.S. Bureau of the Census.*
*For 1974–1981, "Preliminary Estimates of the Population of the United States by Age, Sex, and Race: 1970–1981." Current Population Reports, series P–25, no. 917 (1982). Washington, DC: U.S. Bureau of the Census.*
*For 1982–1984, "Estimates of the Population of the United States by Age, Sex, and Race: 1980–1984." Current Population Reports, series P–25, no. 965 (1985). Washington, DC: U.S. Bureau of the Census.*
*For 1985–1987, "United States Population Estimates by Age, Sex, and Race: 1980–1987." Current Population Reports, series P–25, no. 1022 (1988). Washington, DC: U.S. Bureau of the Census.*

between 1947 and 1955, the beginning and middle of the boom. Because fertility was still increasing during that interval, the proportion of individuals ages 5 to 13 increases from 1960 until around 1968 when it begins to decrease. This also makes sense: 5-year-olds in 1968 were born at the tail end of the boom (1963) when fertility was starting to decline.

This is all easiest to see if only one year is considered. Take 1955 as the peak of the Baby Boom (total fertility rate that year equalled 3.8). In 1960, babies born in 1955 were in the "Under 5" category. Thus, the proportion of people of this age group is highest in 1960. These babies were 10 years old around 1965–1966. Thus, the proportion of people ages 5 to 13 is highest for those two years. These babies were 15 years old in 1970–1971, around which time the proportion of people of this age group nears its maximum (of course, the age group 14 to 17 includes persons older and younger than 15, which makes pinpointing the group born in 1955 difficult).

The general point should be clear: As the Baby Boom cohort ages over time, older age groups grow as a proportion of the American population. Just as Baby Boomers swelled the infant age groups during the 1950s, they swelled the middle-aged groups during the 1980s (and 1990s) and will be a large elderly group in the second decade of the twenty-first century. Because the age structure of American society swells where the Baby Boomers are, this cohort has been described as "a pig in a python," suggesting that its presence will stand out as the group progresses through the years.

Why did the parents of the Baby Boom behave as they did? What made them marry so young and have so many children? It is no surprise that there are many possible answers depending on which demographic explanation one considers (for example, see Cherlin, 1981).

First, a period explanation holds that the 1950s were a time of stable economic conditions and relative prosperity. Men and women who had postponed marriage during World War II were able to marry and begin families once the war ended. The healthy economy was accompanied by unprecedented levels of housing construction, which allowed returning veterans to purchase homes cheaply and newly married couples to form their own families. Tremendous emphasis was placed on home and family life in literature and media. The rapid development of suburbs also fostered traditional family values (Mom stays home and raises the children while Dad commutes to work each day).

Second, a cohort explanation notes that the parents of the Baby Boom grew up during the Great Depression. Fathers then were often unemployed—one-third of the population was out of work. Sons and daughters of these men thus grew up faster than they would have otherwise. Sons, many still quite young, often worked to help sustain their families. Daughters of unemployed men assumed traditional housewife-like roles to help out their families. For both boys and girls, in short, adulthood came early. These young men and women came to value stable families and children, so as adults, they married young and had many offspring.

Finally, there are age explanations. One in particular (Easterlin, 1980) focuses on the very small size of the birth cohorts of the 1920s and 1930s—that is, the parents of the Baby Boom. When these small cohorts entered their early adult years in the late 1940s and early 1950s, the postwar economy was expanding. But with relatively few young adults, employers were forced to pay higher wages to attract a work force. In comparison with the meager life-styles that these individuals had experienced as children and adolescents during the Great Depression, high wages offered them a very comfortable standard of living, enough to satisfy their material desires with enough to allow marriage and children. In short, the small size of the young adult age group entering the 1950s explains the high wages they commanded and the consequent behaviors that led to the Baby Boom.

Which of these explanations is correct is impossible to determine, because all are formulated to explain events of the past. Whether the parents of the Baby Boom held different values and beliefs is not known to us today, although available evidence indicates that attitudes and values concerning children and family life were not vastly different during the Baby Boom than before it. This finding would cast some doubt on the period explanation. With respect to the cohort explanation, many parents of the Baby Boom were too young to be affected significantly by the Depression, and many others lived in families that were not adversely affected by unemployment (Cherlin, 1981). Both points call into question the cohort explanation. Nonetheless, the age group entering adulthood during the Baby Boom *was* quite small and had favorable economic prospects, but this explanation cannot account for all of the behaviors of the Baby Boom parents.

Each explanation can be faulted for being incomplete, and yet each adds one piece to the puzzle of the Baby Boom. That there are several plausible explanations suggests that each accounts for part of the story. Rather than seek one entirely correct explanation, demographers use all three to provide a more complete accounting of demographic trends.

# Explaining Crime and Divorce in the 1970s

Figures 14.1 and 14.2 showed that crime and divorce rates rose sharply from the late 1960s until about 1980, the years in which the children of the Baby Boom were entering young adulthood. By applying the three demographic explanations—period, cohort, and age—we can better understand the trends in both crime and divorce.

## Divorce

**Period Explanations.**     There is some evidence that attitudes toward divorce became more tolerant during the 1970s. Cherlin (1981) reports that national opinion polls between 1968 and 1974 revealed that a growing proportion of Americans believed that obtaining divorce should be easier than it was. Such attitudinal changes may have led people to be more willing to seek divorces, especially when many states in the 1970s enacted no-fault divorce laws that permitted couples to obtain them without having to charge one spouse with an offense such as adultery or cruelty. Some researchers thus believe that easier divorce laws fostered higher rates of divorce.

The problem with such period explanations is that it is not known whether attitudes and laws were the cause or the consequence of higher rates of divorce. Some studies indicate, for example, that divorce rates in no-fault states were no higher in the 1970s than would be expected from the trends in states that did not reform their laws (Cherlin, 1981, p. 49). Furthermore, the sharp increase in divorce rates actually began somewhat before 1968, which possibly suggests that laws were changing in response to rising divorce rates rather than vice versa.

**Cohort Explanations.**     The Baby Boom generation grew up in times of economic prosperity and social stability, but when its members became adults in the late 1960s and 1970s, the economy was in poor shape. Because there were so many members of this cohort, competition for jobs was intense and wages were consequently depressed. Thus, for many Baby Boomers, opportunities were less favorable than they had been for their parents. But these young adults had grown up with a relative abundance of material goods. As adults, therefore, their experience was one of deprivation.

> The relatively unfavorable income position of the young men, combined with their tastes for material goods, meant that many young married couples postponed having children . . . young wives went to work to supplement the family income, . . . and increased marital conflict, fueled by the tight economic situation, led to the sharp increase in divorce (Cherlin, 1981, p. 56).

This explanation for divorce is identical to the cohort explanation for the Baby Boom discussed above and has the same shortcomings.

**Age Explanations.**     Age explanations focus on the relative size of particular age cohorts in society. The median age for divorce in the United States, now as well as in the 1960s and 1970s, is between age 29 and 31 (males and females have slightly different median ages at divorce because males are typically several years older than their wives).

Because most divorces are granted to people in this age group, it is necessary to know its population. When there are relatively few people aged 25 to 35 in the population, few people are "at risk" of divorcing. On the other hand, when there are disproportionately large numbers of persons at risk, the divorce ratio will increase even if the proportion of marriages ending in divorce does not.

Suppose, for example, that 25 percent of marriages made between 1940 and 1950 ultimately end in divorce. Further suppose that a comparable proportion of marriages entered into between 1960 and 1970 ultimately end in divorce. If this were true, there would be no increase in the probability of a marriage ending in divorce. Because most people who divorce are in the 25 to 35 age group, it is clear that if more of these people are around in 1980 than in 1960, the divorce ratio will be higher even though the likelihood of divorce does not increase.

Remember that the divorce ratio divides the number of divorced people by the number of married people. When 25 to 35 year olds are a greater proportion of all Americans (married and divorced), then their experience with divorce, even if no different from previous generations, will make the divorce ratio increase because they constitute a greater proportion of all people. To demonstrate, let us imagine two small societies. In society A, there are 100 married people under age 25, 100 between 25 and 35, and 100 older than 35—a total of 300 married people. Suppose that 20 percent of marriages end in divorce. To make things simple, let us assume that all divorces occur at the median age of divorce—30—and all occur in the same year. After the divorces, there are still 100 married people under age 25, 100 married people older than 35, but only 80 married people ages 25 to 35. The divorce ratio is calculated as 20 (divorced people) divided by 280 (married people) = 0.071, or 71 per 1,000.

In society B, there are also 300 married people, but the age structure is different. In this society, there are 50 married people under age 25, and 50 more than 35, but 200 between ages 25 and 35—that is, a disproportionate number of 25 to 35 year olds. The same proportion of marriages in society B ends in divorce as in society A—20 percent. Using the same simplifying assumptions as for society A, this means that following the divorces, there are still 50 married people under age 25, and 50 more than 35, but 160 married people between 25 and 35 (because 20 percent of 200 is 40 divorced people). The divorce ratio is 40 (divorced people) divided by 260 (married people) = 0.153 or 153 per 1,000—more than twice the figure for society A. This illustration shows that the divorce ratio can more than double, even when the proportion of marriages that end in divorce does not change at all, simply because of different age structures.

When the age structure of the United States is examined (Figure 14.1), the proportion of divorce-prone individuals clearly began a rapid and pronounced increase beginning around 1967–1968, or the same time that the divorce ratio began its rapid increase. In fact, the proportion of Americans aged 25 to 34 grew from 11.7 percent in 1967 to 17.6 percent in 1985, but has not grown appreciably since. The same holds true for the divorce ratio.

The age structure does not account for the entire increase in the divorce ratio since the 1960s. Indeed, demographers have shown that the *probability* of divorce has increased, with between 40 percent and 50 percent of marriages contracted between 1965 and 1975 predicted to eventually end in divorce. Still, the age structure does account for much of the increase in the divorce ratio, and with Baby Boomers no longer in their divorce-prone years, the divorce ratio also is dropping.

This demographic explanation does not account for *why* people in the 25- to 35-year-old age group get divorced, but one of the most commonly accepted explanations today is that women now have considerably more alternatives to marriage. By working, women are able to escape loveless, abusive, or intolerable marriages. Their economic independence provides social independence as well. Because women of the Baby Boom cohort have entered the labor force in unprecedented numbers, their educational attainments and occupational pursuits have allowed them to divorce if their marriages break down. Although the age structure explains part of the increase in the divorce ratio, the entire set of changes associated with the rapid entry of Baby Boom women into the labor force and their higher educational attainments completes the explanation as thoroughly as it can be completed.

## Explaining Crime Rates

We may apply the same reasoning to crime rates that we did to divorce ratios. What explains the rapid increase in crimes from the late 1960s through the 1970s and the subsequent decline since 1980?

**Period Explanations.**    According to some analysts, two period factors are involved in the rise of crime: handgun ownership and drug use. The involvement of handguns in violent crimes is well documented. In fact, the United States is unusual in comparison with other modern nations in allowing the widespread private ownership of handguns. But despite the fact that handguns figure so importantly in violent crimes in this country, handgun ownership did not increase during the 1970s. Approximately one-half of Americans own handguns or other firearms, a figure that has not changed appreciably in the past two decades (National Opinion Research Center, 1972, 1988).

Drugs also have been singled out as a major cause of crime in our society. Many property crimes are motivated by the need for quick cash in order to purchase illegal drugs. Whether drug use was a growing problem during the 1970s is difficult to assess, but conventional thought holds that it was. National surveys revealed growing use of drugs by young people through most of the 1970s, although there has been a drop in those rates since the late 1970s.

Other social phenomena of the 1970s may have had implications for crime rates, including the general disorder associated with the war in Vietnam, student protests, racial unrest, and high-ranking politicians convicted of crimes. In some way, each may have fostered more crime, although showing this to be true is not possible because these were society-wide phenomena. Rather than view these factors as causes of crime, it probably makes more sense to view them as consequences of the same factor that produced more crime. Technically, in other words, the rise in crime and the occurrence of these events may have been spurious—that is, both were caused by a third factor.

**Cohort Explanations.** Most FBI index crimes are committed by young people. In fact, about one-third of these crimes are committed by people under age 18, and another one-third by people ages 18 to 24. Although very few crimes are committed by people under 13, 13 to 17 year olds commit one-quarter of all index crimes in the United States (Federal Bureau of Investigation, 1985). A cohort explanation for the crime rates of the 1970s would seek some common experience that is shared by people ages 13 to 24 that would lead to crime and persist over their lifetimes. Individuals that age in 1970 were born between 1946 and 1957, the beginning to the middle of the Baby Boom. People of that age in 1980 were born between 1956 and 1967, or toward the end of the Baby Boom. In other words, the high crime rates occurred during years in which the Baby Boom cohort was between ages 13 and 24.

A cohort explanation does not work for crime, however, because if the Baby Boom cohort producing the crimes of 1970 were affected by some common experience, then crimes in 1980 would be produced by these same individuals, who would have been ten years older. FBI statistics, however, show clearly that very young people are consistently the perpetrators of crime as much now as in 1970.

**Age Effects.** The age distribution of the United States gives the answer to why the crime rate increased and declined when it did. As just noted, the peak of the Baby Boom cohort (birth year 1955) entered its crime-prone years of ages 13 to 24 in the late 1960s. These people began to exit their crime-prone years around 1979–1980. Since then, the proportion of Americans in the 13- to 24-year-old age group has steadily declined. The crime index rate mirrors closely the progression of the Baby Boom cohort through their teens and early twenties.

Age effects do not explain the entire increase in crime during the 1960s, but just as was true with divorce ratios, age effects explain a large portion of the trend. The rest must be attributed to period effects such as those noted above.

## The Future and the Cohort of 1965–1975

In the same way that historical events can be analyzed by demographic trends, it is possible to make projections for age cohorts. For illustration, consider those individuals born between 1965 and 1975, who will be ages 15 to 25 in 1990. Most of the parents of these children were born during the Baby Boom. Unlike their own parents, the Baby Boomers have had unusually small numbers of children. In fact, their fertility was so low during these years that the period is commonly referred to as the "Birth Dearth."

One explanation for the extraordinarily low fertility of Baby Boomers is that educational and occupational opportunities were open to large numbers of women who opted for careers rather than for large families. Another explanation suggests that Baby Boomers are not foregoing children as much as postponing them. Regardless of the reason, the fact remains that the total number of children born each year between 1965 and 1975 was significantly lower than the number born each year before or after that decade. Figures in Table 14.1 show this clearly.

Members of the Birth Dearth cohort reached the beginning of their crime-prone years in 1978 when those born in 1965 turned 13. The cohort will reach the end of its crime-prone years in 1999 when those born in 1974 turn 24. Its small size should be reflected in the crime rate—a decline beginning around 1978 and continuing for approximately two decades.

Clearly the children of the Birth Dearth face different conditions from those that the children of the Baby Boom faced—in many ways, they are opposite conditions. Their cohort will be smaller than cohorts both older and younger than themselves. This suggests that societal resources—education, recreation, and health care–devoted to children were in greater abundance when this cohort was in its childhood years because there were fewer children in need of them. In a similar fashion, family resources were more abundant for children of the Birth Dearth because the typical family had fewer children. Additionally, the small size of this cohort means that competition for jobs will be lower when they enter the labor market. Starting salaries should be higher for them than for cohorts before or after. Thus, with their higher starting salaries and higher educational attainments, children of the Birth Dearth resemble

**Table 14.1**  Total U.S. Births, 1955 to 1985

| Year | Number of Births |
|------|------------------|
| 1955 | 4,079,000 |
| 1960 | 4,258,000 |
| 1965 | 3,760,000 |
| 1970 | 3,731,000 |
| 1975 | 3,144,000 |
| 1980 | 3,612,000 |
| 1985 | 3,761,000 |

Source:  *Statistical Abstract of the United States,* 1986. Washington, DC: U.S. Bureau of the Census

their grandparents' generation, or the parents of the Baby Boom. Will they have higher fertility? Will they marry younger than earlier cohorts? Will they have low divorce rates? Their grandparents did.

The answers to these questions depend on assumptions that one makes about the future. Demographers who focus on cohort explanations such as those discussed in this chapter see the members of the Birth Dearth cohort responding to demographic trends much the same as their grandparents did. Children of the Birth Dearth grew up in hard economic times, but when they become young adults, they will have good employment prospects and relatively high wages. Hence, some predict, they will marry younger. Because wages will be higher, fewer women will be pushed into the labor force, instead having children and becoming homemakers and mothers much as their grandmothers did. Divorce will become less likely because of the restructuring of the typical family and the decline in economic pressures.

Not all demographers buy this picture of the future, however, particularly those who stress age and period explanations. To them, the basic demographic trends of the late twentieth century are stable and probably will persist. Women, they argue, are unlikely to stop working just because families can survive on their husbands' earnings. Contemporary attitudes about women and their education and occupations probably will not change simply because incomes rise. The trend toward later ages in marriage and lowered fertility, they argue, reflects the changed situation of women in our modern society. Demographic shifts of cohort size, therefore, are not seen as likely to alter such trends. Finally, given the structure of contemporary marriages, divorce rates are not expected to decrease significantly. Unless women drop out of the labor force and fertility increases significantly, these demographers see no reason to predict lower divorce probabilities.

Which of these possibilities is more likely or whether either is likely depends on the response of individuals to their particular circumstances. Demography is no better able to tell the future than any other science, but it can predict the future structure of our society—that is, its size and composition. With such knowledge, predictions are far more likely to be accurate.

# References

Cherlin, Andrew. *Marriage, Divorce, and Remarriage.* 1981. Cambridge, MA: Harvard University Press.

Easterlin, Richard A. *Birth and Fortune: The Impact of Numbers on Personal Welfare.* 1980. New York: Basic Books.

Federal Bureau of Investigation. *Crime in the United States: Uniform Crime Reports.* 1985. Washington, DC: U.S. Department of Justice.

National Opinion Research Center. *General Social Survey.* 1972. Washington, DC: U.S. Bureau of the Census.

National Opinion Research Center. *General Social Survey.* 1988. Washington, DC: U.S. Bureau of the Census.

# Suggested Readings

Cherlin, Andrew. *Marriage, Divorce, and Remarriage.* A sociologist reviews trends in marriage, divorce, fertility, and family patterns over the course of the twentieth century. Age, period, and cohort explanations are advanced for such trends.

# Index